The Legal Answer
Book for
Nonprofit Organizations

Nonprofit Law, Finance, and Management Series

The Art of Planned Giving: Understanding Donors and the Culture of Giving by Douglas E. White

Charity, Advocacy, and the Law by Bruce R. Hopkins

The Complete Guide to Nonprofit Management by Smith, Bucklin & Associates

Developing Affordable Housing: A Practical Guide for Nonprofit Organizations by Bennett L. Hecht

Financial and Accounting Guide for Not-for-Profit Organizations, Fifth Edition by Malvern J. Gross, Jr., Richard F. Larkin, Roger S. Bruttomesso, John J. McNally, Price Waterhouse LLP

Fund-Raising: Evaluating and Managing the Fund Development Process by James M. Greenfield

Fund-Raising Fundamentals: A Guide to Annual Giving for Professionals and Volunteers by James M. Greenfield

Fund-Raising Regulation: A State-by-State Handbook of Registration Forms, Requirements, and Procedures by Seth Perlman and Betsy Hills Bush

Fund-Raising Regulation Report by Bruce R. Hopkins and Betsy Hills Bush

The Law of Fund-Raising, Second Edition by Bruce R. Hopkins

The Law of Tax-Exempt Healthcare Organizations by Thomas K. Hyatt and Bruce R. Hopkins

The Law of Tax-Exempt Organizations, Sixth Edition by Bruce R. Hopkins

The Legal Answer Book for Nonprofit Organizations by Bruce R. Hopkins

A Legal Guide to Starting and Managing a Nonprofit Organization, Second Edition by Bruce R. Hopkins

Modern American Philanthropy: A Personal Account by John J. Schwartz

The Nonprofit Counsel by Bruce R. Hopkins

The Nonprofit Law Dictionary by Bruce R. Hopkins

Nonprofit Litigation: A Practical Guide with Forms and Checklists by Steve Bachmann

The Nonprofit Management Handbook: Operating Policies and Procedures by Tracy Daniel Connors

Nonprofit Organizations' Business Forms: Disk Edition by John Wiley & Sons, Inc.

Partnerships and Joint Ventures Involving Tax-Exempt Organizations by Michael I. Sanders

Planned Giving: Management, Marketing, and Law by Ronald R. Jordan and Katelyn L. Quynn

Reengineering Your Nonprofit Organization: A Guide to Strategic Transformation by Alceste T. Pappas

Reinventing the University: Managing and Financing Institutions of Higher Education by Sandra L. Johnson and Sean C. Rush, Coopers & Lybrand, L.L.P.

Streetsmart Financial Basics for Nonprofit Managers by Thomas A. McLaughlin

Successful Marketing Strategies for Nonprofit Organizations by Barry J. McLeish

The Tax Law of Charitable Giving by Bruce R. Hopkins

Tax Planning and Compliance for Tax-Exempt Organizations: Forms, Checklists, Procedures, Second Edition by Jody Blazek

The United Way Scandal: An Insider's Account of What Went Wrong and Why by John S. Glaser

The Volunteer Management Handbook by Tracy Daniel Connors

The Legal Answer Book for Nonprofit Organizations

Bruce R. Hopkins

JOHN WILEY & SONS, INC.

New York • Chichester • Brisbane • Toronto • Singapore

To
Jim Greenfield,
with admiration for his good works on
behalf of the nonprofit sector over the years—
and thanks for 32 questions

Copyright © 1996 by John Wiley & Sons, Inc.

ISBN 0-471-10606-2

Printed in the United States of America

10 9 8 7 6 5 4

Subscription Notice

This Wiley product is updated on a periodic basis with supplements to reflect important changes in the subject matter. If you purchased this product directly from John Wiley & Sons, Inc., we have already recorded your subscription for this update service.

If, however, you purchased this product from a bookstore and wish to receive (1) the current update at no additional charge, and (2) future updates and revised or related volumes billed separately with a 30-day examination review, please send your name, company name (if applicable), address, and the title of the product to:

Supplement Department
John Wiley & Sons, Inc.
One Wiley Drive
Somerset, NJ 08875
1-800-225-5945

For customers outside the United States, please contact the Wiley office nearest you:

Professional & Reference Division
John Wiley & Sons Canada, Ltd.
22 Worcester Road
Rexdale, Ontario M9W 1L1
CANADA
(416) 675-3580
1-800-567-4797
Fax (416) 675-6599

John Wiley & Sons, Ltd.
Baffins Lane
Chichester
West Sussex, PO19 1UD
UNITED KINGDOM
(44) (243) 779777

Jacaranda Wiley Ltd.
PRT Division
P.O. Box 174
North Ryde, NSW 2113
AUSTRALIA
(02) 805-1100
FAX (02) 805-1597

John Wiley & Sons (SEA) Pte. Ltd.
37 Jalan Pemimpin
Block B # 05-04
Union Industrial Building
SINGAPORE 2057
(65) 258-1157

About the Author

Bruce R. Hopkins is a lawyer with Powers, Pyles, Sutter & Verville, P.C., in Washington, D.C., where he specializes in the representation of nonprofit organizations. He has served as Chair of the Committee on Exempt Organizations, American Bar Association; Chair, Section of Taxation, National Association of College and University Attorneys; and President, Planned Giving Study Group of Greater Washington, D.C. He was accorded the Assistant Commissioner's (IRS) Award in 1984. He also taught a course on nonprofit organizations at The George Washington University National Law Center for 19 years. Currently, he is chairman of the annual conference, sponsored by the Georgetown University Law Center, on "Representing and Managing Tax-Exempt Organizations."

Mr. Hopkins is the series editor of Wiley's Nonprofit Law, Finance, and Management Series. In addition to *The Legal Answer Book for Nonprofit Organizations,* he is the author of *The Law of Tax-Exempt Organizations, Sixth Edition; The Law of Fund-Raising, Second Edition; The Tax Law of Charitable Giving; Charity, Advocacy, and the Law; Nonprofit Law Dictionary;* and *A Legal Guide to Starting and Managing a Nonprofit Organization, Second Edition.* He is also the co-author of *The Law of Tax-Exempt Healthcare Organizations.* In addition, he writes *The Nonprofit Counsel,* a monthly newsletter, and co-writes *Fund-Raising Regulation Report,* a bi-monthly newsletter.

Mr. Hopkins earned his J.D. and L.L.M. degrees at The George Washington University and his B.A. at the University of Michigan.

How to Use This Book

The Legal Answer Book for Nonprofit Organizations is designed for nonprofit executives, board members, fund-raising professionals, lawyers, and accountants who need quick and authoritative answers concerning the law governing nonprofit organizations. It is designed to help the reader not only better understand this law, but more importantly to show how to work with it and within its boundaries, while maintaining and enhancing a tax-exempt organization's activities and effectiveness. This book uses simple, straightforward language and avoids technical jargon when possible. This question-and-answer format offers a clear and useful guide to understanding the complex, but extremely important, area of the statutes, regulations, and other law governing tax-exempt organizations. Citations are provided as research aids for those who need to pursue particular items in greater detail.

Numbering System: The question numbering system has been designed for ease of use. The questions are numbered consecutively within each chapter (e.g., 5:1, 5:2, 5:3).

Listing of Questions: The detailed Listing of Questions that follows the Table of Contents in the front of this book helps the reader locate areas of immediate interest. This listing serves as a detailed table of contents that provides both the question number and the page on which it appears.

Index: The index at the back of this book provides a further aid to locating specific information. All references in the index are to question numbers rather than page numbers.

"I am your interface with the Celestial Library," Ramda said. "My purpose is to access information you request, then present the answer in a way that will enable your knowing."

—*The Celestial Bar*

Preface

Your author has had the pleasure of writing books for John Wiley & Sons for over seventeen years. The point of these endeavors has been to summarize and interpret the vast bodies of law that apply to nonprofit organizations and those who serve them. This book, however, is different from the others—for two reasons.

First, this book is unique in that it is the only one that was someone else's idea. It was, if you will, commissioned. The inspiration for it is the Acquisitions Editor at Wiley who manages this area, Marla J. Bobowick. She requested a book about the real-life issues that arise in my law practice. This time, she asked, don't just write about law—summarize the specific and practical advice given to clients. From the moment she started explaining what she had in mind, I knew exactly what she wanted me to do: Give away the store.

I admit to struggling with this idea for a seemingly interminable amount of time. Looking back, the problem basically was format; I was trying for a new one but could not conjure it up. I wanted this book to be nearly effortlessly useful for the nonprofit manager: a sourcebook that he or she could pick up and, through one mechanism or another, immediately find the item of advice needed.

This dilemma was gracefully resolved by my mother. One evening, during a casual chat, she asked about my writing projects. That being one of my favorite subjects, I brought her up to date on the status of them, including my ongoing trauma with the evolution of this book. Hardly missing a beat, she said, "How about using a question-and-answer approach?" After thinking about it and concluding that it was an excellent suggestion,

I broached the subject with Marla. She gave the proposal her blessing and the format problem was thereby solved.

The second reason that this book is unique is that it was not to be merely a compilation of law on a particular subject. While law summary was unavoidable, the substance of the book needed to be advice. The content and tone had to be much like that used when speaking with clients. Most of the other books may read like written advice (opinion letters); this time, it was to be as Marla asked: Share your thoughts on the nonprofit law issues of the day as if the client was on the other side of your desk.

With the objectives and format in place, the hard work (and, I admit, much fun) began. The first task was to select the subject matter for the chapters; these were distilled to the dozen areas of nonprofit law that generate the most inquiries. Within them, I listed the questions that frequently arise in the practice, coupling them with law summaries in a tone and length used in a meeting or on the telephone with clients. Once the book had crystallized to this point, a group of individuals was asked to supply questions. My "inquisitioners" included Susan Kudla Finn, Carolyn Freeland, James Greenfield, William Peyser, James Terwilliger, and D. Benson Tesdahl. Their contributions were very helpful and are very much appreciated; they, of course, are not responsible for the content of the answers. (Toward the end of the project, Tom Hyatt, one of the lawyers in my office, submitted this question: "When are you going to stop writing books about nonprofit law?" The question was rejected because it was not germane.)

During the writing, I was very sensitive to questions that frequently arose in the office. Questions and answers kept being added and re-ordered down to the last minute.

While lawyers are welcome to purchase and utilize this book, it was written for the nonlawyer. Thus, in addition to some law summary, there is much in the way of general explanation of how things legal in import ought to be done. As to some topics, there is no "law" as such. Your author has been in practice in this branch of the law for over 25 years; a considerable portion of what is in the book is reflective of responses to the same questions that arise year in and year out. Some perspectives and commentary have been included.

The end product has real value only if those who need it can use it to promptly resolve a problem or answer a question before them. To facilitate its usefulness, all of the questions answered in the book are listed at the beginning. There is also an index. Endnotes have been kept to the minimum. (For more, see "How to Use This Book" on p. vii.) Those who need additional information on a matter can turn to one or more of the books in Wiley's Nonprofit Law, Finance, and Management Series.

We are going to do this again. Questions and answers for another dozen subjects are being developed for publication in a second volume. (Send in your questions.) Periodically, each book will be revised, to take account of reactions to it, new questions raised, and changes in the law.

With this book, I have two hopes. One (that is earnestly shared with the other lawyers in the firm) is that clients will continue to call. The other is that managers of nonprofit organizations and others will use it to readily find answers to the basic questions they have.

Writing about the law is not always entertaining; there can be considerable tedium experienced while making one's way through statutes, regulations, and court opinions. This time, the experience was much different: there was much enjoyment in grappling with the questions and formulating responses that are intended to sound "just like being in the office."

Thanks, Marla.

Thanks, as well, to the others who helped in the production of the book, particularly Mary Daniello at Wiley, and Nancy Marcus Land and Maryan Malone at Publications Development Company.

BRUCE R. HOPKINS

Washington, DC
December 1995

Contents

List of Questions   xv

Chapter 1   General Operations of a Nonprofit Organization   1

Chapter 2   Boards of Directors and Conflicts and Liability   27

Chapter 3   Private Inurement and Private Benefit   56

Chapter 4   Lobbying   74

Chapter 5   Political Activities   92

Chapter 6   Public Charity Status   107

Chapter 7   Fund-Raising Regulation   132

Chapter 8   Planned Giving   162

Chapter 9   Fund-Raisers' Inquiries   186

Chapter 10   Unrelated Business Activities   203

Chapter 11   Subsidiaries   224

Chapter 12   IRS Audits of Nonprofit Organizations   241

Endnotes   264

Index   280

List of Questions

CHAPTER 1   General Operations of a Nonprofit Organization

Overview

Q 1:1	What is a nonprofit organization?	2
Q 1:2	Who owns a nonprofit organization?	3
Q 1:3	Who controls a nonprofit organization?	3
Q 1:4	Sometimes the term not-for-profit organization is used instead of nonprofit organization. Are the terms synonymous?	4
Q 1:5	How is a nonprofit organization started?	4
Q 1:6	How does a nonprofit organization incorporate?	5
Q 1:7	Who are the incorporators?	5
Q 1:8	Can the same individuals be the directors, officers, and incorporators?	6
Q 1:9	What about the registered agent?	6
Q 1:10	What does the registered agent do?	6
Q 1:11	Does the registered agent have any liability for the corporation's affairs?	6
Q 1:12	Can the same individual be a director, officer, incorporator, and registered agent?	6
Q 1:13	How does a nonprofit organization decide the state in which to be formed?	7
Q 1:14	How does a nonprofit organization qualify to do business in another state?	7

Q 1:15 What is the legal standard by which a nonprofit
organization should be operated?   8

Q 1:16 What is the standard for an organization that is
tax-exempt and charitable?   8

Q 1:17 What is the rationale for this standard for charities?   8

Q 1:18 What does the term fiduciary mean?   8

Q 1:19 What is the standard underlying fiduciary responsibility?   9

Q 1:20 What is the meaning of the term reasonable?   9

Q 1:21 Who are the fiduciaries of a charitable organization?   9

Q 1:22 What happens as the nonprofit organization grows, achieves
a higher profile, and needs to add individuals to the board?
How do those who created the entity retain control of the
organization? After all their hard work, they definitely don't
want some group to run off with the organization.   10

Q 1:23 Can the founding board have it both ways? Can it retain
control of the organization and, at the same time, have
an expanded and more professional governing board?   10

Q 1:24 What are the rules regarding the development
of chapters?   11

Q 1:25 Do chapters have to be incorporated?   12

Q 1:26 What is the role of a lawyer who represents one or
more nonprofit organizations?   12

Q 1:27 How should the lawyer representing a nonprofit
organization be compensated?   13

Tax Exemption

Q 1:28 Are all nonprofit organizations tax-exempt organizations? 14

Q 1:29 Are all tax-exempt organizations nonprofit organizations? 14

Q 1:30 Concerning tax exemption, what taxes are involved?   14

Q 1:31 How does an organization become tax-exempt?   15

Q 1:32 Are there any exemptions from the recognition requirement? 16

Q 1:33 How does an organization remain tax-exempt?   16

Q 1:34 When might an organization's tax exemption be revoked?   17

Q 1:35 If an organization loses its tax-exempt status, can it
reacquire it?   17

Q 1:36 Are tax-exempt organizations completely immune
from taxation?   18

Q 1:37 In view of the massive amount of government regulation of
nonprofit organizations, why don't they forfeit tax-exempt
status and be treated for tax purposes the same as
for-profit organizations?   18

Q 1:38 What are the basic considerations to take into account in deciding whether an organization should be exempt as a charitable organization or a social welfare organization?   19

Q 1:39 What are the basic considerations to take into account in deciding whether an organization should be exempt as a charitable entity or a business league?   20

Q 1:40 When should a tax-exempt organization consider the establishment of a related foundation?   20

Charitable Giving

Q 1:41 Are all tax-exempt organizations eligible to receive tax-deductible contributions?   21

Q 1:42 What are the rules for deductibility of contributions of money?   22

Q 1:43 What are the rules for deductibility of contributions of property?   23

Q 1:44 What is planned giving?   26

CHAPTER 2 Boards of Directors and Conflicts and Liability

Overview

Q 2:1 What is the origin of a board of directors of a nonprofit organization?   28

Q 2:2 What are the rules concerning the composition of the board of directors?   29

Q 2:3 How does a charitable organization know whether its board of directors is lawfully constituted?   30

Q 2:4 What is the function of the board of directors?   30

Q 2:5 Must the board of directors of a charitable organization be representative of the community?   31

Q 2:6 Can the organization's board be only family members?   31

Q 2:7 Can the family-member directors also be the officers of the nonprofit organization?   32

Q 2:8 In any instance, can the same individual be both a director and an officer?   32

Q 2:9 What is the function of the officers?   32

Q 2:10 Can the same individual hold more than one officer position?   33

Q 2:11 What are the methods by which a board of directors of a nonprofit organization can vote?   34

Q 2:12 Can members of the board of directors of a nonprofit organization vote by proxy? 34

Q 2:13 What material should be in the minutes of meetings of boards of directors of nonprofit organizations? 35

Q 2:14 Is it a concern as a matter of law whether directors are termed trustees? 35

Expenditures of Funds

Q 2:15 How do these rules apply to the expenditures of funds? 36

Q 2:16 What is expected in terms of program expenditures? 36

Q 2:17 What are the rules pertaining to employee compensation? 37

Q 2:18 The management of a charitable organization wants to redecorate the offices of the organization and purchase new furniture. How much money can it spend and how "fancy" can it be? 38

Q 2:19 Does this standard of fiduciary responsibility apply to every expense incurred by a charitable organization? 40

Q 2:20 What are the rules for charitable organizations concerning travel by board members, officers, and employees? 40

Q 2:21 What about spouse travel? 41

Q 2:22 What about the use of hotels? 41

Q 2:23 What about the expenses of meals? 42

Q 2:24 Can a board member borrow money from a charitable organization? 42

Q 2:25 Can a charitable organization purchase or rent property from a board member? 43

Q 2:26 Besides expenses, what else should a charitable organization be concerned about? 43

Self-Dealing and Conflicts of Interest

Q 2:27 What is self-dealing? 45

Q 2:28 Is self-dealing the same as a conflict of interest? 45

Q 2:29 What is the source for a requirement that board members disclose (in writing) any possible conflict of interest they might have with the nonprofit organization they serve? 46

Q 2:30 What language should be contained in a conflict of interest statement? 46

Q 2:31 Is a conflict of interest policy legally binding on the individuals covered by it and/or the nonprofit organization? 47

Q 2:32   How does an individual know when a conflict of interest
is present?   47

Q 2:33   What are the obligations of a board member or officer
when a conflict of interest is disclosed?   48

Q 2:34   How should a nonprofit organization respond to
disclosure of a conflict of interest?   48

Q 2:35   What are the penalties when a conflict of interest
is breached?   48

Q 2:36   Can a nonprofit organization receive contributions
from a corporation or foundation where a board
member has a conflict of interest?   49

Q 2:37   Can a nonprofit organization negotiate for discounted
prices for goods or services to be purchased from a
source where a board member or officer has disclosed
a conflict of interest?   49

Q 2:38   Are there guidelines on or limitations to the extent or
nature of the discount value or percent of purchased
goods or services?   50

Exposure of the Board to Liability

Q 2:39   What happens if the board of directors of a nonprofit
organization makes a mistake?   50

Q 2:40   How likely is it that a member of the board of directors
of a nonprofit organization will be found personally liable
for something done or not done while serving the
organization?   51

Q 2:41   How can a nonprofit organization provide some protection
for its board against the likelihood of personal liability for
the result of something they did or did not do while serving
the organization?   52

Q 2:42   Does a nonprofit organization really have to indemnify its
officers and directors and purchase liability insurance?
Can't they just be certain their acts are always in good faith?   54

CHAPTER 3   Private Inurement and Private Benefit

Overview

Q 3:1   What is private inurement?   57
Q 3:2   When is a person an insider?   58
Q 3:3   What types of tax-exempt organizations are expressly
subject to the private inurement rule?   59

Q 3:4   What is private benefit?   60

Q 3:5   What is the difference between private inurement and
             private benefit?   60

Q 3:6   What happens when a nonprofit organization engages in
             either practice?   60

Private Inurement

Q 3:7   What are the principal types of transactions that
             constitute private inurement?   61

Q 3:8   When is compensation private inurement?   61

Q 3:9   Is payment of a bonus to an employee of a nonprofit
             organization legal?   63

Q 3:10   How should a bonus compensation program for
             employees be defined?   63

Q 3:11   What role should the board of directors play in the
             annual review and approval of bonus awards to employees?   65

Q 3:12   How is the bonus compensation program reported to the
             IRS and disclosed to the public?   65

Q 3:13   Are the seven factors mentioned above the only elements
             to take into account in determining the reasonableness
             of compensation?   65

Q 3:14   How will intermediate sanctions work?   66

Q 3:15   When is a loan private inurement?   68

Q 3:16   When is a rental arrangement private inurement?   69

Q 3:17   Are there other forms of private inurement?   69

Private Benefit

Q 3:18   How is private benefit determined in actual practice?   71

Q 3:19   What is primary private benefit?   71

Q 3:20   What is secondary private benefit?   71

Q 3:21   Is it possible for a donor, when making a gift to a nonprofit
             organization, to realize a private benefit from the gift?   72

Q 3:22   How is incidental private benefit measured?   73

CHAPTER 4   Lobbying

Overview

Q 4:1   What is lobbying?   75

Q 4:2   What is legislation?   76

Q 4:3 Is lobbying a necessary or appropriate activity for a nonprofit organization? 76

Q 4:4 What are the federal tax rules concerning lobbying that are unique to tax-exempt organizations? 76

Q 4:5 How do charitable organizations measure substantiality? 77

Q 4:6 Is there more than one form of lobbying? 77

Q 4:7 What are the various ways by which lobbying can be accomplished? 78

Q 4:8 Are there laws concerning lobbying by nonprofit organizations, other than the federal tax rules? 78

Charities and the Substantial Part Test

Q 4:9 What is the substantial part test? 79

Q 4:10 Can private foundations lobby to the extent of the substantial part test? 79

Q 4:11 Are there exceptions to the prohibition on lobbying under the substantial part test? 80

Q 4:12 What happens when the organization engages in substantial lobbying? 80

Q 4:13 Can a charitable organization that loses its tax exemption because of excessive lobbying convert to another type of tax-exempt organization? 80

Q 4:14 What planning can a charitable organization under the substantial part test engage in to avoid adverse tax consequences because of lobbying? 81

Charities and the Expenditure Test

Q 4:15 What is the expenditure test? 81

Q 4:16 How does this test become applicable to an organization? 82

Q 4:17 Are there exceptions to the term lobbying under this test? 82

Q 4:18 What happens when the organization engages in "too much" lobbying? 83

Q 4:19 Can the charitable organization convert to another type of tax-exempt organization? 83

Q 4:20 What types of lobbying programs are most suitable for the expenditure test? 83

Q 4:21 When should a charitable organization elect the expenditure test? 84

Q 4:22 Under what circumstances would an organization elect to revoke its election to be under the expenditure test? 85

Q 4:23 What planning can a charitable organization under the expenditure test engage in to avoid adverse tax consequences because of lobbying? 85

Social Welfare Organizations

Q 4:24 Are there any restrictions on lobbying by tax-exempt social welfare organizations? 86

Q 4:25 Why don't all lobbying charities convert to social welfare organizations? 86

Q 4:26 How can a public charity utilize a tax-exempt lobbying subsidiary? 87

Trade, Business, and Professional Associations

Q 4:27 Are there any restrictions on lobbying by tax-exempt trade and other associations? 87

Q 4:28 How does the member know how to calculate the dues deduction? 88

Q 4:29 What happens if the association makes an error in the calculation of the dues deduction ratio? 88

Q 4:30 Are there any exceptions to these rules? 89

Q 4:31 Is the concept of lobbying the same as it is for public charities? 89

Veterans' Organizations

Q 4:32 Are there any restrictions on lobbying by tax-exempt veterans' organizations? 90

Q 4:33 Aren't the tax rules for veterans' organizations unfair in relation to those for charitable organizations? 90

Reporting Requirements

Q 4:34 Are any reporting requirements imposed on tax-exempt organizations that lobby? 90

Q 4:35 What are the reporting requirements under the substantial part test? 91

Q 4:36 What are the reporting requirements under the expenditure test? 91

CHAPTER 5   Political Activities

Overview

Q 5:1 What are political activities? 93

Q 5:2 What are the rules, for tax-exempt organizations, concerning political activities? 93

Q 5:3 What do participation and intervention mean? 94

Q 5:4 Can a charitable organization educate the public about candidates and issues in the setting of a political campaign? 95

Q 5:5 Does the law differentiate between the political positions of organizations and those of individuals associated with them? 96

Q 5:6 When is an individual a candidate? 97

Q 5:7 When does a campaign begin? 97

Q 5:8 What is a public office? 98

Charities and Political Activities

Q 5:9 Is there a substantiality test for charitable organizations concerning political activities? 98

Q 5:10 What happens when a public charity engages in a political campaign activity? 99

Q 5:11 Do these rules apply to churches and other religious organizations? 100

Q 5:12 Are these rules enforced against religious organizations? 100

Q 5:13 Is the prohibition against political campaigning by religious organizations constitutional? 100

Q 5:14 What happens when a private foundation engages in a political campaign activity? 101

Q 5:15 Can a charitable organization utilize a political action committee without adversely affecting its tax exemption? 101

Other Exempt Organizations and Political Activities

Q 5:16 What is a political organization? 102

Q 5:17 Aren't political action committees affiliated with other tax-exempt organizations? 103

Q 5:18 Is the tax imposed on political organizations confined to those organizations? 103

Q 5:19 What are the rules concerning political activities by social welfare organizations? 103

Q 5:20 What are the rules concerning political activities by trade and business associations? 104

Q 5:21 To what extent can exempt organizations other than charities utilize political action committees? 104

Q 5:22 What do the terms hard money and soft money signify? 105

Q 5:23 How do the federal election laws interrelate with the federal tax laws? 105

Reporting Requirements

Q 5:24 What are the reporting requirements for
charitable organizations?   106

Q 5:25 What are the reporting requirements for other
tax-exempt organizations?   106

CHAPTER 6 Public Charity Status

Overview

Q 6:1   What is a public charity?   107
Q 6:2   What is a private foundation?   108
Q 6:3   What are the categories of public charities?   108
Q 6:4   How does an organization acquire public
charity status?   109
Q 6:5   How does an organization maintain its public
charity status?   109
Q 6:6   Why is it so important to be classified as a public
charity and avoid private foundation status?   109

Publicly Supported Charities

Q 6:7   What is a donative publicly supported
charitable organization?   111
Q 6:8   What is a service provider publicly supported
charitable organization?   112
Q 6:9   What is an advance ruling?   113
Q 6:10 At the end of the advance ruling period, will the
IRS automatically request more information regarding the
organization's public support, or does the organization
need to initiate contact with the IRS?   115
Q 6:11 What is a definitive ruling?   115
Q 6:12 Does it matter which category of publicly supported
charity an organization uses?   116
Q 6:13 What happens when an organization ceases to be a
publicly supported charity?   117
Q 6:14 What should an organization do when it realizes, during
the course of its advance ruling period, that it will not
qualify as a publicly supported organization as of the
close of that period?   117

Supporting Organizations

Q 6:15 What is a supporting organization?   118

Q 6:16 What are the requisite relationships between a
        supporting organization and a supported organization?   119

Q 6:17 What are the functions of a supporting organization?   122

Q 6:18 Does the supported organization have to be identified in the
        organizational document of the supporting organization?   123

Q 6:19 How many supported organizations can a supporting
        organization support?   124

Q 6:20 Can a supporting organization support or benefit a
        charitable organization or other person, in addition to
        one or more specified supported organizations?   125

Q 6:21 Can a supporting organization support another
        supporting organization?   126

Q 6:22 Can a charitable organization be a supporting
        organization with respect to a tax-exempt organization
        that is not a charitable one?   126

Q 6:23 Are any limitations placed on the composition of the
        board of directors of a supporting organization?   127

Q 6:24 Should a supporting organization be separately incorporated?   128

Q 6:25 Should a supporting organization have bylaws?   128

Q 6:26 Who elects or appoints the directors of a supporting
        organization?   129

Q 6:27 Can a supporting organization maintain its own financial
        affairs (such as by means of a separate bank account
        and separate investments)?   129

Q 6:28 What financial reports and disclosure should a supporting
        organization make to the supported organization?   130

Q 6:29 What oversight should the supported organization perform?   131

CHAPTER 7 Fund-Raising Regulation

Overview

Q 7:1   How does the federal government regulate fund-raising for
        charitable purposes?   132

Q 7:2   How do the state governments regulate fund-raising for
        charitable purposes?   133

Q 7:3   Are these state laws constitutional?   133

Federal Law Requirements

Q 7:4 What are the IRS audit practices as applied to fund-raising charitable organizations? 134

Q 7:5 How do the charitable giving rules apply? 135

Q 7:6 What are the charitable gift substantiation requirements? 136

Q 7:7 Do these rules apply with respect to benefits provided to donors after the gifts were made, where there was no prior notification of the benefit, such as a recognition dinner? 137

Q 7:8 How do the substantiation rules apply to gifts made by means of charitable remainder trusts, charitable lead trusts, and pooled income funds? 137

Q 7:9 What are the quid pro quo contribution rules? 138

Q 7:10 What is a good faith estimate? 139

Q 7:11 Are there any exceptions to the quid pro quo contribution rules? 139

Q 7:12 How does a charitable organization value the involvement of a celebrity for purposes of the quid pro quo contribution rules? 140

Q 7:13 What are the appraisal requirements? 141

Q 7:14 What does the IRS look for with respect to new charitable organizations? 141

Q 7:15 How do the reporting rules apply? 142

Q 7:16 Do the unrelated business income rules apply in the fund-raising setting? 143

Q 7:17 Are there limitations on the use of the royalty exception in the fund-raising setting? 144

Q 7:18 Are there fund-raising disclosure requirements for noncharitable organizations? 145

Q 7:19 Are there any other federal law requirements as to fund-raising? 145

State Law Requirements

Q 7:20 What are the elements of a typical state charitable solicitation act? 147

Q 7:21 Do these laws apply to all charitable solicitations? 149

Q 7:22 How do these laws apply to professional fund-raisers? 150

Q 7:23 How do these laws apply to professional solicitors? 150

Q 7:24 Do these laws place limitations on the fees paid to professional solicitors? 152

Q 7:25 What is a charitable sales promotion and how do the state laws apply to it? 152

Q 7:26 What is the significance of the portions of these laws concerning prohibited acts? 153

Q 7:27 Are there any exceptions to these laws? 154

Q 7:28 What provisions are generally required in a contract between a charitable organization and a professional fund-raiser or professional solicitor? 155

Q 7:29 When does a charitable organization have to comply with one of these laws? 155

Q 7:30 When does a professional fund-raiser or a professional solicitor have to comply with one of these laws? 156

Q 7:31 When does a charitable organization have to comply with more than one of these laws? 156

Q 7:32 Are solicitations of merely a few individuals subject to these state laws? 157

Q 7:33 When does a professional fund-raiser or professional solicitor have to comply with more than one of these laws? 157

Q 7:34 What happens when a charitable organization, professional fund-raiser, or professional solicitor violates one of these laws? 157

Q 7:35 What is the rationale for these state laws? 158

Q 7:36 Are these state laws effective? 159

Q 7:37 To be in compliance with these laws, what type of management system should a charitable organization have? 159

Q 7:38 How does state law regulation interrelate with the oversight activities of the watch-dog agencies? 161

CHAPTER 8   Planned Giving

Overview

Q 8:1 What is planned giving? 162

Q 8:2 What are remainder interests and income interests? 164

Q 8:3 How are these interests created? 164

Q 8:4 What are the tax advantages for a charitable gift of a remainder interest? 165

Q 8:5 It was said that the trust generally is tax-exempt. Why the qualification? 165

Q 8:6 What is a charitable remainder trust? 166

Q 8:7   What is a pooled income fund?   168

Q 8:8   What is a charitable lead trust?   170

Q 8:9   What is a charitable gift annuity?   170

Q 8:10   What about gifts of life insurance?   172

Q 8:11   Are there other ways to make deductible gifts of remainder interests?   173

Charitable Remainder Trusts

Q 8:12   What types of charitable organizations can be remainder interest beneficiaries of remainder trusts?   173

Q 8:13   How does the makeup feature work?   173

Q 8:14   What types of property are suitable for charitable remainder trusts?   174

Q 8:15   What happens if the donated property is encumbered with debt?   175

Q 8:16   What happens when an option is transferred to a charitable remainder trust?   175

Q 8:17   What happens when an item of tangible personal property is transferred to a charitable remainder trust?   176

Q 8:18   Can there be adverse consequences where the income payment term is very short?   177

Q 8:19   Who can be a donor to a charitable remainder trust?   178

Q 8:20   Who can be a trustee of a charitable remainder trust?   178

Q 8:21   When should a charitable remainder trust be used rather than another planned giving technique?   179

Q 8:22   What are the disadvantages of using a charitable remainder trust in relation to other planned giving techniques?   179

Pooled Income Funds

Q 8:23   What types of charities can be remainder interest beneficiaries of pooled income funds?   180

Q 8:24   What types of property are suitable for pooled income funds?   180

Q 8:25   How is the rate of return calculated for a new pooled income fund?   181

Q 8:26   Who can be a donor to a pooled income fund?   181

Q 8:27   Who can be a trustee of a pooled income fund?   182

Q 8:28   What happens when a charitable organization that has a pooled income fund ceases to qualify as a type of public charity that can maintain a pooled income fund?   182

Q 8:29   When should a pooled income fund be used rather than
          another planned giving technique?   182
Q 8:30   What are the disadvantages of using a pooled income
          fund in relation to other planned giving techniques?   183

Starting a Program

Q 8:31   How does a charitable organization start a planned
          giving program?   183

CHAPTER 9   Fund-Raisers' Inquiries

Overview

Q 9:1   Is there a charitable contribution deduction for a gift
          of services?   186
Q 9:2   Is there a charitable contribution deduction for a gift
          of the right to use materials, equipment, or facilities?   187
Q 9:3   What are the obligations of a charitable organization
          regarding a restricted gift or bequest received in a prior
          year for a program that has since been discontinued?   187
Q 9:4   How does a nonprofit organization establish the gift
          value for a contribution of securities?   188

Auctions

Q 9:5   Is an auction conducted by a charity considered one
          of the types of special events?   189
Q 9:6   Why is the revenue from a charity auction not taxed?   189
Q 9:7   Do those who donate items to an auction receive a
          federal income tax charitable contribution deduction
          for the gift?   190
Q 9:8   Does an individual who acquires an item at a charity
          auction receive a charitable contribution deduction as
          a result of the transaction?   191
Q 9:9   How do the charitable gift substantiation rules apply
          in the auction setting?   193
Q 9:10   How do the quid pro quo rules apply in the auction setting?   193
Q 9:11   Does the sales tax apply to purchases made at an auction?   194
Q 9:12   How are the proceeds of a charity auction reported
          to the IRS?   194

Volunteers

Q 9:13   Should volunteers be included in the directors' and
          officers' liability insurance coverage?   195

Q 9:14 What is the law regarding the conduct of volunteers representing nonprofit organizations? 195

Q 9:15 Can a volunteer sign a contract for services on behalf of a nonprofit organization? 196

Q 9:16 Are there any requirements or guidelines on length of service for volunteers serving as board members? 196

Other Matters

Q 9:17 What role should the professional fund-raiser have in connection with the charity's annual information return? 197

Q 9:18 How does a fund-raising charitable organization go about selecting a lawyer? 198

Q 9:19 How will some of the recent scandals involving public charities affect fund-raising? 199

Q 9:20 What can the professional fund-raising community do to curb the increasing amount of government regulation? 201

CHAPTER 10 Unrelated Business Activities

Overview

Q 10:1 A tax-exempt organization often needs more money than it can generate through gifts, grants, and dues. Management of the organization is thinking about raising money by charging fees for some products or services, but it is concerned about taxation. Where does it begin? 203

Q 10:2 How does an organization measure what is primary? 204

Q 10:3 How does an exempt organization know whether an activity is a related one or an unrelated one? 205

Q 10:4 What is the rationale underlying the unrelated income rules? 205

Q 10:5 Are these claims of unfair competition leading to anything, such as law changes? 206

Q 10:6 What is the trade or business requirement? 207

Q 10:7 Does this mean that the law considers the programs of exempt organizations as businesses? 207

Q 10:8 When the federal tax law regards an exempt organization as a composite of businesses, isn't that different from how nonprofit organizations see themselves? 208

Q 10:9 Why would a tax-exempt organization object to that additional element of the definition, concerning a profit motive? Wouldn't that rule always favor exempt

organization, causing some activities to not be
businesses in the first instance? 208

Q 10:10 What are some of the other elements being engrafted
onto this definition? 209

Q 10:11 What is a commercial activity? 209

Q 10:12 What are the statutory and regulatory references to the
commerciality doctrine? 210

Q 10:13 What are the rules as to whether a business activity is
regularly carried on? 210

Q 10:14 How is regularity measured? 211

Q 10:15 Are there any other aspects of this level of analysis? 211

Q 10:16 What are the other two aspects of regularity? 211

Q 10:17 Do some operations get converted into regular ones by
using that approach? 212

Q 10:18 What about the third level of analysis, concerning the
substantially related requirement? 212

Q 10:19 How is relatedness determined? 213

Q 10:20 What are some examples of these judgments? 213

Q 10:21 Are there any other aspects of the substantially related test? 214

Q 10:22 How is the unrelated business income tax calculated? 216

Exceptions

Q 10:23 What types of activities are exempt from unrelated income
taxation? 217

Q 10:24 What types of income are exempt from unrelated
income taxation? 218

Q 10:25 How can the royalty exclusion be most effectively utilized? 220

Q 10:26 Are there any exceptions to the rules stating these exclusions? 220

Q 10:27 Are there any exceptions to these exceptions? 221

Specific Applications

Q 10:28 What are the contemporary unrelated business issues
for hospitals and other health care providers? 222

Q 10:29 What are the contemporary unrelated business issues
for colleges and universities? 222

Q 10:30 What are the contemporary unrelated business issues
for museums? 222

Q 10:31 What are the contemporary unrelated business issues
for trade, business, and professional associations? 222

Q 10:32 How do the unrelated business rules apply in the
context of charitable fund-raising?   223

Q 10:33 How is the unrelated income tax reported?   223

CHAPTER 11 Subsidiaries

Overview

Q 11:1 What is a subsidiary in the nonprofit law context?   225

Q 11:2 Why would a tax-exempt organization establish a subsidiary?   225

Q 11:3 How does a nonprofit organization control a subsidiary?   225

Q 11:4 What body can act as the incorporator or corporate
member to establish a subsidiary?   227

Q 11:5 Is there a minimum number of board members required
for a subsidiary?   227

Q 11:6 What legal requirements should be followed in maintaining
the parent–subsidiary relationship?   227

Q 11:7 What are the powers and oversight requirements of the
parent organization?   228

Q 11:8 How is revenue from a for-profit subsidiary taxed?   228

Q 11:9 What are the tax consequences of liquidation of a
subsidiary into its parent organization?   229

Q 11:10 What are the federal tax reporting requirements with
respect to subsidiaries?   230

Q 11:11 What are the state law reporting requirements with
respect to subsidiaries?   231

Tax-Exempt Subsidiaries

Q 11:12 Why would a tax-exempt organization establish a
tax-exempt subsidiary?   232

Q 11:13 What are some of the common uses of tax-exempt
subsidiaries?   232

Q 11:14 Is it necessary for a tax-exempt subsidiary to obtain
separate recognition of tax-exempt status?   233

Q 11:15 Should the tax-exempt status of the subsidiary be as a
charitable entity or as a supporting organization?   234

Q 11:16 What are the reporting requirements between the parent
and subsidiary organizations?   234

Q 11:17 If a tax-exempt subsidiary can raise money in its own
name, what disclosure requirements should it observe
with respect to the parent organization?   234

Q 11:18 What formal action is required to transfer funds between a tax-exempt parent and a tax-exempt subsidiary?   235

Q 11:19 Can a tax-exempt subsidiary raise funds for an endowment and hold these funds separate from the parent?   235

For-Profit Subsidiaries

Q 11:20 Why would a tax-exempt organization establish a for-profit subsidiary?   236

Q 11:21 What are some of the common uses of for-profit subsidiaries?   237

Q 11:22 Are there limits on the use of tax-exempt assets to capitalize a for-profit subsidiary?   239

Q 11:23 Can a supporting organization have a for-profit subsidiary?   239

Q 11:24 Can a private foundation have a for-profit subsidiary?   240

CHAPTER 12   IRS Audits of Nonprofit Organizations

Overview

Q 12:1 How is the IRS organized from the standpoint of its audit function?   241

Q 12:2 Where does the IRS derive its audit authority?   242

Q 12:3 What issues are addressed in an exempt organization's audit?   243

Q 12:4 How is an IRS audit initiated?   243

Q 12:5 Why is an IRS audit initiated?   243

Q 12:6 What items of a tax-exempt organization will the IRS review on audit?   244

Q 12:7 Are there different types of IRS audits?   245

Q 12:8 How does the IRS determine whether to use the coordinated examination procedure?   246

Q 12:9 How does an exempt organization cope with IRS personnel during an audit?   246

Q 12:10 What does the IRS do after the audit has been completed?   246

Q 12:11 What is the likelihood that a tax-exempt organization will be audited by the IRS?   247

IRS Audits of Health Care Organizations

Q 12:12 What is the IRS audit program for hospitals and other health care organizations?   247

Q 12:13 What is the focus of the IRS concerning the tax-exempt status of nonprofit hospitals? 248

Q 12:14 What is the emphasis by the IRS in this area on private inurement and private benefit? 249

Q 12:15 What is the interest of the IRS in this area with respect to joint ventures? 251

Q 12:16 How do the private inurement rules interrelate with the federal antikickback laws? 251

Q 12:17 What types of financial analyses is the IRS likely to make in these audits? 253

Q 12:18 What are the rules for analyzing a hospital's balance sheet? 254

Q 12:19 Are there any special rules for hospitals in connection with package audits? 255

Q 12:20 What unrelated business income issues involving health care institutions arise on audit? 257

Q 12:21 How is the IRS using closing agreements in the health care context? 257

Colleges and Universities

Q 12:22 What is the focus of the IRS as to the tax-exempt status of colleges and universities? 259

Q 12:23 How does the IRS approach an audit of a college or university? 259

Q 12:24 What internal items of a college or university will the auditing agent review? 260

Q 12:25 What other information is the agent likely to evaluate? 260

Q 12:26 What issues are likely to be reviewed during this type of audit? 261

Q 12:27 Do the rules pertaining to lobbying and political campaign activity get reviewed in these audits? 262

Q 12:28 What unrelated business income issues involving colleges and universities arise on audit? 262

Q 12:29 What other issues can arise in these audits? 263

CHAPTER 1

General Operations of a Nonprofit Organization

A lawyer representing nonprofit organizations faces, on a daily basis, a barrage of questions about the rules governing the organizations' formation, administration, operation, and management. Some of these questions may be answered using state law rules, some with federal law rules. More frequently than nonlawyers might suspect, there is no law on the particular point.

These questions may require answers from an accountant, a fundraiser, an appraiser, or a management consultant, rather than a lawyer. For example, a lawyer is not professionally competent to answer these questions: "How much can I be paid?" or "How much is this gift property worth?" Even regarding matters that are within the lawyer's province, however—legal standards—the law is often very vague. Much of the applicable law is at the state level, so there can be varied answers to questions. Yet, federal law on the subject is building.

Here are the questions most frequently asked by clients about general operations of a nonprofit organization, the matter of fiduciary responsibility, acquiring and maintaining tax-exempt status, and the basics of deductible charitable giving—and the answers to them.

OVERVIEW

Q 1:1   What is a nonprofit organization?

The term *nonprofit* organization is a misleading term; regrettably, the English language lacks a better one. It does *not* mean that the organization cannot earn a profit. Many nonprofit organizations are enjoying profits. An entity of any type cannot long exist without revenues that at least equal expenses.

The easiest way to define a nonprofit organization is to first define its counterpart, the *for-profit organization.* A for-profit organization exists to operate a business and to generate profits (revenue in excess of costs) from that business for those who own the enterprise. As an example, the owners of a for-profit corporation are stockholders, who take their profits in the form of dividends. Thus, when the term for-profit is used, it refers to profits acquired by the owners of the business, not by the business itself. The law, therefore, differentiates between profits at the *entity level* and profits at the *ownership level.*

Both for-profit and nonprofit organizations are allowed by the law to earn profits at the entity level. But, only for-profit organizations are permitted profits at the ownership level. Nonprofit organizations rarely have owners; these organizations are not permitted to pass along profits (net earnings) to those who control them.

Profits permitted to for-profit entities but not nonprofit entities are forms of *private inurement* (see Chapter 3). That is, private inurement refers to ways of transferring an organization's net earnings to persons in their private capacity. The purpose of a for-profit organization is to engage in private inurement. By contrast, nonprofit organizations may not engage in acts of private inurement. (Economists call this fundamental standard the *nondistribution constraint.*) Nonprofit organizations are required to use their profits for their program activities. In the case of tax-exempt nonprofit organizations, these activities are termed their *exempt functions.*

NOTE: The prohibition on private inurement does not mean that a nonprofit organization cannot pay compensation to its employees and others. The law does require, however, that these payments be reasonable.

Consequently, the doctrine of private inurement is the essential dividing line, in the law, between nonprofit and for-profit organizations.[1]

Q 1:2   Who owns a nonprofit organization?

For the most part, a nonprofit organization does not have owners who would be comparable to stockholders of a for-profit corporation or general partners in a partnership. There are some exceptions: a few states allow nonprofit corporations to be established with the authority to issue stock.

NOTE: This type of stock does not pay dividends, because that would contravene the prohibition on private inurement (see Q 1:1). However, the stock can be transferred to others, by sale, gift, or otherwise.

Stock in a nonprofit organization is used solely for purposes of ownership. Any "person" (an individual, a business entity, or another nonprofit organization) can be a shareholder under this arrangement.

TIP: When a nonprofit organization is being established and those forming it want to ensure their control of it, irrespective of the composition of the board of directors, setting up a stock-based nonprofit organization often is the answer (see Q 1:23).

Q 1:3   Who controls a nonprofit organization?

It depends on the nature of the organization. Usually, control of a nonprofit organization is vested in its governing body, frequently termed a board of directors or board of trustees. Actual control may lie elsewhere—with the officers or key employees, for example. It is unlikely that control of a large membership organization would be with the membership, because that element of power is too dissipated. In a small membership entity, such as a coalition, control may well be with the membership.

Q 1:4   Sometimes the term not-for-profit organization is used instead of nonprofit organization. Are the terms synonymous?

As a matter of law, no. People use the two terms interchangeably in good faith, but the proper legal term is *nonprofit* organization.

The law uses the term *not-for-profit* to apply to an activity rather than to an entity. For example, the federal tax law denies business expense deductions for expenditures that are for a not-for-profit activity.[2] Basically, this type of activity is not engaged in with a business or commercial motive; a not-for-profit activity is essentially a hobby.

The term not-for-profit is often applied in the nonprofit context by those who do not understand or appreciate the difference between profit at the entity level and profit at the ownership level (see Q 1:1).

Q 1:5   How is a nonprofit organization started?

Nearly every nonprofit organization is a creature of state law (or District of Columbia law). (A few nonprofit organizations are chartered under a federal statute.) Thus, a nonprofit organization is started by creating it under the law of a state.

There are only three types of nonprofit organizations: (1) corporations, (2) unincorporated associations, and (3) trusts. The document by which a nonprofit organization is formed is generally known as its *articles of organization.* For a corporation, the articles are called articles of incorporation. For an unincorporated association, the articles are in the form of a constitution. The articles of a trust are called a trust agreement or a declaration of trust.

Most nonprofit organizations also have a set of *bylaws*—the rules by which they are operated. Some organizations have additional rules: codes of ethics, manuals of operation, employee handbooks, and the like.

A nonprofit organization formed as a corporation commences its existence by filing articles of incorporation with the appropriate state. Some states require the filing of trust documents. It is rare for a state to require the filing of a constitution or a set of bylaws as part of the process of forming the organization. (Bylaws and similar documents may have to be filed under other state laws, however.)

NOTE: These observations pertain to the filing of the document as part of the process of creating the nonprofit organization. An entity that is soliciting contributions is likely to have to file its articles of organization and bylaws in every state in which it is fund-raising, as part of the solicitation registration requirements (see Chapter 7).

Following the creation (and, if necessary, the filing) of the articles of organization, the newly formed entity should have an organizational meeting of the initial board of directors. At that meeting, the directors will adopt a set of bylaws, elect the officers, pass a resolution to open a bank account, and attend to whatever other initial business there may be.[3]

Q 1:6   How does a nonprofit organization incorporate?

The state usually has a form set of articles of incorporation. A lawyer who knows something about nonprofit organizations can prepare this document or the incorporators can do it themselves. They need to agree on the organization's name, state the corporate purposes, list the names and addresses of the directors, name a registered agent, and include the names and addresses of the incorporators. The incorporators are the individuals who sign the articles.

TIP: This is not entirely a matter of state law. What is in or not in a set of articles of organization (Q 1:5) can be determinative of whether the organization is able to become tax-exempt under federal law. The two most important elements are the statement of the organization's purpose and, in the case of charitable entities, the inclusion of a clause preserving income and assets for charitable purposes.

Q 1:7   Who are the incorporators?

Under the typical legal requirement around the country, anyone who is 18 years of age and a U.S. citizen can incorporate a nonprofit corporation. Each state's law should be confirmed on the point, however. The initial board members can be the incorporators. Many states require three incorporators.

Some groups are very sensitive to the matter of who is listed as an incorporator. They see the articles of organization as being of great significance to the organization—a document to be preserved and trea-sured for posterity (like the U.S. Constitution). Others prefer to let the lawyers working on the case be the incorporators. No particular legal sig-nificance is attached to service as an incorporator.

Q 1:8   Can the same individuals be the directors, officers, and incor-porators?

Generally, yes. Again, the law of the appropriate state should be reviewed.

Q 1:9   What about the registered agent?

Typically, the registered agent must be either an individual who is a res-ident of the state or a company that is licensed by the state to be a com-mercial registered agent.

Q 1:10   What does the registered agent do?

The registered agent functions as the corporation's point of communica-tion to the outside world. Any formal communication for the corporation as a whole is sent to the registered agent. Thus, if the state authorities want to communicate with the corporation, they do so by contacting the agent. If someone wants to sue the corporation, the agent is served with the papers.

Q 1:11   Does the registered agent have any liability for the corpora-tion's affairs?

No. The registered agent, as such, is not a director or officer of the cor-poration. Thus, the agent has no exposure to liability for the corpora-tion's activities. The agent would be held liable for his or her own offenses, such as breach of contract.

Q 1:12   Can the same individual be a director, officer, incorporator, and registered agent?

Yes, unless state law expressly forbids such a multirole status, which is unlikely. The registered agent—if an individual—must be a resident of the state in which the entity is functioning (Q 1:9), but the requirement of residency is not applicable to the other roles.

Q 1:13   How does a nonprofit organization decide the state in which to be formed?

Generally, a nonprofit organization is formed in the state in which it is to be headquartered. Most frequently, this is the state in which those who are forming the entity and who will be operating it are residents and/or maintain their offices. An organization can be formed in only one state at a time.

Occasionally, however, another state's law contains attributes that are desirable for those who are forming a nonprofit organization. For example, only a few states permit the creation of a nonprofit corporation that can issue stock. An organization seeking this feature can be formed in one of those states and then qualified to conduct its activities in the state where its principal operations will be (see Q 1:23).

TIP: A nonprofit organization (particularly a nonprofit corporation) must be qualified to *do business* in every state in which it has an operational presence. In some states, for purposes of this qualification, the solicitation of gifts (irrespective of the means) is considered doing business.

An entity that is formed in one state (the domestic state) and is doing business in another state (the foreign state) is regarded, by the latter state, as a *foreign* organization.

Q 1:14   How does a nonprofit organization qualify to do business in another state?

A nonprofit organization qualifies to do business in another state by filing for a *certificate of authority* to do business in the state. The process of obtaining this certificate is much like incorporating in a state. Also, the entity is required to have a *registered agent* in each state in which it is certified to do business (as well as in the domestic state).

TIP: The law of each state should be checked to see what persons qualify to be registered agents (Q 1:9). An organization that is doing business in several states may find it more efficient to retain the services of a commercial firm licensed to function as a registered agent in all of the states.

Q 1:15   What is the legal standard by which a nonprofit organization should be operated?

It depends on the type of organization. If the nonprofit organization is not tax-exempt, the standard is nearly the same as that for a for-profit entity. If the nonprofit organization is tax-exempt, but is not a charitable organization, the standard is higher. The legal standard is highest for a tax-exempt charitable organization. In general, the standard is easy to articulate, but often difficult to implement.

Q 1:16   What is the standard for an organization that is tax-exempt and charitable?

The legal standard by which all aspects of operations of the organization should be tested requires *reasonableness* and *prudence*. Everything the organization does should be undertaken in a reasonable manner and to a reasonable end. Also, those working for or otherwise serving the charitable organization should act in a way that is *prudent*.

The federal tax exemption granted to charitable and certain other forms of tax-exempt organizations can be revoked if the organization makes an expenditure or engages in some other activity that is deemed to be not reasonable. The same is likely true at the state level: unreasonable behavior may cause the attorney general to investigate the organization.

Q 1:17   What is the rationale for this standard for charities?

The principles underlying the laws concerning charitable organizations, both federal and state, are taken from the English common law, principally those portions pertaining to trusts and property. The standards formulated by English law hundreds of years ago for the administration of charitable trusts were very sound and very effective, and they underpin the laws today. The heart of these standards is the *fiduciary* relationship.

Q 1:18   What does the term fiduciary mean?

A *fiduciary* is a person who has special responsibilities in connection with the administration, investment, and distribution of property, where the property belongs to someone else. This range of duties is termed *fiduciary responsibility*. For example, guardians, executors, receivers, and the like are fiduciaries. Trustees of charitable trusts are fiduciaries. Today, a director or officer of a charitable organization is a fiduciary.

Indeed, the law can make anyone a fiduciary. As an illustration of the broad reach of this term, in a few states, professional fund-raisers are deemed, by statute, fiduciaries of the charitable gifts raised during the campaigns in which they are involved.

Q 1:19   What is the standard underlying fiduciary responsibility?

In a word, *prudence;* a fiduciary is expected to act, with respect to the income and assets involved, in a way that is *prudent*. This standard of behavior is known as the *prudent person rule*. This rule means that fiduciaries are charged with acting with the same degree of judgment—prudence—in administering the affairs of the organization as they would in their personal affairs. Originally devised to apply in the context of investments, this rule today applies to all categories of behavior—both commissions and omissions—undertaken in relation to the organization being served.

Q 1:20   What is the meaning of the term reasonable?

The word *reasonable* is much more difficult to define than *prudence*. A judge, attorney general, IRS agent, and the like will say that the word is applied on a case-by-case basis. In other words, the term describes one of those things that one "knows when one sees it," much like obscenity.

The term *reasonable* is basically synonymous with *rational*. A faculty of the mind enables individuals to distinguish truth from falsehood and good from evil by deducing inferences from facts. Other words that can often be substituted for reasonable are *appropriate, proper, suitable, equitable,* and *moderate*. Whatever term is used, an individual in this setting is expected to use this faculty and act in an appropriate and rational manner.

Q 1:21   Who are the fiduciaries of a charitable organization?

The principal fiduciaries of a charitable organization are the directors. The officers are also fiduciaries. Other fiduciaries may include an employee who has responsibilities similar to those of an officer, such as a chief executive officer or a chief financial officer who is not officially a director or officer. Outsiders, such as people who are hired to administer an endowment fund or pension plan, are fiduciaries with respect to the organization. Each of these individuals has what is known as *fiduciary responsibility* (see Q 1:19). ·

Q 1:22   What happens as the nonprofit organization grows, achieves a higher profile, and needs to add individuals to the board? How do those who created the entity retain control of the organization? After all their hard work, they definitely don't want some group to run off with the organization.

That is certainly true. This is a very common problem. An illustration is an organization that provides scholarships. Over time, the gift support and scholarships increase, as does the number of benefited students and grateful family members. More people will take interest in the organization. Some donors may ask whether they can join the board. Others will encourage the original board members to add individuals to the board who are professional educators and can bring expertise to the organization. Some private foundations interested in making grants may want the organization's board to be more reflective of the community.

Suppose, for example, that there are four educators in the community who are very suitable for inclusion on the board—and they are willing to serve. The three founders freely acknowledge they could use the help. But, with a board of seven, the original three would probably lose control. The educators could vote the three out of their directors' seats and out of their offices. After all of their hard work and success, the founders of the organization could be completely excluded from its operations.

The three existing board members have understandable worries.

Q 1:23   Can the founding board have it both ways? Can it retain control of the organization and, at the same time, have an expanded and more professional governing board?

Yes. There are four ways to do this.

1. Be certain that the other board members are friends and other colleagues who will not subsequently attempt to wrest control of the organization away from the founders. This approach works only to the extent the loyalty remains.

2. Have two classes of members, with the founders in one class and all other board members in the other. The governing documents then provide that certain decisions can be made only after a majority vote of both classes.

3. Use the membership feature. The founding individuals become members of the organization. The governing documents then provide that certain decisions can be made only by the members and/or that all board members can be removed by the members.

4. Issue stock, if permitted. In a few states, nonprofit organizations can be created with the authority to issue stock. The controlling individuals become stockholders. The governing documents then provide that certain decisions are reserved to the stockholders and/or that all board members can be removed by the stockholders.

TIP: Before any of these approaches is utilized in a particular case, the law of the appropriate state(s) should be examined to be certain it is permissible.

Q 1:24   What are the rules regarding the development of chapters?

There is very little law on this topic. A nonprofit organization that wants to have chapters is free to do so. The principal legal question for an organization with chapters is whether the chapters are separate legal entities or are part of the "parent" organization.

Thus, the rules as to chapters are likely to be confined to those the principal organization devises. A good practice for the main organization is to develop criteria for the chapters and then "charter" them according to the criteria. Some parent organizations execute a contract with their chapters, to be in a position to enforce the criteria. To some extent, then, the proper process for the creation and maintenance of a chapter program is akin to franchising in the for-profit setting.

There are no rules—other than those that an organization devises for itself—regarding the jurisdiction of chapters. A chapter can encompass a state, a segment of a state, or several states. There is no legal need for uniformity on this point; chapters can be allocated on the basis of population.

Q 1:25   Do chapters have to be incorporated?

No, there is no legal requirement that chapters be incorporated. (Basically, there is little law mandating that any nonprofit organization be incorporated.) However, it is a good practice to cause them to be corporations, so as to minimize the likelihood of liability for the parent organization and the boards of directors of the chapters.

Again, this pertains to the question of whether the chapters are separate legal entities (Q 1:24). A chapter can be a separate legal entity without being incorporated; for example, a chapter can be an unincorporated association. (It is not likely that the chapter would be in trust form.) (See Q 1:5.) In most instances, chapters are separate legal entities. This means, among other elements, that they must have their own identification number (they should not use the parent organization's number) and pursue their own tax exemption determination letter (unless they are going to rely on the group exemption).

Q 1:26   What is the role of a lawyer who represents one or more nonprofit organizations?

Overall, the role of a lawyer for a nonprofit organization—sometimes termed a *nonprofit lawyer*—is no different from that of a lawyer for any other type of client. The tasks are: to know the law (and avoid malpractice), represent the client in legal matters to the fullest extent of one's capabilities and energy, and otherwise zealously perform legal services without violating the law or breaching professional ethics.

The typical lawyer today is a specialist, and the nonprofit lawyer is no exception. Nonprofit law is unique and complex; the lawyer who dabbles in it does so at peril. A lawyer may be the best of experts on labor or securities law, and know nothing about nonprofit law. The reverse is, of course, also true: the nonprofit lawyer is likely to know nothing about admiralty or domestic relations law.

The first task listed above is "to know the law." That is literally impossible: no lawyer can know all of the law. The nonprofit lawyer, like any other lawyer, needs to be just as aware of what he or she does *not* know as to what is known. The nonprofit lawyer may be called in as a specialist to assist another lawyer, or, occasionally, a nonprofit lawyer may turn to a specialist in other fields that can pertain to nonprofit entities, such as environmental or bankruptcy law.

The nonprofit lawyer basically needs to know the nonprofit law of the state(s) in which he or she is licensed to practice, and the federal tax law that pertains to nonprofit organizations as tax-exempt entities. Among the other bodies of law that the nonprofit lawyer should know are the rules pertaining to charitable giving, fund-raising regulation, and the applicable postal laws. Still other fields of law may fall within the ambit of the nonprofit lawyer's practice—such as antitrust, education, estate planning, health care delivery, and unfair trade practice. Some nonprofit lawyers have a practice in litigation; most do not.

Some lawyers represent nonprofit organizations that have a significant involvement in a field that entails a considerable amount of federal and/or state regulation. This is particularly the case with trade, business, and professional organizations. These lawyers may know much about the regulatory law in a particular field, yet know little about the law pertaining to nonprofit organizations as such.

Q 1:27   How should the lawyer representing a nonprofit organization be compensated?

There is nothing unique about the compensation arrangements for lawyers representing nonprofit organizations (other than the fact that the compensation may be comparatively lower). Most lawyers representing nonprofit organizations will determine their fee solely on a hourly rate for the time expended. In these circumstances, the client is entitled to a statement (usually monthly) that clearly reflects the time expended, how it was expended, who expended it (including paralegals), and the hourly rates. These statements usually itemize expenses to be reimbursed.

It is good practice to provide the nonprofit organization client, at the outset of the relationship, with a letter that spells out the billing practices.

Some lawyer–client relationships in the nonprofit realm are based on a retainer fee arrangement. The client pays the lawyer a fixed fee for a stated period, irrespective of the volume of services provided. The retainer arrangement gives the nonprofit organization a budgeting advantage: it knows what its legal fee exposure will be for the period. The lawyer gains an advantage of cash flow. Both parties should monitor the arrangement on an ongoing basis—the lawyer to ward off undercompensation and the nonprofit organization to avoid overcompensation.

The fee arrangement may blend a retainer with additional hourly rate fees for specified services.

Other fee relationships include bonuses and contingencies. A nonprofit organization should always be mindful of the private inurement constraint—the rule that compensation, including legal fees, must always be reasonable (see Q 1:16).

TAX EXEMPTION

Q 1:28   Are all nonprofit organizations tax-exempt organizations?

No. The concept of the *nonprofit organization* (see Q 1:1) is different from that of the *tax-exempt organization*. The term tax-exempt organization usually is used to mean an organization that is exempt, in whole or in part, from the federal income tax (see Q 1:30).[4]

To be tax-exempt, it is not sufficient that an organization be structured as a nonprofit organization. The organization must meet specific statutory and other regulatory criteria to qualify for the tax-exempt status (see Q 1:31).

Some nonprofit organizations cannot qualify as certain types of tax-exempt organizations under the federal tax law. For example, a nonprofit organization that engages in a substantial amount of lobbying cannot be a tax-exempt charitable organization (see Chapter 4). Some nonprofit organizations are ineligible for any category of tax exemption. For example, an organization that provides a substantial amount of commercial-type insurance cannot be a tax-exempt charitable or social welfare organization, and may not fit within any other classification of exempt entities.[5]

Q 1:29   Are all tax-exempt organizations nonprofit organizations?

No. However, in almost all cases, a tax-exempt organization is a nonprofit entity. An example of an exception is an instrumentality of the U.S. government, which is likely to have been created by statute rather than as a nonprofit organization.[6]

Q 1:30   Concerning tax exemption, what taxes are involved?

The term *tax-exempt organization* usually is used to mean an organization that is exempt, in whole or in part, from the federal income tax (see

Q 1:28). There are other federal taxes for which there may be an exemption, such as certain excise and social security taxes. (See Q 1:36.)

State laws have several bases enabling an organization to qualify for a tax exemption. Taxes may be levied, at the state level, on income, franchise, sales, use, tangible property, intangible property, and real property. The law varies dramatically from state to state as to the categories of exemptions that are available.

Q 1:31   How does an organization become tax-exempt?

To be tax-exempt, an organization must meet the specific statutory and other regulatory criteria for the tax-exempt status it is seeking. This is true for both federal and state tax exemptions.

The process for acquiring one or more state tax exemptions varies from state to state. Usually, the procedure entails filing a form, accompanied by an explanation of the organization's programs, so the tax authorities can assess the suitability of the organization for the exemption(s) being sought. The criteria for a tax exemption, however, are basically established by a statute.

The federal income tax exemption is available to organizations that satisfy the appropriate criteria stated in applicable provisions of the Internal Revenue Code. Thus, Congress ultimately grants the federal income tax (and other federal tax) exemption. The Internal Revenue Service[7] does not grant tax-exempt status; the IRS grants *recognition* of tax-exempt status.

This recognition process, which is mandatory for nearly all charitable organizations, is commenced by filing an application for recognition of tax-exempt status with the IRS.[8] The application for charitable organizations is on Form 1023; the application for most other organizations is on Form 1024.

NOTE: Throughout, when the word *charitable* is used, it includes educational, religious, and scientific organizations.

This application includes a description of the purposes and activities of the organization, its fund-raising plans, the composition of its board of directors, and financial information. The organization's articles of organization and bylaws must be attached.

NOTE: It is important to use the current IRS applications: Form 1023 is dated July 1993, and Form 1024 is dated August 1993. However, in late 1995, both of these forms were in revision.

An applicant organization should allow at least three months for the IRS to process the application. For charitable organizations, this procedure also involves classification as charitable entities for purposes of the charitable giving rules (see Q 1:41–Q 1:44) and categorization as public charities or private foundations (see Chapter 6).

Q 1:32   Are there any exemptions from the recognition requirement?

Yes. The following *charitable* organizations can be tax-exempt without having to file an application for recognition of tax exemption: (1) organizations (other than private foundations) that have gross receipts that normally are not in excess of $5,000 annually, and (2) "churches" (including synagogues and mosques), interchurch organizations, local units of a church, conventions and associations of churches, and integrated auxiliaries of churches.[9]

Most other types of tax-exempt organizations are not *required* to obtain recognition of exempt status. In this category are social welfare organizations, labor organizations, trade and business associations, social clubs, fraternal groups, and veterans' organizations.[10] However, these entities may nonetheless seek recognition of tax-exempt status.

TIP: An organization that is not required to obtain recognition of tax-exempt status should think about doing it anyway. For the most part, the considerations are the same as those underlying the potential for any other ruling request. That is, the organization may simply want the comfort of having the IRS on record as agreeing with its qualification for tax exemption.

Q 1:33   How does an organization remain tax-exempt?

The simple answer is that an organization remains tax-exempt by staying in compliance with the rules governing the particular category of tax exemption. These rules are the most pronounced for charitable organizations.

Thus, for a charitable organization to remain tax-exempt, it must meet a variety of tests on an ongoing basis, including the organizational requirements, the private inurement and private benefit limitations (see Chapter 3), the lobbying restrictions (see Chapter 4), the political campaign activities prohibition (see Chapter 5), and avoidance of too many unrelated business activities (see Chapter 10).

Q 1:34   When might an organization's tax exemption be revoked?

In general, an organization's tax exemption is revoked when the IRS determines that the organization was materially out of compliance with one or more of the requirements underlying its tax-exempt status. For example, in the case of a charitable organization, the IRS may have concluded that it engaged in a private inurement transaction or a political campaign activity.

The IRS learns of bases for revocation of tax exemption in a variety of ways. The information may come to it as the result of an audit. Someone may have provided to the IRS information involving some wrongdoing. Often, the IRS obtains information leading to a revocation from the popular media (see Q 9:19, Q 12:5).

Q 1:35   If an organization loses its tax-exempt status, can it reacquire it?

Generally, yes. An organization qualifies for tax-exempt status if it meets the statutory criteria for the particular category of exempt organization involved (Q 1:31). If it fails to satisfy the criteria, it no longer qualifies for exemption (Q 1:34). If it resumes qualification, then its tax-exempt status must be restored. These analyses are made on a year-by-year basis.

For example, if a tax-exempt social welfare organization lost its tax-exempt status for a year because it earned too much unrelated business income, it could reacquire that exempt status for subsequent years by sufficiently reducing the amount of unrelated income or by transferring the unrelated business(es) to a for-profit subsidiary (see Chapter 11).

For tax-exempt organizations that *must* seek recognition of tax-exempt status (Q 1:31), such as charitable organizations, the process is more complex. When these exempt organizations lose their tax exemption, they can reacquire it, but they must reapply for recognition of exemption.

For example, if a charitable organization lost its tax-exempt status for a year because of too much lobbying activity, it could reacquire an exempt status for subsequent years by sufficiently reducing its attempts to influence legislation or by transferring the lobbying function to a related social welfare organization (see Q 4:14, Chapter 11). However, the organization would have to formally reapply for its exempt classification.

TIP: A charitable organization in this circumstance may be able to remain tax-exempt for the years in which its revocation of exemption as a charity are in effect. The organization undoubtedly could qualify as a social welfare organization during that period, and social welfare organizations are not required to seek recognition of tax-exempt status. Classification as a social welfare organization would be replaced by classification as a charitable organization once the new determination letter took effect. But, contributions to the organization would not be deductible as charitable gifts during the period it was categorized as a tax-exempt social welfare organization.[11]

Q 1:36   Are tax-exempt organizations completely immune from taxation?

No. Despite the term, a tax-exempt organization is not completely free from the prospect of taxation. Thus, nearly all exempt organizations are subject to tax on their unrelated business taxable income (see Chapter 10). Many types of tax-exempt organizations are subject to a tax if they engage in certain types of political activities (see Q 5:18). Public charities can be taxable if they undertake a substantial amount of lobbying activities (Q 4:12, Q 4:18) or if they participate in a political campaign (Q 5:10). Private foundations must pay an excise tax on their net investment income and are susceptible to a host of other excise taxes (see Q 6:6). Organizations such as social clubs, political organizations, and homeowners' organizations[12] are taxable on their net investment income. State law also can impose taxes on entities otherwise classified as tax-exempt organizations.

Q 1:37   In view of the massive amount of government regulation of nonprofit organizations, why don't they forfeit tax-exempt status and be treated for tax purposes the same as for-profit organizations?

For some nonprofit organizations, this course of action could be taken, looked at purely from a tax standpoint. This is because, for most of these entities, their expenses equal or exceed their income, so that there would not be any net taxable income in any event. Nonetheless, these organizations are not legally functioning on a *for-profit* basis (see Q 1:1). At the same time, an organization can be nonprofit and yet taxable.

Charitable and other organizations that are eligible to receive tax-deductible contributions would forfeit this tax feature if they were to convert to for-profit status (assuming they could as a matter of law). However, gifts are not forms of income,[13] so contributions would not be taxable income should a charitable entity choose to be a non-exempt organization.

CAUTION: There are special rules in this regard for membership groups.[14] A non-exempt membership organization is not permitted to simply net all income with all expenses for tax purposes. Instead, expenses can only be deducted against income to which they functionally relate. Where expenses of a certain function exceed the income generated by that function, the excess expenses may not be offset against income from the function. This can cause taxable income where there would not be taxable income if all expenses were netted against all income.

Q 1:38   What are the basic considerations to take into account in deciding whether an organization should be exempt as a charitable organization or a social welfare organization?

The essential distinction between a charitable (including educational, scientific, and the like) organization and an entity qualifying as a social welfare organization is that the charitable entity is operated primarily for philanthropic and similar purposes, while the social welfare organization is likely to be an advocacy entity. Thus, the principal function of a social welfare organization may well be attempts to influence legislation or other programs designed to shape the outcome of public policy on one or more issues, such as by written materials (including propaganda), demonstrations, and boycotts. While a charitable organization may be able to engage in forms of advocacy to a certain extent, the social welfare organization usually is one that undertakes more advocacy than the

federal law will tolerate for charitable organizations. Nearly every charitable organization can qualify as an exempt social welfare organization;
the reverse is often not the case.

Under the federal tax laws, both types of organizations are tax-
exempt. However, only the charitable entities are eligible to receive tax-
deductible charitable contributions (see Q 1:41).

Q 1:39   What are the basic considerations to take into account in de-
ciding whether an organization should be exempt as a charitable entity or a business league?

The essential distinction between a charitable (including educational,
scientific, and the like) organization and an association qualifying as a
business league is that the charitable entity is operated primarily for the
benefit of the public, or a considerable segment of it, while the business
league is operated principally for the advancement of its members. Thus,
for example, although an organization such as a bar association or medical society may have some public benefit programs (such as community
services or the maintenance of a library), in the view of the IRS its primary purpose is to improve practice conditions for lawyers or physicians.
Thus, there is often a presumption that an association of members who
are individuals is a business league.

In fact, however, a membership structure should not be the determining factor. An organization can be principally charitable in nature
and still have a membership. This fact is evidenced by a wide variety of
religious, educational, and scientific organizations (the latter including
professional societies).

Under the federal tax laws, both types of organizations are tax-
exempt. However, only the charitable entities are eligible to receive tax-
deductible charitable contributions (see Q 1:41).

Q 1:40 · When should a tax-exempt organization consider the estab-
lishment of a related foundation?

In most instances, an exempt organization that establishes a related foundation is a noncharitable tax-exempt entity. It is most common for social
welfare organizations and business leagues to do this, although nearly
every type of exempt organization can have a related "foundation." The

purpose of the foundation is to house charitable, educational, and similar functions in a separate entity, so that these functions can be supported by grants and deductible contributions. Another model is for the charitable and similar programs to be conducted in the noncharitable exempt "parent," with the foundation functioning essentially as a fund-raising vehicle.

NOTE: There is no reason why a foundation of this nature should be a private foundation. These entities usually are publicly supported charities or supporting organizations (see Chapter 6).

Thus, the prime reason for use of a related foundation is to best utilize the federal tax law distinctions, but the parent organization may have other reasons for establishing the foundation. For example, a second reason may be concentration of the fund-raising function in a separate entity that has its own governing board and bank account. Because the fund-raising program may be better managed with this approach, many charitable organizations (such as universities and hospitals) utilize separate fund-raising (or development) foundations.

A third reason for this approach may be that the foundation's public charity tax status is preferable to that of the parent organization. For example, the parent charitable organization may be ineligible to maintain a pooled income fund, while the charitable foundation has that eligibility (Q 8:23).[15]

CHARITABLE GIVING

Q 1:41 Are all tax-exempt organizations eligible to receive tax-deductible contributions?

No. The list of organizations that are eligible for exemption from the federal income tax is considerably longer than the list of organizations that are eligible to receive contributions that are deductible under the federal tax law as charitable gifts.

Five categories of nonprofit organizations are charitable donees for this purpose:

1. Charitable (including educational, religious, and scientific) organizations.

2. A state, a possession of the federal government, a political subdivision of either, the federal government itself, and the District of Columbia, as long as the gift is made for a public purpose.

3. An organization of war veterans, and an auxiliary unit of or foundation for a veterans' organization.

4. Many fraternal societies that operate under the lodge system, as long as the gift is to be used for charitable purposes.

5. Membership cemetery companies and corporations chartered for burial purposes as cemetery corporations.[16]

Generally, contributions to other types of tax-exempt organizations are not deductible.

NOTE: The range of charitable organizations for deductible charitable giving purposes is the same as the range of these organizations for income tax exemption purposes, with one minor exception. Organizations that test for public safety are charitable, but only for exemption purposes.[17]

TIP: Although contributions to exempt organizations other than those in these five categories are not deductible, this limitation is rather easily sidestepped by the creation of a related charitable entity, often loosely termed a *foundation*. Tax-exempt organizations that effectively use related foundations for purposes of attracting charitable gifts include trade, business, and professional associations; social welfare organizations; labor unions and similar organizations; and social clubs (see Q 1:40). In some instances, an otherwise nonqualifying organization may be allowed to receive a deductible charitable gift where the gift property is used for charitable purposes.

Q 1:42   What are the rules for deductibility of contributions of money?

A charitable contribution is often made with money. Some prefer the word *cash*. While this type of gift is usually deductible, there are limitations on the extent of deductibility in any one tax year.

NOTE: For a contribution of money to be deductible by an individual under the federal income tax law, he or she must itemize deductions.

For individuals, where a charitable gift is made with money and the charitable donee is a public charity (see Q 6:1) or a select type of private foundation, usually a private operating foundation (see Q 6:13), the extent of the charitable deduction under the federal income tax law cannot exceed 50 percent of the donor's adjusted gross income.[18] The limitation for other charitable gifts of money to charity (such as to most private foundations and fraternal organizations) generally is 30 percent.[19] In either instance, the excess portion can be carried forward and deducted over a period of up to five subsequent years.[20] Thus, for example, if an individual had adjusted gross income of $100,000 for a particular year and made gifts of money to public charities in that year totaling $40,000, the gifts would be fully deductible (unless other limitations apply) for that year. If all of these gifts were instead made to typical private foundations, the deduction for the year of the gifts would be $30,000; the excess $10,000 would be carried forward to later years.

The charitable contribution deduction for individuals is subject to the 3 percent limitation on overall itemized deductions.[21] A gift of money may have to be substantiated (see Q 7:6) and/or may be a quid pro quo contribution (see Q 7:9). A planned gift can be made in whole or in part with money (see Chapter 8).

A for-profit corporation may make a charitable gift of money. That contribution may not exceed, in any tax year, 10 percent of the corporation's taxable income.[22] Carryover rules are available.[23]

Q 1:43   What are the rules for deductibility of contributions of property?

The rules pertaining to charitable contributions of property are more complex than those involving gifts of money (Q 1:42). This type of gift is usually deductible, but there are several limitations on the extent of deductibility in any tax year.

NOTE: For a contribution of property to be deductible by an individual under the federal income tax law, he or she must itemize deductions.

One set of these limitations states percentage maximums, applied in the same fashion as with gifts of money (Q 1:42). For individuals, where a charitable gift consists of property and the charitable donee is a public charity (see Q 6:1) or a select type of private foundation (see Q 6:13), the extent of the charitable deduction under the federal income tax law cannot exceed 30 percent of the donor's adjusted gross income.[24] The limitation for other charitable gifts generally is 20 percent.[25] For example, if an individual had adjusted gross income for a year in the amount of $100,000, and made gifts of property to public charities in that year totaling $25,000, the gifts would be fully deductible (unless other limitations apply) for that year. If all of these gifts were instead made to typical private foundations, the deduction for the year of the gifts would be $20,000. In either instance, the excess portion can be carried forward and deducted over a period of up to five subsequent years.[26]

One of the appealing features of the federal income tax law in this context is that a charitable contribution of property that has appreciated in value often is deductible based on the full fair market value of the property.[27] The capital gain inherent in the appreciated property, which would be taxable had the property instead been sold, goes untaxed.

NOTE: When this benefit is available, the property must be *capital gain property* rather than *ordinary income property.* As a generalization, the distinction is based on the tax treatment of the revenue that would result if the property were sold. That is, the revenue would either be long-term capital gain, or ordinary income or short-term capital gain. (Generally, long-term capital gain property is a capital asset held for at least 12 months.[28]) Where the property is ordinary income property, the charitable contribution deduction must be reduced by the amount of gain that would either be ordinary income or short-term capital gain; in other words, the deduction is confined to the donor's cost basis in the property.[29]

As an illustration, an individual purchased an item of property for $20,000 and it is now worth $40,000. He or she contributes this property to a public charity and receives a charitable contribution deduction of $40,000. The capital gain of $20,000 escapes taxation. (By reason of the percentage limitation, this gift would yield, for a gift year, a charitable deduction of $30,000 and a carryforward of $10,000.)

TIP: This rule pertaining to the favorable tax treatment for gifts of appreciated property is equally applicable in the planned giving setting (see Chapter 8). In many situations (but not all), the deductible remainder interest is based on the full fair market value of the contributed property, and the appreciation element is not taxed.

If the property contributed is tangible personal property and the charitable donee uses the property for a noncharitable purpose, the contribution deduction must be reduced by the amount of the long-term capital gain inherent in the property.[30] This deduction reduction rule also applies where the charitable donee is a private foundation (with limited exceptions).[31]

NOTE: The most important of these exceptions concerns *qualified appreciated stock,* which essentially means publicly traded securities.[32] This type of stock could formerly be contributed to a private foundation, with the deduction based on the full fair market value of the stock (as long as all of the inherent gain is long-term capital gain). However, this favorable rule expired at the close of 1994. Legislation to retroactively resurrect the rule and extend it through 1997 is expected to pass Congress late in 1995.

A gift of property may have to be substantiated (see Q 7:6), may be a quid pro quo contribution (see Q 7:9), and/or may be subject to appraisal requirements (see Q 7:13). A planned gift can be made in whole or in part with property (see Chapter 8).

A for-profit corporation may make a charitable gift of property. That contribution may not exceed, in any tax year, 10 percent of the corporation's taxable income.[33] The carryover rules apply.[34] For corporations, there are special rules limiting the deductibility of gifts of inventory (somewhat enhanced when the property is to be used for the care of the ill, the needy, or infants)[35] and gifts of scientific property for purposes of research.[36] In most cases involving these two circumstances, the allowable charitable contribution deduction is an amount equal to as much as twice the corporation's basis in the property.

Q 1:44 What is planned giving?

The phrase *planned giving* addresses techniques of charitable giving where the contributions (usually of property) are large in amount and are normally integrated carefully with the donor's (or donors') financial and estate plans. For this reason, this giving is termed *planned* giving, because of the time and planning devoted to designing the gift transaction by both donor and charitable donee. (Planned giving is the subject of Chapter 8.)

CHAPTER 2

Boards of Directors and Conflicts and Liability

For a nonprofit organization, the board of directors is (or should be) the critical body that determines the entity's programs and investments, and provides management guidance. The role of the officers and employees is important, but the board of directors has the responsibility to frame the organization's overall policy directions and objectives. The governing board is also the locus of ultimate responsibility for the organization's activities—and can be a prime target when matters of liability arise.

The board is particularly significant for charitable organizations. In this context, the members of the board are fiduciaries; they are charged with treating the organization's assets and other resources with the same degree of care and sustenance that they would their own. When there is wrongdoing or misguided practices are revealed, the abuse is all too frequently traceable to an inattentive or passive—or captive—board of directors. More frequently than before, government regulators are placing greater duties and responsibilities on the board of directors, in the hope of averting misdeeds.

Here are the questions most frequently asked by clients about the role of the board of directors and officers, the rules as to proper expenditures of funds, self-dealing and conflicts of interest, and board members' liability—and the answers to them.

OVERVIEW

Q 2:1   What is the origin of a board of directors of a nonprofit organization?

There are many ways for the board of directors of a nonprofit organization to originate. Often, these individuals are elected by a membership. In some instances, they are appointed by another body, such as the board of directors of a related nonprofit or for-profit organization. They may be *ex officio* directors—on the board because of a position they hold with another entity.

TIP: The term *ex officio* means "by reason of the office." The phrase has nothing to do with the individual's ability to vote. All too frequently, it is assumed that *ex officio* board members, for that reason, cannot vote; many sets of bylaws have been written on that premise. However, the assumption is wrong. It is, therefore, a good practice to state in the bylaws whether any *ex officio* board members may vote.

It is common to have a self-perpetuating board—one whose members periodically elect themselves and/or others to the board position. The origin of the board of directors of a nonprofit organization may be a blend of these options.

NOTE: This is largely a state law matter. The law of the appropriate state should be checked before any option in this regard is selected.

In many states, the names and addresses of the members of the board of a nonprofit corporation must be stated in the articles of incorporation. It is usually appropriate to provide in the same document how the board of directors is derived.

NOTE: Sometimes, the terminology of this topic is confusing. The governing board of a nonprofit organization may be termed a board

---

of directors, board of trustees, board of governors, or some other title. The name itself rarely has any legal significance. The use of *trustees* is normally associated with charitable organizations. When a charitable organization is closely affiliated with another organization (whether or not tax-exempt), misunderstanding can be eliminated by terming the board of the charitable entity a board of trustees; the other board can then be the board of directors or given another title.

Q 2:2   What are the rules concerning the composition of the board of directors?

For the most part, the law does not contain rules of this nature (see Q 2:3). Most frequently, the rules governing the composition of the board of directors of a nonprofit organization are those imposed by the organization itself. Some of these outcomes, of course, are attributable to the type of organization involved. For example, a broad-based membership organization is likely to have a different governing structure than a private foundation with two or three trustees. Likewise, where one nonprofit organization controls another nonprofit organization, the relationship usually is structured by means of interlocking directorates; the governing instruments of the controlled entity will spell out how the controlling entity selects the board of the controlled entity.

There may be some federal tax implications in this area. In a few situations, the tax law imposes rules concerning board composition. For example, in the law concerning supporting organizations (see Chapter 6), there are rules that mandate certain forms of overlapping board and limitations on the extent to which disqualified persons can control the organization. The rules of the facts and circumstances test (see Q 2:5, Q 6:7) address board composition. The IRS is becoming more aggressive in requiring certain board compositions. As illustrations, the IRS will not allow a tax-exempt hospital's board of directors to be dominated by the medical staff physicians,[1] and the participation of a public charity in a limited partnership may be conditioned on the requirement that representatives of other partners are not on the board of the charitable organization.[2] Moreover, the IRS did not hesitate to, in a closing agreement with a nonprofit hospital, observe that the board of directors of the institution failed to adequately be aware of, review, and assert control over certain of the hospital's actions.[3] A byproduct of intermediate (Q 3:14) sanctions may be the expansion of boards of directors of some charitable and social welfare organizations. But, for the most part, the federal tax law is silent on the composition of the board of directors of a nonprofit organization.

Q 2:3   How does a charitable organization know whether its board of directors is lawfully constituted?

The subject of board composition is essentially a matter of state law. Most states' laws contain the criteria for members of the board of nonprofit organizations, particularly nonprofit corporations. For example, the law in most jurisdictions requires at least three directors and specifies that each of them must be at least 18 years of age. There usually are no other limitations. Some states require only one director.

There may be some federal tax requirements that bear on this point (Q 2:2).

Q 2:4   What is the function of the board of directors?

There is considerable disagreement on this point. The ideal standard is: setting of policy, objectives, and general direction for the nonprofit organization. The board is there to *direct* but only in an overarching, "big picture" sense. That body should not micromanage the entity.

In practice, a board's degree of involvement has every sort of gradation. The size of the board and the frequency of its meetings can be determining factors. Many boards of directors retain ongoing management authority between board meetings by means of executive committees. These committees, however, tend to be composed of individuals who are also officers, so the role of that group also shares in the role of the officers (Q 2:11).

Particularly in the case of charitable organizations, the members of the board are *fiduciaries* (see Q 1:18). Because of this standard, these individuals are required to act with the same degree of judgment—prudence—in administering the affairs of the organization as they would in their personal affairs (see Q 1:19).

The officers and key employees should administer the nonprofit organization on a day-to-day basis, not the board of directors. But, in actuality, board members often inject themselves into the details of administration. The law basically is powerless to draw lines here; the degree of management involvement by an individual board member usually is a function of the tolerance of the other board members, the energy and personality of the board member, and the amount of time he or she has available for the pursuit.[4]

Q 2:5   Must the board of directors of a charitable organization be representative of the community?

For the most part, no. Neither federal nor state law dictates the characteristics of a nonprofit board to that extent. There are a few exceptions (Q 2:2) but, to date at least, they are minor. Nearly all charitable organizations are free to have on the governing board anyone the board wants.

The principal exception on this topic is a rule in the facts and circumstances test (see Q 6:7). This test looks to whether the organization has a governing body that represents the "broad interests of the public," rather than the personal or private interests of a few individuals. Qualifying boards are those that are composed of (1) community leaders, such as elected or appointed officials, members of the clergy, educators, civic leaders, or other such individuals representing a broad cross-section of the views and interests of the community; (2) individuals having special knowledge or expertise in the particular field or discipline in which the organization is operating; (3) public officials acting in their capacities as such; (4) individuals selected by public officials acting in their capacities as such; and (5) in the case of a membership organization, individuals elected pursuant to the organization's governing instrument or bylaws by a broadly based membership.[5]

Also, the rules concerning supporting organizations can determine the composition of the board of directors of a supporting organization (see Q 6:25).

Q 2:6   Can the organization's board be only family members?

Yes. It is common for a nonprofit organization—charitable or otherwise—to be founded by one or two individuals. In the beginning, these individuals may comprise or dominate the board of directors and also be the officers of the organization. This type of organization is the nonprofit equivalent of what is known in the for-profit sector as a *closely held corporation*. Close governance in the nonprofit sector is completely in conformity with the law.

TIP: Despite the fact that a close board is wholly legal, it likely will subject the organization to a greater degree of scrutiny by government officials, particularly when they are concerned about private inurement or private benefit (see Chapter 4). The IRS occasionally will balk at a close board when considering recognition of tax-exempt status, although technically the IRS has no general authority to preclude one.

It is common, for example, for a private foundation to be structured in this fashion; it is the principal reason these entities are considered *private* charities (Q 6:2).

In most jurisdictions, as few as three directors are required for a nonprofit corporation. (The minimum number of directors for a nonprofit corporation varies from state to state. Some states require only one.) If an entity is to be a corporation and it has the requisite number of directors, this approach is fully lawful.

Q 2:7   Can the family-member directors also be the officers of the nonprofit organization?

Yes. The law in most states requires a president, a treasurer, and a secretary. Board members can also be officers. One individual can hold two officer positions, except that the same individual cannot be both president and secretary. (Frequently, an organization's documents must be signed by the president and attested to by the secretary. The law does not recognize as effective an attestation of one's own signature (Q 2:10).)

Q 2:8   In any instance, can the same individual be both a director and an officer?

Yes. There is no legal prohibition against the dual role. In fact, in both nonprofit and for-profit organizations, some or all of the officers are quite commonly members of the board as well.

Q 2:9   What is the function of the officers?

The law is rather vague on this point. An officer usually is expected to provide more "hands-on" management than a director but not as much as a key employee. These distinctions often become muddled, particularly when the same individual plays two or more of these roles (Q 2:4, Q 2:10). Further, the degree of involvement by an officer is likely to be determined by whether he or she is a volunteer or is an employee.

Specifically, the function of the *president* is to serve as the chief executive officer of the organization. It is common to state in the entity's bylaws that, subject to the overall supervision of the board of directors, the president shall perform all duties customary to that office.

The function of the *treasurer* is to have custody of and be responsible for all funds and assets of the organization. He or she keeps or causes to be kept complete and accurate accounts of receipts and disbursements of the organization. The treasurer is responsible for the deposit of moneys in such banks or other depositories as the board of directors may designate. He or she is to periodically render a statement of accounts to the board. It is common to state in the entity's bylaws that, subject to the overall supervision of the board of directors, the treasurer shall perform all duties customary to that office.

NOTE: Proper management practice is to obtain a security bond to protect the organization should the treasurer abuse that position for personal gain.

The functions of the *secretary* are to keep an accurate record of the proceedings of all meetings of the board of directors, and to give notice of meetings and other events as the law or the bylaws may require. It is common to state in the entity's bylaws that, subject to the overall supervision of the board of directors, the secretary shall perform all duties customary to that office.

Q 2:10   Can the same individual hold more than one officer position?

It depends on the positions. For example, it is common for the same individual to be the secretary and treasurer. By contrast, it is not a good idea to have the same individual be the president and secretary. The law often requires the signatures of both of these officers on legal documents and contemplates two individuals. The laws of some states prohibit an individual from being both president and secretary of a nonprofit corporation.

Q 2:11   What are the methods by which a board of directors of a non-profit organization can vote?

The methods by which a board of directors of a nonprofit organization can vote is a subject of state law; nearly every state's nonprofit corporation act addresses the subject. Obviously, the board members can meet and cast votes while they are together (assuming a quorum is present). Most states allow these boards to act by written consent in lieu of a meeting, although the members must be unanimous on any decision so made. If state law approves (and, in some instances, if provided for in the bylaws), the members can hold a meeting by conference call, as long as all of them can hear each other. Thus, for example, unless state law expressly permits the practice, members of the board of directors of a nonprofit organization cannot vote by mail ballot.

CAUTION: That observation does not apply to members of the organization itself. Most state laws allow them to vote by mail.

Q 2:12   Can members of the board of directors of a nonprofit organization vote by proxy?

No, unless state law expressly provides for voting in this manner (and few do). This is a form of voting that is fairly common in the nonprofit sector, yet technically is not proper. (This means that board decisions made by proxy voting may, if challenged, be void and unenforceable.)
    The reason for this is that the concepts underlying the functioning of a nonprofit organization's board of directors are derived from common law precepts pertaining to charitable trusts. The law contemplates that trustees of these trusts will meet and debate in formulating policies for the organization. Since they can only have a meaningful dialog if they are interacting in person (in the days before the telephone and video conferencing), the law discourages decision-making other than that following in-person deliberations. The dictates of fiduciary responsibility require personal attendance on occasions when the organization's course for the future is being shaped. Thus, only those statutory exceptions to this common law principle can render lawful means of voting without assembly of the board. But even contemporary statutory law

frowns on voting forms that are least likely to draw the board together: proxies and mail ballots.

Q 2:13   What material should be in the minutes of meetings of boards of directors of nonprofit organizations?

There is no particular rule of law that applies to the contents of minutes of directors' meetings. These minutes should be complete, in that they reflect all material subjects discussed at the meeting, and accurate. Statements that are defamatory, willful misrepresentations of fact, or incriminating should be avoided. Corporate minutes should not be replicas of former Senator Bob Packwood's diary.

These minutes should tell the substantive story of what transpired at the meeting; they should not be verbatim transcripts of the dialog or otherwise be in exhaustive detail. They should enable someone looking at them years later to glean the essence of the meeting and the decisions made at it. Those looking at the minutes may not be confined to subsequent boards; other readers can be representatives of government or the media. Thus, how matters are stated can be as important as what is said. In one instance, a public charity described a series of apparent private inurement transactions in a set of board minutes, which the IRS reviewed on audit; the contents of the minutes were cited by the IRS as a factor in revoking the organization's tax-exempt status.[6] Ultimately, it is a question of judgment as to what goes in and what stays out of corporate minutes; there is no bright line of distinction as to what is suitable for inclusion in the document. This is a judgment that can easily be questioned with the benefit of hindsight.

Q 2:14   Is it a concern as a matter of law whether directors are termed trustees?

No. Nearly all state laws use the term *directors*. However, the words director and trustee are essentially synonymous. If an organization wants to be certain of avoiding adverse technicalities, it need only reference the word *director* once in its bylaws and then note that the term to be used thereafter is *trustee*.

The word trustee is usually utilized where the entity is a charitable one (although the word is often also used to describe an individual who oversees a pension or similar fund). *Trustee* carries with it a higher degree of panache and dignity than does *director;* sometimes, it is preferred for that purpose alone. On a more practical level, the terms can be functionally used in the case of related organizations, to avoid confusion. For example, in the case of a business association and its related foundation, the board members of the association can be labeled directors and those of the foundation's governing body trustees.

EXPENDITURES OF FUNDS

Q 2:15 How do these rules apply to the expenditures of funds?

The board of directors of a nonprofit organization, as part of its overall role in setting policy and direction (Q 2:4), should establish a budget, which governs the basic parameters of the expenditures of the organization's funds. This pertains to outlays for program, management, and fundraising.

Q 2:16 What is expected in terms of program expenditures?

The primary purpose of a nonprofit organization is to carry out its program function—termed the *exempt function* in the case of tax-exempt organizations. Thus, the law expects that the primary expenditures of a nonprofit organization will be for its program activities.

However, there are no mechanical tests for measuring what is *primary* or, as is often the term, *substantial.*[7] A tax-exempt organization can have some unrelated business activity but there is no precise standard as to how much; unrelated business obviously cannot dominate the organization's affairs (see Chapter 10, particularly Q 10:2). The states cannot regulate charitable fund-raising on the basis of the amount of the charity's fund-raising costs (see Chapter 7, particularly Q 7:4). The blend of the three types of outlays will vary according to the type of organization and the particular circumstances it is in.

TIP: From time to time, the IRS will apply what it terms the *commensurate test* to the activities of a charitable organization. This involves an analysis as to whether the organization is engaging in adequate exempt functions, in relation to the resources that it has.[8] For example, the most recent application of this test (which the IRS subsequently abandoned) was to assert that an organization that allegedly devoted too much of its income to fund-raising should lose its tax exemption because of transgression of the commensurate test.[9]

Q 2:17 What are the rules pertaining to employee compensation?

The subject of key employee compensation is under intense scrutiny at the IRS, the Department of the Treasury, and on Capitol Hill. There is great interest in enactment of a body of tax law to clarify the rules concerning employee compensation. These rules, which would be known as *intermediate sanctions,* would impose an excise tax on amounts of excess compensation and would require the employee to repay the employer organization the amount of compensation that is considered unreasonable (see Q 3:14). The rules are termed *intermediate* because, in most instances, they would be applied instead of revocation of the organization's tax-exempt status. The IRS would be expected to provide more guidance than it has to date on how a nonprofit organization assesses whether compensation is reasonable or excessive.

In the meantime, the rules on employee compensation remain vague. As now written, they are built on the concept of *reasonableness* (see Q 1:20). A charitable organization's ongoing tax-exempt status (federal and state) is predicated on the assumption that the compensation of all employees is reasonable. The current focus is primarily on executive compensation. For an employee who is an *insider* with respect to the organization, excessive compensation is a form of *private inurement* and can be a basis for revocation of exempt status (see Chapter 3). If the employee is not an insider and the amount of excess compensation is more than incidental, the result is *private benefit,* which also is a ground for loss of tax-exempt status.

Whether an individual's compensation is reasonable is a question of fact, not law. Lawyers cannot credibly opine on that subject. There are, however, compensation experts who can legitimately advise on the appropriateness of amounts of compensation. In many instances, prudence can lead an organization to procure a formal opinion from one of these experts as to the reasonableness of the compensation of one or more employees.

What lawyers can do is evaluate an individual's compensation using the various criteria that the law has devised for assessing reasonableness. (These tests are summarized at Q 3:8.)

The lawyer's lot in these situations can be illustrated by the following example. A client charitable organization was hiring a new executive director, and the lawyer was asked to review the proposed contract and advise the organization accordingly. Nothing in the contract was separately inappropriate, but it was the lawyer's judgment that the overall package of salary and benefits was much too generous, to the point of being excessive. This was completely a judgment call, the use of intuition. Three aspects of the proposed arrangement were particularly troubling:

1. The incoming executive's compensation package was twice that of the outgoing executive director.
2. The salary alone was one-eighth of the organization's annual budget.
3. The individual being hired was a member of the board of directors of the organization.

To further worsen the situation, the new executive director was given express authority to consult (for fees) and to earn other forms of outside income.

The lawyer was obligated to advise the client that there was a substantial likelihood that the compensation package would be considered excessive by federal or state government authorities, and that the organization's tax exemption may be endangered. The lawyer could not point to anything specific; the client was provided with a judgment, based on an understanding of the case law. The client (specifically, the chairman of the board of directors) was very unhappy with the lawyer's position. The board went ahead and hired the individual as planned; the lawyer's days of representing that particular organization are over.

Q 2:18   The management of a charitable organization wants to redecorate the offices of the organization and purchase new furniture. How much money can it spend and how "fancy" can it be?

A precise monetary amount cannot be provided for this sort of thing. There is no mechanical standard for determining the extent of these types of expenditures. Those involved, as *fiduciaries,* can lawfully use the organization's income and assets for office decoration, furniture, and so forth, as long as they stay within the bounds of what is *reasonable* and *prudent* (Q 1:18–Q 1:20, Q 2:5–Q 2:6). To use other words that are easy to articulate, but often difficult to apply, they should avoid outlays that are *lavish* or *extravagant.*

An example may help clarify this matter. In 1994, the State of New York concluded an examination of a charitable organization, which culminated in a settlement.[10] This three-year investigation led to a document concerning what the attorney general referred to as the "financial administration and spending practices" of the organization. The state concluded that the board of trustees of this organization "failed to exercise appropriate cost controls in its management" of the entity. This finding specifically referred to the construction and furnishing of the entity's headquarters.

The New York attorney general found that the organization incurred "excessive" costs in furnishing the offices. The settlement required the trustees of this charity to, in the future, "exercise cost consciousness at all times" when making spending decisions. An expense policy document observed that, "[a]s it is not always possible to apply hard-and-fast rules to every situation, all trustees and employees are expected to use common sense in the disbursement of" the organization's funds. This "standard" is nothing more than another iteration of the doctrines of *reasonableness* and *prudence.* The standard used in the settlement was that of *cost consciousness.*

NOTE: This settlement with the attorney general in New York required each of the organization's 14 trustees to pay $10,000 to the organization as restitution for the excessive costs incurred in constructing and furnishing the headquarters.

These guidelines are very useful in testing the wisdom of decisions by the leadership of charitable organizations.

TIP: This settlement agreement is not *law.* It only applies to the parties and only involves the State of New York. (The document specifically states that there was no admission of any wrongdoing.) It is being emphasized only because of the pertinence of its provisions and the lack of such specific guidance elsewhere.

Equally useful is the *front-page-of-the-newspaper test.* Envision how a director of a charity would feel if a story about the organization's fiscal practices appeared on the front page of the community's newspaper. A classic example of the disasters that can be created when the front-page test is failed is the series of experiences suffered by the United Way of America because of the doings of its then-president.[11]

Q 2:19 Does this standard of fiduciary responsibility apply to every expense incurred by a charitable organization?

Yes. For example, the settlement in New York (Q 2:18) also pertained to travel, hotel accommodations, location of board meetings, and use of consultants.

Q 2:20 What are the rules for charitable organizations concerning travel by board members, officers, and employees?

The New York settlement agreement (Q 2:18) is useful as a guideline. The standard to be used is *cost consciousness.* When the directors of the organization are prudent, they authorize spending of the organization's money as if it were their own. For example, if a director travels via a commercial airline at his or her own personal expense, does he or she fly first-class? If not, it is very hard to justify first-class travel at the expense of the organization.

NOTE: First-class air travel while pursuing a charity's affairs is not illegal or otherwise inherently impermissible. Only justification of the practice is involved.

Thus, the attorney general, in the New York settlement, required the charitable organization to use the "most economic available" airfares. The organization was largely prohibited from paying or reimbursing for first-class airfares and using chartered airplanes. Generally, the use of limousines was also prohibited unless "international officials or other dignitaries" are involved.

Q 2:21   What about spouse travel?

This is a very difficult and sensitive subject. The settlement in New York generally prohibited the organization from paying or reimbursing travel expenses for spouses or other close family members. The only exception is when the individual provides a "specific contribution for the program for which the travel is incurred through an active participation in a scheduled program." Moreover, where the spouse or family member is that of an employee, prior approval of the chief executive officer is required; where a trustee is involved, prior approval of the chairman of the audit committee is required.

Also, federal tax law relates to this subject. There is no income tax deduction for amounts paid or incurred with respect to a spouse (or dependent or other individual) accompanying an individual (or an officer or employee of the business) on business travel, unless the accompanying individual is an employee of the taxpayer, the travel of the accompanying individual is for a bona fide business purpose, and the travel expenses would otherwise be deductible by the accompanying individual.[12] However, the business expense deduction is available where the payment is treated as compensation to the employee.[13] A tax-exempt organization is not concerned with these rules as to tax deductions. However, it would seem that, where an exempt organization pays for the travel expenses of a spouse, that payment is additional income to the employee of the organization, unless the purpose of the presence of the spouse is the performance of programmatic, administrative, or other services that further the organization's exempt purposes.

Q 2:22   What about the use of hotels?

A tax-exempt organization can pay for the use of hotels for conferences, board meetings, and so forth. As always, the standard to follow is (Q 2:18), *reasonableness.* The New York settlement guidelines, with their emphasis on *cost consciousness,* generally require the use of "available corporate and discount rates," and prohibit the payment of "deluxe or luxury" hotel rates and the use of hotel suites. These guidelines pertain only to the use of hotels by trustees and employees; they do not specifically apply to the use of hotels for conferences and other programmatic purposes. The only exception is when a suite is used for business purposes; even then, the use requires the prior approval of the chief executive officer. The guidelines expect avoidance of locations where a sports competition or other special event is taking place, or where a particular hotel is hosting a major convention or similar event.

Q 2:23   What about the expenses of meals?

As a general proposition, a charitable organization can pay for meals for the board, employees, and the like, where done in a business context. The standards are *reasonableness* and *cost consciousness*. There should not be payment or reimbursement for meals that are lavish or extravagant. There should be appropriate documentation of the amounts incurred and the business purpose for them.

Q 2:24   Can a board member borrow money from a charitable organization?

In general, the answer is yes. However, there are several aspects to keep in mind. One is the matter of perception. A form of behavior may be legally permissible, yet still look bad. Remember the *front-page-of-the-newspaper test* (Q 2:18). This type of transaction also has the negative connotation of *self-dealing.* Nearly all charitable organizations can lawfully engage in forms of self-dealing, but they must be prepared to withstand charges of potential wrongdoing.

Once again, the standard of *reasonableness* applies. There will not be private inurement in a loan to a board member if the features of the transaction are reasonable. The factors governing reasonableness in this situation are the reason for the loan, the likelihood of repayment, the amount of the loan, whether it is memorialized in a note, the rate of interest, the extent and amount of security, the arrangements for repayment, and the length of the borrowing term. From the standpoint of the organization, the borrowing is an investment, but those same dollars could be invested in a more conventional and secure manner. The state attorney general is likely to look closely at this type of borrowing, particularly where the loan is not being paid according to the terms of the note.

NOTE: Special rules in this regard pertain to private foundations (see Chapter 6).[14]

Q 2:25 Can a charitable organization purchase or rent property from a board member?

Again, the simple answer is yes. These circumstances have to be tested against the same considerations as those involving a loan to a board member (Q 2:24). The standard is one of reasonableness and the transaction would be a form of self-dealing.

The factors governing reasonableness in these situations are the specific reasons for rental of that particular property, the amount of the rent, whether the arrangement is memorialized in a lease, and the length of the lease term.

NOTE: Special rules in this regard pertain to private foundations (see Chapter 6).

Q 2:26 Besides expenses, what else should a charitable organization be concerned about?

The tests of what is *reasonable* and *prudent* are overarching; they apply to all expenditures, including legal and fund-raising fees.

There are two other areas of some sensitivity: (1) the location of board meetings and (2) competitive bidding.

Expenses for board meetings are the subject of the New York settlement discussed in Q 2:18. The guidelines there are quite useful in setting general parameters. The settlement document states that the primary factors to be considered in selecting locations for board meetings (including meetings of committees) are the programs, purposes, and costs of the meetings. The charitable organization is to take into account the programmatic benefits of the location, whether it has existing facilities already available, the cost of travel and hotel accommodations, seasonal factors, the feasibility of having only a delegation of the board attending the meeting instead of the full board, the feasibility of paying for program participants to travel to the organization rather than having the board travel to their location, and the scheduling of committee or board meetings on consecutive days. The board must approve in advance the location of all of its meetings.

NOTE: This matter of the full board attending meetings or educational functions can be problematic, particularly where the surroundings are luxurious. On one occasion, all seven members of the board of a charitable organization attended a seminar held at a fine resort. All of them were having lunch at the same table, as part of a group luncheon, when they were joined by one of the morning's speakers, an assistant attorney general of the state. Early into the meal, this government official realized that the seven were attending the seminar at the behest of the same charity (some were members of the same family). There was palpable unpleasantness during the balance of the meal.

Where a committee meeting is held at a time other than a full meeting of the board, the committee must approve the site and date of the meeting in advance. The meeting minutes must specify the purpose of any meeting held and the reason for the site selected, if the meeting is not held at a facility of the organization.

Concerning competitive bidding, there are no legal requirements other than the very general one of *prudent behavior.* The New York settlement documents require that all contracts, including leases and contracts for professional services, be procured via competitive procedures to the maximum extent feasible. Moreover, the awards are to go to firms whose "experience and capabilities are most advantageous" to the organization.

The New York settlement requires that these contracts be in writing and state the fees or rates to be charged, the time for completion, and the estimated total cost. All contracts in excess of $50,000 must be the subject of written proposals or competitive bids. When the organization evaluates proposals from qualified vendors, the primary consideration is to be cost. Other factors to be taken into account are prior experience, reputation, location, and minority participation.

The organization's vice president for finance must prepare an analysis of the basis on which a vendor was chosen, irrespective of whether the contract was awarded following competitive bidding or on a single-source basis. This analysis must be reported to the organization's audit committee.

SELF-DEALING AND CONFLICTS OF INTEREST

Q 2:27   What is self-dealing?

Self-dealing occurs when a person is engaged in a transaction with a nonprofit organization while at the same time having a significant relationship with the organization. The person is on both sides of the deal, hence the term. For example, self-dealing occurs where a nonprofit organization purchases an item of property from a business that is controlled by an individual who is on the board of directors of the nonprofit organization.

   The term self-dealing is particularly used in the private foundation rules (see Chapter 6). There, the person self-dealing with a foundation is termed a *disqualified person*.[15] In the realm of public charities, such a person is known as an *insider* (Q 3:2). For charities, an insider is likely to be about the same as a fiduciary (Q 1:18).

   In the private foundation setting, a disqualified person includes each member of the board of directors or trustees, each of the officers, key employees who have duties and responsibilities similar to those of officers, substantial contributors, members of the family of the foregoing, and corporations, trusts, and estates that are controlled by disqualified persons.

Q 2:28   Is self-dealing the same as a conflict of interest?

No. The concept of a conflict of interest is broader than the concept of self-dealing. One common characteristic that these terms have, however, is that both are derogatory. Neither practice is necessarily illegal. (If a disqualified person with respect to a private foundation engages in an act of self-dealing, he or she will likely become subject to one or more federal excise taxes imposed as penalties (see Q 6:6).)

   A conflict of interest presents itself when a person who has a significant relationship with a nonprofit organization also is deriving, or may be in a position to potentially derive, a benefit from something the nonprofit organization is doing or may be doing. The person may be able to obtain some personal benefit from these circumstances; because of the duality of interests, the person is conflicted. An act of self-dealing between a nonprofit organization and an insider with respect to it also is an instance of a conflict of interest. However, a conflict of interest can be present without a specific transaction or arrangement having yet arisen. Also, insiders are not always directly involved in a conflict of interest situation. For example, a charitable organization may be contemplating making a research grant to a scientific institution; a board member of the grantor entity has a conflict of interest if his or her brother or sister is a researcher at the grantee institution.

A conflict of interest transaction is a transaction with the nonprofit organization, or any of its affiliates, in which an individual connected with the organization (usually its directors and officers) has a direct or indirect interest.

NOTE: A conflict of interest can often be resolved by disclosure of the conflict to the board of directors of the nonprofit organization. Indeed, some nonprofit organizations have formal policies to this end (Q 2:27). However, problems associated with self-dealing usually cannot be remedied merely by disclosure.

Q 2:29   What is the source for a requirement that board members disclose (in writing) any possible conflict of interest they might have with the nonprofit organization they serve?

This requirement generally is not in the law; at most, it may appear in the law of a particular state. Thus, in nearly all instances, the source of this obligation will be in a conflict of interest policy developed by the nonprofit organization. The most common form of this policy is a written statement of the policy adopted by the board of directors of the nonprofit organization.

NOTE: Some of the watchdog agencies (such as the Philanthropic Advisory Service of the Council of Better Business Bureaus and the National Charities Information Bureau) require the adoption of a conflict of interest policy as a condition of their approval of a charitable organization. (See Q 7:38).

Q 2:30   What language should be contained in a conflict of interest statement?

A conflict of interest policy should annually elicit from each individual covered by it the disclosure of any organization that does business with or is in competition with the organization, where the individual (and/or any of his or her immediate family members) serves as a director or officer of that other entity. Similar disclosure should be made with respect to an individual's participations in partnerships, consulting arrangements, and other circumstances where the individual has significant influence over management decisions.

Moreover, the same type of disclosure should be made where the individuals receive compensation from another entity over a certain threshold (such as $10,000) or where there is an equity or debt relationship over a certain threshold (such as 10 percent).

The conflict of interest statement should obligate the director, officer, or any other individual to disclose a conflict of interest to the board of directors of the organization. It should require that the disclosure be reflected in the minutes of the board meeting, along with the potential adverse consequences to the organization.

The board of directors of the organization should be required to determine whether the disclosure was made adequately and forthrightly (which may require some questioning and other discussion at the board meeting), and whether the organization should proceed with the transaction involving the conflict (if that is the case). A conflict of interest transaction should be subject to approval by the board by a process more stringent than would otherwise be the case (such as by a two-thirds vote when normally only a majority vote would be required). The interested director or officer should not be counted in ascertaining the presence of a quorum for the meeting or in the vote itself. It is preferable that this individual not be present at the time of the voting.

Q 2:31   Is a conflict of interest policy legally binding on the individuals covered by it and/or the nonprofit organization?

It should be. If the policy is adopted by the organization's board of directors in conformance with the requirements of state law and the organization's bylaws, usually pursuant to board resolution, the policy is legally binding. It is in the nature of a contract between the directors and officers of the organization and the organization itself, and between and among these individuals.

Q 2:32   How does an individual know when a conflict of interest is present?

For the most part, the conflict of interest policy—most likely stated on the conflict of interest disclosure form that is annually prepared by the covered individuals—will spell out what the conflicts are. Still, some judgment may be required in determining whether there is a conflict. For example, it may not be clear whether an individual has a "significant influence over management decisions" (Q 2:30). The initial determination may rest with the covered individual. The most prudent practice is: When in doubt, disclose the matter to the board of directors.

Q 2:33   What are the obligations of a board member or officer when a conflict of interest is disclosed?

The principal obligation is met when the disclosure is made. The other obligations should be to be subject to questions by the board as to the conflict (actual, potential, or perceived), to answer those questions, to disclose to the organization any adverse consequences resulting from the conflict of which the individual is aware, and to refrain from voting on the transaction involved (if any), from being included in the quorum for the meeting, and from being present during that voting (even if the policy may not specifically require absence (Q 2:30)).

Q 2:34   How should a nonprofit organization respond to disclosure of a conflict of interest?

The disclosure should be made only to the board of directors (Q 2:30). As soon as is reasonably possible following the disclosure, the board of directors should discuss the matter at a board meeting. If a particular transaction is involved, the board should vote on the conflict before considering the transaction. It is the responsibility of a board of directors to determine whether there is a conflict of interest and, if so, whether to proceed with the transaction or to use other means to reconcile the conflict.

Q 2:35   What are the penalties when a conflict of interest is breached?

The penalties, whatever they may be, would be levied by the board of directors on the individual who breached the conflict of interest policy. The range of these penalties is likely to be determined by state law and the organization's bylaws. The options include a gentle rebuke, a serious rebuke, a censure, and/or removal from office.

NOTE: Some organizations state in their conflict of interest policy
that a transaction may be void or voidable if not approved by the
board of directors in accordance with the conflict of interest policy.
This practice is quite suitable when the only parties to the transaction
are the nonprofit organization and one or more individuals covered by
the policy (for example, a lease between the organization and a company wholly owned by a board member). However, where the transaction involves other parties who are not covered by the conflict of
interest policy, a voiding of the transaction pursuant to the policy
could be an illegal breach of contract that would subject the organization (and perhaps one or more board members) to a lawsuit.

Q 2:36   Can a nonprofit organization receive contributions from a cor- poration or foundation where a board member has a conflict of interest?

In general, yes. It is unlikely that these contributions would be inappropriate as a matter of law. For the most part, gifts from this source would
not contravene the conflict of interest policy of the organization because
money is flowing to it, rather than from it. However, there is always a
possibility that the recipient organization could find itself in an awk-
ward or embarrassing position as a consequence of these gifts (remember the front-page-of-the-newspaper test (Q 2:18)). Prudence is always
in order in this context.

Q 2:37   Can a nonprofit organization negotiate for discounted prices for goods or services to be purchased from a source where a board member or officer has disclosed a conflict of interest?

Absolutely. The essence of the requirements in this area is disclosure,
not a prohibition. The transaction may proceed if the conflict of interest
is fully disclosed and considered by the board of directors, and the
board decides that (1) the transaction would be reasonable with respect
to the organization and (2) the presence of the conflict did not significantly influence the action of the board with respect to the conflict.
These determinations should be reflected in the minutes of the relevant
board meeting (Q 2:13).

TIP: A conflict of interest does not automatically mean that private inurement or private benefit has occurred (see Chapter 3). However, the potential for difficulties of that nature is greater, and the parties should act with caution. If the nonprofit organization is a private foundation and the transaction is with one or more disqualified persons with respect to the organization, the application of the private foundation rules (particularly those pertaining to self-dealing) should be carefully checked (see Chapter 6).

Q 2:38 Are there guidelines on or limitations to the extent or nature of the discount value or percent of purchased goods or services?

No. The emphasis in this area is on disclosure and on whether to proceed with the transaction. The greater the discount or the smaller the percentage of purchased goods and services, the more likely the transaction will be deemed fair and reasonable to the nonprofit organization.

EXPOSURE OF THE BOARD TO LIABILITY

Q 2:39 What happens if the board of directors of a nonprofit organization makes a mistake?

The answer depends on the nature of the "mistake."

1. Was the mistake an "honest" one or did it involve the kind of behavior that the board knew or should have known was inappropriate or insufficient? The action or decision should be tested against the principles of *fiduciary responsibility* (Q 1:19). Whose interests were being pursued, the organization's or those of one or more individuals? Did the mistake entail a violation of a law? Is it a civil or criminal violation? Did the board seek the advice of a lawyer or other appropriate professional before undertaking the transaction? In essence, the question always is: Did the board members act *reasonably?* In this context, that means: Did they act in *good faith?*

2. Did the mistake damage the organization or any other person?

3. How easily can the mistake be undone?

4. What protections were in place to shield the organization and the directors from liability?

For example, the board of the organization involved in the New York settlement (see Q 2:18) was charged with the mistake of condoning lavish and extravagant expenditures. Their "mistake" damaged the organization, but corrective action could and was taken: the New York attorney general mandated that each member of the board was to pay the organization $10,000 as restitution for his or her misconduct. A few other states will surcharge the directors for similar behavior.

When an action by a board of directors of a nonprofit organization causes damage, either to the organization or to someone else, most consequences do not include personal liability on the part of the directors. Instead, the offensive activity is considered by the law to be a responsibility of the organization itself. Thus, the likelihood that the members of the board of directors of a nonprofit organization will be punished in some way because they did something they should not have done (a commission) or they failed to do something they should have done (an omission) is remote.

But suppose that (1) a board approves a significant investment that was speculative, (2) the organization incurs a substantial economic loss as a result, and (3) it is subsequently shown that the board should have known that the investment was inappropriate. In these circumstances, there could be adverse consequences. An attorney general may pursue a surcharge of the board and/or proceedings to remove and replace one or more board members.

Still, it is unusual for members of the board of a nonprofit organization to be found personally liable for something done or not done involving the organization. This is particularly true where the transaction or other behavior is outside the realm of investment decisions. Yet, it can happen. In one case, some members of the board of a charitable organization were found to have conspired to discharge an employee on the basis of racial discrimination. Their acts violated civil rights laws and the individuals were found personally liable. Personal liability can also arise in the areas of defamation, antitrust, and fund-raising regulation. (For the latter, see Chapter 7.)

Q 2:40   How likely is it that a member of the board of directors of a nonprofit organization will be found personally liable for something done or not done while serving the organization?

The likelihood is not great because the law first regards the action or nonaction as that of the organization. Even if there is liability, the liability almost always is that of the organization. This is particularly true where the organization is a corporation (Q 2:41).

Still, a member of the board of directors (or an officer) who is held personally liable will not find solace in knowing that he or she stands with a select few. Personal liability may attach where the conduct is wrongful and willful, continuous, and not due to reasonable cause. (See Q 2:42.)

Q 2:41   How can a nonprofit organization provide some protection for its board against the likelihood of personal liability for the result of something they did or did not do while serving the organization?

Basically, there are four means of protection. One of them is to incorporate the organization. The law recognizes corporations as separate legal entities, and the corporate form usually serves as a shield against personal liability. For corporations, liability is generally confined to the organization and does not extend to those who manage it. In those extreme cases that are the exception to this rule, the jargon is that the corporate shield has been pierced.

Today, when a nonprofit organization is formed, the resulting entity is usually a corporation. Most lawyers advise their individual clients not to sit on the board of directors of a nonprofit organization that is not incorporated.

The second form of protection is *indemnification*. A nonprofit organization should provide in its articles or bylaws that it will pay the judgments and related expenses (including legal fees) incurred by the directors and officers (and perhaps others), when those expenses are the result of a commission or omission by those persons while acting in the service of the organization. The indemnification cannot extend to criminal acts and may not cover certain willful acts that violate a civil law.

NOTE: Because the resources of the organization are involved, the true value of an indemnification depends on the economic viability of the organization. In times of financial difficulties for a nonprofit

organization, an indemnification of its directors and officers can be
a classic "hollow promise."

Indemnification is often confused with *insurance,* the third form of
protection. However, instead of shifting the risk of liability from individuals to the organization, insurance shifts the risk of liability to an independent third party—an insurance company. The resources of the
insurer, rather than those of the insured, are then used to resolve the
dispute. Some risks, such as those arising from violation of a criminal
law, cannot be shifted to an insurer.

There is one caution here: an officers' and directors' liability insurance contract is likely to contain an extensive list of civil law transgressions that are *excluded* from coverage. These may include offenses such
as libel and slander, employee discrimination, and antitrust activities—
the most prevalent types of liability in the nonprofit context. Thus, when
reviewing a prospective insurance contract that seems to offer the necessary coverage, the "exclusions" paragraphs should be carefully reviewed.

This type of insurance can be costly. Premiums can easily be thousands of dollars annually, even with a sizable deductible. Although the
costs of these premiums have dropped in recent years, many nonprofit
organizations still cannot afford them.

NOTE: Because of the inadequate coverage and high cost of currently available insurance, in some states, nonprofit organizations
are being created for the purpose of facilitating smaller nonprofit organizations' access to various types of insurance. However, these
organizations—because they have this insurance-related function—
cannot qualify for tax-exempt status.

Unfortunately, due to rampant litigiousness in our society, the risks of liability usually are too great for any organization that functions without
this protection. The premium for this type of insurance simply must be
regarded as a "cost of doing business."

It is critical that the organization purchase officers' and directors'
liability insurance. A lawyer will likely recommend to any individual that
he or she not serve on the board of a nonprofit organization that does
not have adequate insurance of this nature.

The fourth of these protections is the newest of them: *immunity.* This form of protection is available when the applicable state law provides that a class of individuals, under certain circumstances, is not liable for a particular act or set of acts or for failure to undertake a particular act or set of acts. Several states have enacted immunity laws for officers and directors of nonprofit organizations, protecting them in case of asserted civil law violations, particularly where these individuals are serving as volunteers.

Q 2:42   Does a nonprofit organization really have to indemnify its officers and directors and purchase liability insurance? Can't they just be certain their acts are always in good faith?

Unfortunately, reliance on assumptions of good faith can prove traumatic and expensive. A lawyer will recommend both an indemnification clause and officers' and directors' liability insurance.

However, there is no question that the most important protection against legal liability is to act in ways that ward off liability. There are several ways to avoid personal liability while fulfilling the spirit and the rules of fiduciary responsibility. They are:

1. Learn about the legal form of the organization and its structure. For example, if the organization is a corporation, obtain copies of its articles of incorporation and bylaws—and read them. Compare the organization's operating methods with the structure and procedures that are reflected in these documents.

2. Learn how and why the organization operates—the purposes of its programs, their number, possible overlap of efforts, and the nature of its membership and/or other support.

3. Committees, subsidiaries, directors' "pet projects," members' personal interests or contacts, or community needs may have introduced activities (and corresponding budget outlays) that were not authorized in the normal way. Some may deserve more recognition and support, while others may be (albeit innocently) endangering the organization's tax-exempt status. Find out exactly what the organization is *doing.*

4. Directors should never be afraid to ask about any arrangements or information that is unclear to them. An individual with fiduciary responsibilities (Q 1:19) should not fret about asking what

may seem to them to be "dumb questions" in the presence of the other directors; many of them are likely to have the same questions on their minds.

5. Magazine articles and books describing the proper role for directors and officers of nonprofit organizations will help to update the individual's knowledge as to permissible and innovative practices. Officers and directors should periodically attend a seminar or conference to further their understanding of and effectiveness in their roles.

6. This is both the easiest and hardest rule to follow: The director or officer should, at all times, engage in behavior that prevents (or at least significantly minimizes) the possibility of personal liability even if the organization itself is found liable. The individual, being a fiduciary, has a duty to act in a prudent manner (Q 1:19). Constant awareness of that duty offers no small measure of self-protection.[16]

CHAPTER 3

Private Inurement and Private Benefit

The private inurement doctrine is the most fundamental principle of law applicable to nonprofit organizations. The rule is inherent in the very definition of the word *nonprofit* organization (see Chapter 1). The doctrine exists to preclude application of a nonprofit organization's income or assets to private ends. The rule, read literally, would prevent inurement of "net earnings" (profits), but, in practice, the reach of the doctrine is far more wide-ranging. A private inurement transaction must involve a person who is an insider with respect to the organization. The private inurement doctrine is most pronounced for charitable organizations.

The rules as to private benefit are much more vague and expansive than the private inurement doctrine. A private benefit transaction can occur where an insider is not involved. However, incidental private benefit will be disregarded for tax purposes, which is rarely the case in the realm of private inurement.

Here are the questions most frequently asked by clients about the doctrines of private inurement and private benefit, including the emerging rules as to intermediate sanctions—and the answers to them.

OVERVIEW

Q 3:1   What is private inurement?

Private inurement is a term used to describe a variety of ways of transferring some or all of an organization's resources (income and/or assets) to persons in their private capacity. Private inurement is supposed to occur with for-profit organizations; in these organizations, profit (net earnings) is intended to be shifted from the entity to the private persons (usually the owners of the organization). By contrast, nonprofit organizations may not engage in forms of private inurement; that is the essence of the term *nonprofit*. Thus, the doctrine of private inurement is the fundamental dividing line between nonprofit and for-profit organizations. (See Q 1:1.) It is a particularly critical factor for charitable organizations in acquiring and maintaining tax-exempt status.

In the nonprofit setting, the private inurement standard references transfers of *net earnings*.[1] On its face, this phraseology suggests that private inurement transactions are akin to the payment of dividends. However, that is not the case; the law has evolved to the point where many types of transactions are considered forms of private inurement even though there is no transmission of "net earnings" in a formal accounting sense.

TIP: The IRS provided its view of the term's contemporary meaning: private inurement "is likely to arise where the beneficial benefit represents a transfer of the organization's financial resources to an individual solely by virtue of the individual's relationship with the organization, and without regard to accomplishing exempt purposes."[2] On another occasion, the IRS was more blunt: the prohibition on inurement means that an individual "cannot pocket the organization's funds."[3]

As the first of these quotes indicates, one of the ways the law determines the presence of private inurement is to look to the ultimate purpose of the organization. If the organization is benefiting individuals in their private capacity and not doing so in the performance of exempt functions, private inurement likely is present. If so, the organization may not qualify as a tax-exempt organization or, for that matter, a nonprofit organization.

The private inurement law does not prohibit transactions with in-siders. (These transactions may well be accorded greater scrutiny by the IRS or a court, however.) Thus, a nonprofit organization—including a public charity—can pay an insider compensation, rent, interest on loans, and the like. At the same time, the amount paid must be reason-able—that is, it must be comparable to similar payments in the com-mercial setting.

NOTE: This aspect of private inurement differs from the self-dealing rules applicable to private foundations; in general, they have no arm's-length standard. Even transactions with insiders that are beneficial to a foundation are largely prohibited under the private foundation rules.

Private inurement focuses on types of transactions (Q 3:8–Q 3:16). It also requires the involvement of one or more *insiders* of the organiza-tion (Q 3:2). Although it is the view of the IRS that the private inurement rule is absolute, some courts have suggested that there is some form of a de minimis floor underlying it.[4] (However, any such de minimis thresh-old may not be as generous as the insubstantiality test underlying the private benefit doctrine (Q 3:22).)

Q 3:2   When is a person an insider?

A person is an *insider* of a nonprofit organization when he, she, or it has a special relationship with the organization. (The federal tax law borrowed the term from the federal securities law, which prohibits, among other practices, "insider trading.") Usually, the special relationship arises out of a governance arrangement; that is, an organization's insiders include its directors, trustees, and officers. Key employees can be embraced by the term if their duties and responsibilities are akin to those of an officer.

TIP: The rules concerning private inurement are quite similar to those involving self-dealing in the private foundation setting (see Chapter 6). In that setting, insiders are termed *disqualified persons.*[5] In the foundation context, the equivalent term for insiders described above is *foundation managers.*

A person can be an insider because of some other relationship with the nonprofit organization. A founder of the entity, a substantial contributor, or a vendor of services could be an insider, particularly where, because of that relationship, he or she has a significant voice in the policy making or operations of the organization.

There are attribution rules in this area. Controlled businesses and family members may also be treated as insiders.

TIP: Although they are not controlling outside the private foundation context, the rules concerning disqualified persons can provide a useful analogy in defining substantial contributors, family members, and affiliated persons such as corporations, trusts, and estates.

There is no statutory definition of the term insider. This leaves the IRS and the courts free to apply the doctrine as circumstances warrant from their viewpoint. For example, it is the position of the IRS that all physicians on the medical staff of a hospital are insiders with respect to that hospital, irrespective of whether they are directors or officers of the hospital.[6]

Q 3:3   What types of tax-exempt organizations are expressly subject to the private inurement rule?

Under the federal income tax law, the types of tax-exempt organizations that are bound by the private inurement rule are charitable (including educational, religious, and scientific) organizations, business leagues (including trade, business, and professional associations), social clubs (including country clubs, and golf and tennis clubs), and veterans' organizations.[7]

NOTE: Tax-exempt social welfare organizations are not expressly subject to the private inurement rules. Certain activities by some of these organizations have brought this fact to the attention of Congress. Legislation to engraft the private inurement rule onto the law pertaining to social welfare organizations is expected to pass Congress late in 1995.

Q 3:4   What is private benefit?

The term *private benefit*, unlike *private inurement*, is not part of the definition of a nonprofit organization (Q 3:1). Rather, private benefit is a term used in the context of tax-exempt organizations, principally charitable entities. It is a part of the operational test, which looks to determine whether a tax-exempt charitable organization is being operated primarily for exempt purposes.[8] The essence of the private benefit requirement is that the entity is not supposed to be operated for private ends, other than insubstantially.

Q 3:5   What is the difference between private inurement and private benefit?

There are two principal differences between private inurement and private benefit:

1. A private inurement transaction must be with an insider. A private benefit transaction can involve anyone. Thus, the private benefit doctrine has a much broader sweep than does the private inurement doctrine. Any transaction or arrangement that may constitute private inurement also is a form of private benefit.

2. In the view of the IRS, the private inurement doctrine is absolute; that is, there is no de minimis threshold. (The courts have suggested that there is some threshold in this setting, albeit a rather small one (Q 3:1).) By contrast, insubstantial private benefit does not cause any violation of the private benefit limitation.

Q 3:6   What happens when a nonprofit organization engages in either practice?

If a form of private inurement is caused by a charitable organization or other tax-exempt organization to which the doctrine applies, the organization loses its ability to be categorized as tax-exempt under the federal income tax law. More fundamentally, the organization would violate the state law definition of a nonprofit organization and may lose its nonprofit designation under state law.

If a substantial amount (or more than an insubstantial amount) of private benefit is caused by a charitable organization, the organization loses its ability to be tax-exempt as a charity.

PRIVATE INUREMENT

Q 3:7   What are the principal types of transactions that constitute private inurement?

Among the many and varied types of private inurement that the IRS and the courts have identified over the years, the most predominant are unreasonable (excessive) compensation, unreasonable borrowing arrangements, and unreasonable rental arrangements. In this context, the emphasis once again is on transactions that are reasonable. (See Q 1:16.)

Q 3:8   When is compensation private inurement?

This is one of the most often-asked questions. The answer as a matter of law is easy to articulate. An item or package of compensation is private inurement when it is paid to an insider and it is unreasonable and excessive. However, the process by which reasonableness is determined and the factors that must be taken into account are vague. The determination depends very much on the material facts and circumstances.

The court cases in this area focus on egregious violations, and, because they are fact-specific, they offer little guidance. The IRS has offered no particular assistance in illuminating this topic. A push for intermediate sanctions, however, is clarifying the matter of the factors and to some extent is addressing the matter of the process (Q 3:14).

There are seven general factors that can be used to ascertain whether an item or package of compensation is reasonable. Before enumerating them, however, a preliminary aspect of this matter must be stated. The compensation of an individual by a nonprofit organization must take into account the complete compensation package, not just the salary component. In addition to the base salary, these elements include any bonuses or commissions, incentive compensation, fringe benefits, consulting fees, and retirement and pension plans.

The determining factors are:

1. The amount and type of compensation received by others in similar positions.
2. The compensation levels paid in the particular geographic community.
3. The amount of time the individual is spending in the position.

4. The expertise and other pertinent background of the individual.

5. The size and complexity of the organization involved.

6. The need of the organization for the services of the particular individual.

7. Whether the compensation package was approved by an independent board.

The first two factors are based on commonality: What are others in similar positions in similar locales being paid? The geographic factor is relatively easy to isolate; the other aspects may not be. If the comparison is of association executives or foundation trustees, the exercise may be relatively mechanical. In other instances, the basis of comparison may not be so clear. For example, in ascertaining the reasonableness of the compensation of a televangelist, should the comparison be with a local member of the clergy or a television personality?

The third factor—the amount of time devoted to the position—is very important. A compensation arrangement may be quite reasonable where the individual is working full-time, but excessive where he or she is working for the organization less than full-time. Thus, the analysis must take into account whether the individual is receiving compensation from other sources and, if so, the amount of time being devoted to them (see Q 2:17).

NOTE: The annual information return filed by most tax-exempt organizations[9] requires that the details of compensation received by a director, officer, or key employee of the filing organization be disclosed when (1) more than $100,000 was paid by the organization and one or more related organizations, and (2) more than $10,000 of the compensation was provided by a related organization.

The sixth factor relates to a topic the IRS is currently addressing to a considerable extent. The IRS is generally approving, albeit reluctantly, of incentive programs. There has been a crackdown on tax-exempt hospitals that are providing inducements to physicians to attract them away from their private practice and onto the hospitals' medical staffs.[10] The principles being laid down in this setting are spilling over into aspects of the compensation practices of other nonprofit organizations.

The seventh factor is notable for a variety of reasons. This element is giving the IRS an opportunity to have a greater say in determining who is to sit on the board of directors of a nonprofit organization. Where an independent board is in place, the founders or other principals of the organization lack control. (See Q 1:22–Q 1:23.) Thus, this element strongly advances the thought that ostensibly "high" compensation, when derived from a controlled board, is presumptively unreasonable.

TIP: There may be some other avenues to travel with respect to this last factor. One approach is to create an independent compensation committee of the board, which would make recommendations in this area to the board. The other is to seek the opinion of a qualified firm that has expertise in ascertaining the reasonableness of individuals' compensation.

TIP: In mid-1994, the IRS revoked the tax-exempt status of a health care organization because of alleged private inurement and private benefit. This case involved many forms of compensatory and other categories of alleged inurement. The matter presently is pending in court; the outcome of the case could have a significant bearing on this aspect of the law.[11]

Q 3:9   Is payment of a bonus to an employee of a nonprofit organization legal?

Yes. There is no prohibition on the payment of bonuses by a nonprofit organization to its employees. The only requirement is that the bonus be reasonable. In making that analysis, all of the compensation paid to the employee will be taken into account (Q 3:8).

Q 3:10   How should a bonus compensation program for employees be defined?

There need not be any formally defined plan. That is, the management of the organization could simply decide that the merits of an individual's work warrant additional compensation.

If a bonus compensation program is defined, the management of the organization could be allowed, by the board of directors, to make additional payments of certain amounts at a specified time, such as at year-end. The board may want to set parameters for these bonuses, stated as ranges of absolute amounts or percentages of overall compensation.

If bonuses are stated as percentages, additional care should be exercised, particularly where the compensation is a function of an element other than the individual's preexisting compensation. For example, the compensation of a fund-raiser could be, in whole or part, a percentage of the amount of contributions raised during a particular period. Percentages of this nature can trigger special scrutiny because the compensation arrangement may be a distribution of net earnings, which is prohibited by the doctrine of private inurement (Q 3:1). These compensatory programs are often more like commissions than bonuses.

An instance of the problems a percentage arrangement can generate was the net revenue stream sales that were recently popular in the health care community. The IRS essentially has stopped these sales. Tax-exempt hospitals would calculate the net revenue (profit) to be incurred by a particular department for a year and sell that revenue package to a partnership consisting of physicians who were on the hospital's medical staff and were practicing in that department. The arrangement's advantages to the hospitals were: it pleased the physicians, so that they stayed on the medical staff, and it enabled the hospitals to receive the net revenue from the department's operations much sooner than would have otherwise been possible. The advantages to the physicians were: they could administer the department more efficiently and generate more net revenue than originally calculated, and they were able to retain the resulting increment of earnings.

The IRS concluded that the arrangement was a form of private inurement, in that the physicians—as insiders (Q 3:2)—were obtaining a portion of the hospital's net earnings. The IRS basically forced the hospital community to discontinue this practice. Private inurement was found to be inherent in the percentage feature, termed *per se* private inurement. The IRS refused to allow this flow of revenue to be tested against a standard of reasonableness.[12]

However, this type of revenue was more in the nature of investment income than individual compensation. There is no absolute prohibition on the use of percentages in computing an employee's compensation, even where the employee is an insider.

TIP: If a form of percentage compensation is deemed appropriate, one feature to consider to avoid private inurement is a ceiling on the amount to be paid. This ceiling is a safeguard against a windfall. Use of this type of ceiling makes it easier to justify the compensation as being reasonable.

Q 3:11   What role should the board of directors play in the annual review and approval of bonus awards to employees?

The federal tax law is evolving to the point where it is being expected that the board of directors of a nonprofit organization, particularly a charitable one, will fix the parameters of all compensation programs, not just those pertaining to bonuses. Thus, as part of the exercise of its fiduciary responsibility (Q 1:19), the board should set policy for each component of the organization's compensation plan.

In instances of private inurement, it is becoming a more common practice for the IRS and the attorneys general to fault the board for its lack of involvement and to force the board to develop policies for the ongoing review of the organization's compensation practices.

Q 3:12   How is the bonus compensation program reported to the IRS and disclosed to the public?

There is no express requirement that a bonus compensation program or similar program be specifically reported to the IRS or disclosed to the public. However, the compensation of the five highest paid employees of a public charity (Q 6:1) must be identified on the organization's annual information return filed with the IRS.[13] Information on this return is accessible to the public. A bonus or similar amount paid to one of these employees should be reported as part of his or her total compensation.

Q 3:13   Are the seven factors mentioned above the only elements to take into account in determining the reasonableness of compensation?

No. The seven factors referenced above (Q 3:8) are the ones basically used in nearly every case. However, other factors may be taken into account. These include whether there is a percentage factor in the calculation of compensation (Q 3:10). The data gleaned from national compensation surveys may be important. The location of the organization is a factor, as is (in the compensation context) the existence of written offers from similar organizations competing for the services of an individual.

Q 3:14   How will intermediate sanctions work?

It must be stressed that—except in the private foundation setting—there is (as of late 1995) no intermediate sanctions system in the law in the private inurement context. If enacted, it would be an alternative to the present-day sole sanction, which is revocation of the tax exemption of an organization that participates in a private inurement transaction.

NOTE: Under legislation currently working its way through Congress, the version of intermediate sanctions discussed next would be effective as of September 14, 1995.

One version of this set of rules would impose excise taxes, rather than loss (in most instances) of exempt status, on the participants in a private inurement transaction.[14] This proposal would impose penalty excise taxes as an intermediate—or alternative—sanction in cases where an organization exempt from tax as a charitable organization (other than a private foundation) or a social welfare organization engaged in an *excess benefit transaction.* In this case, intermediate sanctions could be imposed on certain disqualified persons who improperly benefited from the transaction and on managers of the organization who participated in the transaction knowing that it was improper.

An excess benefit transaction would include any transaction in which an economic benefit is provided to, or for the use of, any disqualified person if the value of the economic benefit exceeds the value of consideration (including the performance of services) received by the organization for providing the benefit.

A rebuttable presumption would arise to the effect that a transaction was not an excess benefit one if the exempt organization's board had (1) delegated authority to make decisions with respect to the transaction to those board members who did not have a conflict of interest; (2) considered specific information relevant to the decision, including as much information on comparable transactions as could be collected through reasonable efforts; (3) documented the basis for its decision; and (4) approved the transaction, including a limit on the total amount that could be transferred to the controlling person in advance of its occurrence.

A disqualified person who benefited from an excess benefit transaction would be subject to a first-tier penalty tax equal to 25 percent of the amount of the excess benefit (in an instance of unreasonable compensation, the amount of the compensation that is excessive). Organization managers who participated in an excess benefit transaction knowing that it was improper would be subject to a first-tier penalty tax of 10 percent of the amount of the excess benefit (subject to a maximum tax of $10,000).

Additional, second-tier taxes could be imposed on a disqualified person if there was no correction of the excess benefit transaction within a specified time period. In this case, the disqualified person would be subject to a penalty tax equal to 200 percent of the amount of the excess benefit. For this purpose, the term *correction* would mean undoing the excess benefit to the extent possible, establishing safeguards to prevent future excess benefit, and, where a full undoing of the excess benefit is not possible, taking such additional corrective action as would be prescribed by federal tax regulations.

The intermediate sanction for excess benefit transactions could be imposed by the IRS in lieu of or in addition to revocation of the tax-exempt status of the errant organization. If more than one disqualified person or manager is liable for a penalty excise tax, then all such persons would be jointly and severally liable for the tax. The IRS would have the authority to abate the excise tax penalty if it was established that the violation was due to reasonable cause and not to willful neglect, and that the transaction at issue was corrected within the allowed correction period.[15]

CAUTION: This intermediate sanctions scheme is not as benign as it may appear; one entangled in it could face heavy taxes and disgorgement obligations. Suppose an individual was compensated by a public charity in the annual amount of $200,000 and the IRS determined that $50,000 of the compensation was an excess benefit. First, the individual would be assessed a tax of $12,500 (25 percent of $50,000). Second, the individual would be expected to timely correct the transaction, which is to say return the excess compensation

($50,000) to the exempt organization before the first-tier tax is assessed or a deficiency notice mailed. How is an individual making $200,000 annually going to come up with $62,500 in this relatively short time period? Third, if the transaction is not timely corrected, there would be a second-tier tax of $100,000 (200 percent of $50,000). Now the individual owes the exempt organization and the government $162,500, plus interest. Further suppose that, as is often the case, the audit is for a three-year period. The tab then becomes nearly $500,000 ($487,500, to be precise) plus interest.

Needless to say, this would be a substantial hardship where the individual acted in good faith and has already spent the salary; unable to satisfy the disgorgement and tax requirement (and related legal fees), bankruptcy (to shed non-tax debt) may be the only resort. Meanwhile, one or more board members could also be taxed and the organization could have its tax exemption revoked.

Q 3:15   When is a loan private inurement?

A loan to an insider, by a nonprofit organization that is subject to the private inurement doctrine, can be private inurement. That would be the case where the terms of the loan are unreasonable.

The factors to be taken into account in assessing the reasonableness of a loan include the amount of the loan in relation to the organization's resources, whether the terms of the loan are reduced to writing (such as a note), the amount of any security, the rate of interest, the term of the note, and how the transaction is reflected on the books and records of the lender and borrower. The latter factor is significant in determining the intent of the parties, especially whether it was really expected that the loan would be repaid. (If not, the "loan" would be regarded as additional compensation.) Thus, another factor would be the zealousness of the organization in securing payments or levying against the security, should the borrower cease making timely payments.

TIP: While all of these factors are important, the interest rate is particularly significant. If the rate is not reasonable (such as a point or two over the prime rate), the transaction may well be questioned. A no-interest loan to an insider would—absent the most extenuating of circumstances—be private inurement.

As with compensation, the test usually is one of commonalities (Q 3:8): What would the elements of a similar loan be if made in the commercial setting?

Q 3:16 When is a rental arrangement private inurement?

The rental of property from an insider, by a nonprofit organization that is subject to the private inurement doctrine, can be private inurement. That would be the case where the terms of the rental are unreasonable.

The factors to be taken into account in assessing the reasonableness of a rental arrangement include the amount of the rent, whether the terms of the transaction are reduced to writing (such as a lease), the term of the rental, and the need of the organization for the particular property. Regarding the latter element, the ability of the nonprofit organization to rent similar property from an unrelated party may be a factor in the analysis.

There can also be private inurement where a nonprofit organization rents property to an insider. The first of the above three factors is also relevant in this setting. Another factor to be applied would be the extent to which the organization pursued rent collection where the tenant (an insider) fell behind in rent payments.

TIP: While all of these factors are important, the amount of the rent is particularly significant. If the rental rate is not reasonable, the transaction may well be questioned. An excessive amount of rent paid to an insider would be a classic form of private inurement.

As with compensation, the test usually is one of commonalities (Q 3:8): What would be the elements of a similar rental transaction if made in the commercial setting?

Q 3:17 Are there other forms of private inurement?

Yes. One form of private benefit is the provision of services to insiders. Here, it is essential to separate exempt functions from the possibility of private inurement. For example, an organization operated to advance the arts can be a charitable entity; if it is an art gallery that exhibits and sells its members' works, it may be engaging in private inurement.

Likewise, the rendering of housing assistance for low-income families qualifies as a charitable undertaking; private inurement may be taking place where housing is provided to some of the charitable organization's key employees.

The participation by a nonprofit organization, particularly a charitable one, in a partnership or joint venture may raise issues of private inurement.[16] The IRS is especially concerned about a situation where a public charity is considered to be running a business (such as a partnership) for the benefit of private interests. The scrutiny in this area is most intense where the charitable organization is the (or a) general partner in a limited partnership and some or all of the limited partners are insiders with respect to the organization.

The position of the IRS as to public charities in limited partnerships at this time is this: To avoid loss of tax-exempt status, the organization must be a general partner in the partnership for the purpose of advancing its charitable purposes, it must be protected against the day-to-day duties of administering the partnership, and the payments to the limited partners cannot be excessive.

The IRS is more relaxed as to the involvement of charities in general partnerships and joint ventures. There, the test largely is whether the organization is furthering exempt ends. If it is, tax-exempt status is not likely to be disturbed.

TIP: One way to assess whether a transaction involves private inurement is to see whether it would constitute an act of self-dealing under the private foundation self-dealing rules.[17] If it is self-dealing, it is likely to be private inurement.

CAUTION: The foregoing tip is a generalization. In one instance serving as an exception to this guideline, a mortgage loan to a key employee was ruled by the IRS to be self-dealing when extended by a museum classified as a private foundation, but was held to not be private inurement when the museum became a public charity because the value of the loan was included in an overall reasonable compensation package.[18] (Special rules in the foundation setting prevented treatment of the loan as an item of compensation.)

PRIVATE BENEFIT

Q 3:18   How is private benefit determined in actual practice?

The law on this point is particularly vague. The range of transactions embraced by the private benefit doctrine is not as precise as that captured by the private inurement doctrine. However, as noted, every instance of private inurement is also a form of private benefit (Q 3:5).

Because there is no requirement of the presence of an insider to bring the private benefit doctrine into play, the doctrine can become applicable with respect to any type of circumstance and any type of person. It is a fall-back, catch-all concept that is used to prevent the resources of a charitable organization from being misapplied—that is, applied for noncharitable ends.

There is some authority for the proposition that two types of private benefit exist: primary private benefit and secondary private benefit.

Q 3:19   What is primary private benefit?

The concepts of primary and secondary private benefit have been illustrated by a case involving a nonprofit school.[19] The purpose of the school was to train individuals to be political campaign managers and consultants. The court was troubled by the fact that the graduates of the school ended up working for candidates of the same political party. Although the school's programs did not constitute political campaign activities (see Chapter 5), nor violate any other then-existing rule barring tax exemption, the court nonetheless wanted to deny tax-exempt status to the school.

The court achieved this objective by conjuring up the idea of these two levels of private benefit. The first level of private beneficiaries—those enjoying *primary private benefit*—were the students of the school. However, this type of private benefit could not be employed to deny tax-exempt status because it was also an exempt educational function. To prevent the school from acquiring tax exemption, the court turned to secondary private benefit.

Q 3:20   What is secondary private benefit?

Secondary private benefit is private benefit that flows to one or more persons as the consequence of the provision of private benefit to the primary beneficiaries. It is not clear whether secondary private benefit is taken into account if primary private benefit is of a nature that would cause denial or revocation of exemption.

The court in the above-described case (Q 3:19) ruled that, although the primary private benefit did not prevent tax exemption, the secondary private benefit did. The secondary private benficiaries were the political candidates who received the services of the school's graduates. This type of private benefit was held to be more than incidental.

NOTE: The concept of secondary private benefit has not been applied since this opinion was issued. It is a troublesome rule of law because of its reach. Taken literally, every school has secondary private beneficiaries: those who employ its graduates and thus acquire the benefits of the knowledge and skills the school taught. For example, the partners of a law firm who utilize the training of newly graduated associates are secondary private beneficiaries to a far greater economic and other extent than the political candidates who hire trained campaign managers and consultants.

Q 3:21   Is it possible for a donor, when making a gift to a nonprofit organization, to realize a private benefit from the gift?

No private benefit is inherent in this type of a transaction, even where the donor is an insider. The benefits that flow from forms of donor recognition are not private benefit that would adversely affect tax-exempt status. For example, a gift transaction where a building or a scholarship fund is named after the contributor does not involve an extent of private benefit that would threaten the donee's tax exemption. It either is not considered this type of private benefit at all or is regarded as so incidental and tenuous as to be ignored for tax purposes.

However, it is quite possible for a donor to receive a private benefit in exchange for a contribution, in the form of a good or service. For example, an individual could give to a charity a contribution to be used in constructing a building that would house the charity's offices. If the contributor was provided free office space in the building in exchange for the gift, that would be private benefit. The private benefit, if more than incidental (Q 3:22), could cause the charity to lose its tax exemption. (The donor would usually have to reduce the charitable contribution deduction by the value of the good or service received.)

Q 3:22 How is incidental private benefit measured?

There is no precise, mechanical test for assessing private benefit. A facts-and-circumstances test must be applied in each case. The private benefit doctrine is a very subjective legal concept. It enables the IRS or a court to assert private benefit in nearly every instance in which misdirection of the resources of a charitable, and perhaps other nonprofit, organization is occurring.

CHAPTER 4

Lobbying

Lobbying—principally, attempts to influence legislation—is a practice protected by the Constitution and necessary to provide information to legislatures. Yet, lobbying is often considered a disreputable act and the term is frequently used in a derogatory manner. Because it is common for nonprofit organizations to operate in furtherance of one or more causes, they frequently engage in lobbying. The unseemliness of lobbying is sometimes amplified when done by nonprofit entities; there are feelings in some quarters that tax-exempt organizations—particularly public charities—should not lobby.

There are, therefore, restraints in the federal tax law on the extent to which charities and some other tax-exempt organizations can lobby. Public charities are held to a standard of insubstantiality; private foundations are not supposed to lobby at all. Trade and business associations are somewhat affected by the tax law in this regard: the portion of dues paid to them that is attributable to lobbying is not deductible as a business expense. Other exempt organizations, notably social welfare entities, can lobby without restriction. A burgeoning practice for some exempt organizations is to place their lobbying functions in a separate, but related, exempt organization.

Here are the questions most frequently asked by clients about lobbying by nonprofit organizations, the various tax rules surrounding attempts to influence legislation (including new rules as to dues deductibility)—and the answers to them.

OVERVIEW

Q 4:1   What is lobbying?

The word *lobbying* derives from the caricature of someone hanging around in a lobby, waiting for the opportunity to whisper in the ear of a government official in an effort to influence the official's decision or vote. In its broadest sense, lobbying is an attempt to influence the public policy and issue-resolving functions of a regulatory, administrative, or legislative body. However, the term is generally used to describe efforts to influence the voting of one or more members of a legislative body on one or more items of legislation. The legislative body may be a federal, state, or local one. Although lobbying is often regarded as an unsavory practice, it has a constitutional law basis: it is a form of free speech as a petitioning of a government for a redress of grievances. The U.S. Supreme Court observed that the "very idea of a government republican in form implies the right on the part of its citizens to meet peaceably for consultation in respect to public affairs and to petition for redress of grievances."[1]

The Federal Regulation of Lobbying Act defines the term to mean an attempt by a person, who receives compensation or other consideration for the effort, to influence the passage or defeat of legislation.[2] The federal income tax law, concerning lobbying by public charities that are under the expenditure test (Q 4:15), defines the phrase "influencing legislation" as meaning "(a) any attempt to influence any legislation through an attempt to affect the opinions of the general public or any segment thereof, and (b) any attempt to influence any legislation through communications with any member or employee of a legislative body, or with any government official or employee who may participate in the formulation of the legislation."[3] Essentially the same definition is used in the tax regulations pertaining to lobbying by public charities that are under the substantial part test (Q 4:9),[4] and in the federal tax statutes concerning lobbying by private foundations[5] and lobbying for purposes of the business expense deduction (Q 4:27).[6]

However, with respect to the business expense deduction rules, the term lobbying also includes efforts to influence the President of the United States, the Vice President, Cabinet members, and top White House staff.[7] The federal law proscriptions on lobbying, however, generally do not pertain to lobbying of members of an executive branch or of independent regulatory agencies.[8]

Q 4:2   What is legislation?

In general, the word *legislation* means a bill or resolution that has been introduced in a legislative body; it may or may not be considered by that body. The term is defined in the federal tax law, for purposes of the expenditure test (Q 4:15), as "action with respect to acts, bills, resolutions, or similar items by the Congress, any state legislature, any local council, or similar governing body, or the public in a referendum, initiative, constitutional amendment or similar procedure."[9] For purposes of the substantial part test (Q 4:9), the term is similarly defined in the federal tax regulations.[10]

Q 4:3   Is lobbying a necessary or appropriate activity for a nonprofit organization?

For many nonprofit organizations, lobbying not only is a necessary activity, it is a critical one. It is a matter of policy as to whether it is appropriate for them to engage in that activity, particularly when they are tax-exempt. There is nothing inherently illegal about lobbying by nonprofit organizations. Indeed, these organizations have the constitutional right to petition the government. However, the U.S. Supreme Court has held that it is not unconstitutional for the law to deprive charitable organizations of tax-exempt status if they engage in substantial lobbying.[11]

There is a belief among many policy makers that it is inappropriate for charitable organizations to engage in lobbying. This view is largely based on the precept that a person should not be able to receive an income tax deduction for a gift to a charity which is used to advance that person's views on legislation; this is seen as a subsidy of one person's viewpoint by others. Consequently, public charities are constrained as to how much lobbying they can engage in without loss of tax exemption (Q 4:12, Q 4:18).

Q 4:4   What are the federal tax rules concerning lobbying that are unique to tax-exempt organizations?

The principal rule is that public charities may engage in lobbying activities only to the extent they are not substantial.[12] A public charity that engages in substantial attempts to influence legislation is considered an *action organization*[13] and is likely to have its tax exemption denied or revoked. Private foundations are basically constrained from any lobbying

(Q 4:10). Some tax-exempt organizations can have lobbying as their principal or even their sole function; these include social welfare organizations and trade and business associations (Q 4:24–Q 4:31). However, members of an association are likely to have their dues deductions reduced to the extent the organization lobbies (Q 4:27).

Q 4:5   How do charitable organizations measure substantiality?

In general, there is no precise formula for measuring whether lobbying activities are substantial. It is common practice, however, to evaluate the extent of lobbying in terms of a percentage of total funds expended in a period of time or total time expended over a particular period. These are merely informal guidelines, however; the IRS will not commit to any specific percentages. On occasion, substantiality is found as a consequence of an organization's impact on a legislative process, irrespective of outlays of funds or time. The case law makes it clear that this is a case-by-case determination.[14] The decision that an organization has engaged in a substantial amount of lobbying is usually made in hindsight, after the particular legislative process has concluded.

In other areas of the federal tax law, precise percentages are available for defining what is substantial. For example, certain rules concerning supporting organizations define the term to mean at least 85 percent (Q 6:16). In the setting of the business expense deduction, the phrase *substantially all* means at least 90 percent (Q 4:30). Thus, a rough guide would be to define *substantial* as meaning at least 85 percent and *incidental* as meaning no more than 15 percent. However, the federal tax law generally treats the determination of substantiality as being a facts-and-circumstances test. The exception is the expenditure test, which contains some safe harbor percentage limitations (Q 4:15).

Q 4:6   Is there more than one form of lobbying?

Generally, the law regards lobbying as being *direct* or *grass roots*.

Direct lobbying occurs when the lobbying organization communicates, for purposes of influencing legislation, with a member of a legislative body, an individual who is on the staff of such a member, or an individual who is on the staff of a committee of a legislative body. For purposes of the expenditure test (Q 4:15), there is a direct lobbying communication only where the communication refers to specific legislation and reflects a view on the legislation.[15] In the setting of the business expense deduction, direct lobbying includes communications with certain members of the federal executive branch (Q 4:31).[16] When the results of research are used in lobbying, the research activities themselves are automatically considered lobbying. Whether research activities in other settings constitute lobbying is a matter determined on a facts-and-circumstances basis.

Grass roots lobbying takes place when the lobbying organization communicates, for purposes of influencing legislation, with the general public, or a segment of it, in an effort to induce the persons contacted to communicate with a legislative body for the purpose of influencing legislation. Under the expenditure test (Q 4:15), a grass roots lobbying communication takes place only where the communication refers to specific legislation, reflects a view on the legislation, and encourages the recipient of the communication to take action with respect to the legislation.[17] This latter element is known as a *call to action.*

Q 4:7   What are the various ways by which lobbying can be accomplished?

Lobbying is communication. It can be accomplished using any means of communication between human beings. Forms of direct lobbying (Q 4:6) include personal contact, correspondence, telephone calls, facsimiles, telegrams, position papers and other publications, contact via the Internet, and formal testimony. Grass roots lobbying (Q 4:6) includes these forms, along with television, radio, and print media advertisements.

Q 4:8   Are there laws concerning lobbying by nonprofit organizations, other than the federal tax rules?

Yes. The principal law outside the federal tax context is the Federal Regulation of Lobbying Act. Those who lobby for compensation as a principal portion of their activities must register with and report to the Clerk of the House of Representatives and the Secretary of the Senate.[18] The Byrd Amendment prohibits the use of federal funds received as grants, contracts, loans, or cooperative agreements for attempts to influence an officer or employee of a governmental agency in connection with the awarding, obtaining, or making of any federal contract, grant, loan, or cooperative agreement.[19] Regulations published by the Office of Management and Budget provide that costs associated with most forms of

lobbying activities do not qualify for reimbursement by the federal government.[20] Most states have laws regulating lobbying by nonprofit and
other organizations.

CHARITIES AND THE SUBSTANTIAL PART TEST

Q 4:9   What is the substantial part test?

The federal tax law does not allow tax-exempt charitable organizations
to attempt to influence legislation to the extent that the lobbying activities are a substantial part of their total activities.[21] Public charities are
permitted to lobby to the extent that the lobbying is incidental—or at
least not substantial. This limitation is known as the *substantial part test.*

There is no mechanical formula for measuring what is substantial
in this context (Q 4:5). Both expenditures and time can be taken into account; for example, the time of volunteers is considered under this test.
The substantial part test is applicable on a year-by-year basis.

Nothing in the substantial part test specifically applies to lobbying
by related organizations. For example, a public charity with chapters
(separate entities) that are charitable organizations would not normally
have the chapters' lobbying attributed to it. However, a grant by the public charity to one or more of its chapters for lobbying would be a lobbying
expenditure for the grantor.

Q 4:10   Can private foundations lobby to the extent of the substantial part test?

Private foundations, even though they are charitable organizations, cannot lobby to the extent of the substantial part test. Basically, private foundations are not allowed to engage in any lobbying.[22] If prohibited lobbying
takes place, the foundation becomes liable for one or more federal excise
taxes.[23] There are certain exceptions to this general rule. A private foundation can (1) make available the results of nonpartisan analysis, study,
or research, and (2) appear before or otherwise communicate with a legislative body with respect to a possible decision of that body that might
affect the existence of the foundation, its powers and duties, its tax-
exempt status, or the deductibility of contributions to the foundation.[24]
This second item is known as the *self-defense exception.*

Q 4:11   Are there exceptions to the prohibition on lobbying under the substantial part test?

Yes. A public charity will not lose its tax-exempt status because of lobbying activities where the lobbying was the result of an invitation from a legislative body or a committee of that body.[25] Also, activities that are *educational* in nature are not considered lobbying, nor is the mere monitoring of and reporting on legislation. The statutory exceptions that are part of the expenditure test generally do not apply with respect to the substantial part test (Q 4:17).

Q 4:12   What happens when the organization engages in substantial lobbying?

If a public charity subject to the substantial part test engages in a substantial amount of legislative activities in a tax year, it is supposed to have its tax exemption revoked. The organization is also liable for a 5 percent excise tax on the lobbying expenditures.[26] A tax in this amount may also be imposed on the managers of the organization, who are held responsible for knowing that the expenditures would likely result in loss of the organization's tax-exempt status. These two results happen from time to time, but a charitable organization is much more likely to settle the matter with the IRS, often through an agreement to not engage in substantial lobbying activities in the future. Usually, this type of agreement is evidenced by what the IRS terms a *closing agreement* (see Q 12:21).[27]

Q 4:13   Can a charitable organization that loses its tax exemption because of excessive lobbying convert to another type of tax-exempt organization?

Yes, if it is an organization that is covered by the substantial part test. A public charity that has lost its tax-exempt status because of the extent of its lobbying activities can prospectively become a tax-exempt social welfare organization.[28] This change of status would allow it to continue to attempt to influence legislation to a substantial extent and remain tax-exempt, although contributions to it would no longer be deductible as charitable gifts. Another approach would be to transfer the lobbying function to a related social welfare organization (Q 4:26).

Q 4:14   What planning can a charitable organization under the substantial part test engage in to avoid adverse tax consequences because of lobbying?

A public charity should evaluate its activities in this regard to ascertain whether one or more of them may not technically constitute lobbying. They may instead be educational or monitoring activities, or the organization may be able to shelter some of them by procuring an appropriate request for them (Q 4:11). The organization should have in place an adequate record-keeping system with respect to its lobbying endeavors and should follow generally accepted accounting principles in allocating joint costs (Q 4:35).

A public charity should make an effort to keep its annual outlays for lobbying to a level below 10 to 15 percent (Q 4:5). If volunteers are used for lobbying, the total amount of time expended on attempts to influence legislation in a year must be evaluated. However, these precautions will not necessarily prevent an assertion by the IRS, successful or not, that lobbying activities were or are substantial. If a significant amount of lobbying is to be or is being undertaken, a public charity should consider electing the expenditure test rules (Q 4:15), placing its lobbying activities into a tax-exempt lobbying subsidiary (Q 4:26), or converting to a tax-exempt social welfare organization (Q 4:13).

A private foundation must avoid lobbying altogether, other than the forms of lobbying that are allowed by exceptions (Q 4:10).

CHARITIES AND THE EXPENDITURE TEST

Q 4:15   What is the expenditure test?

The *expenditure test* is a scheme devised by Congress to provide public charities a means to determine how much lobbying is allowable without loss of tax-exempt status, by application of precise percentages of total expenditures.[29] The test permits a public charity to expend, for lobbying, 20 percent of its first $500,000, 15 percent of the next $500,000, 10 percent of the next $500,000, and 5 percent of the remaining expenditures. There is an annual ceiling of $1 million for lobbying outlays. Grass roots lobbying may not exceed 25 percent of total allowable lobbying. These limitations are known as the *direct lobbying allowable amount* and the *grass roots lobbying allowable amount.* These percentages are applicable to the organization's expenditures during the most recent four years.

Not all public charities may utilize this test (Q 4:16), and private foundations cannot avail themselves of it (Q 4:10). Lobbying by certain affiliated organizations is attributed to the charitable organization for purposes of the expenditure allowance. For example, an organization with chapters is likely to have this attribution rule applied to its expenditures for lobbying.

Q 4:16   How does this test become applicable to an organization?

A public charity must elect to come within the expenditure test.[30] This is done by filing an IRS form.[31] This filing can be made at any time during the organization's fiscal year; when done, it causes the expenditure test to be applicable with respect to that entire year.

Certain public charities are not permitted to elect the expenditure test. These are churches, associations of churches, conventions of churches, integrated auxiliaries of churches, and supporting organizations with respect to tax-exempt organizations other than public charities.[32] Private foundations cannot make this election because of the general prohibition on lobbying by them (Q 4:10).

Q 4:17   Are there exceptions to the term lobbying under this test?

Five categories of activities are excepted from the scope of lobbying for purposes of the expenditure test:

1. Making available the results of nonpartisan analysis, study, or research.
2. Providing technical advice or assistance to a governmental body or legislative committee in response to a written request by the body or committee.
3. Appearing before, or communicating with, any legislative body with respect to a possible decision by that body that might affect the existence of the organization, its powers and duties, its tax-exempt status, or the deduction of contributions to it. This is known as the *self-defense exception.*

4. Effecting communications between the organization and its members with respect to legislation that is of direct mutual interest.

5. Communicating in a routine manner with government officials or employees.[33]

Q 4:18   What happens when the organization engages in "too much" lobbying?

If an organization exceeds the direct lobbying allowable amount or the grass roots lobbying allowable amount (Q 4:15), it is subject to a 25 percent excise tax on the excessive portion of the outlay.[34] If an organization exceeds either lobbying expenditure limitation by 150 percent or more, it is supposed to have its tax exemption revoked.[35] A public charity in this circumstance is not subjected to the excise tax for engaging in substantial legislative activities (Q 4:12).

   If a public charity has lost its tax-exempt status under these circumstances, it could alter its lobbying practices and reapply for recognition of tax exemption. To achieve tax exemption again, it would have to (1) reduce its lobbying expenditures for the future, to be in compliance with either the substantial part test or the expenditure test; (2) restructure its lobbying program to make effective use of one or more of the exceptions to the lobbying rules (Q 4:17); or (3) conduct some or all of its lobbying activities in a tax-exempt subsidiary (Q 4:23).

Q 4:19   Can the charitable organization convert to another type of tax-exempt organization?

As a practical matter, no. If a public charity subject to the expenditure test engages in substantial legislative activities to the extent that its tax exemption is revoked, it cannot thereafter convert to a tax-exempt social welfare organization.[36] However, it could convert to another type of tax-exempt entity, such as a business league, but that is usually not a suitable alternative.

Q 4:20   What types of lobbying programs are most suitable for the expenditure test?

The expenditure test is most appropriate for a public charity that is engaging, or wants to engage, in lobbying activities that are or would be *substantial,* as that term is defined under the substantial part test. The test is, therefore, often necessary for a charitable organization that would otherwise be considered an action organization (Q 4:4). (This assumes that (1) the lobbying activities are not so extensive as to be not tolerated under the expenditure test, and (2) the public charity in this circumstance is one that can make this election (Q 4:16).)

Because of the allowable lobbying amounts, the expenditure test is more beneficial to direct lobbying than to grass roots lobbying (Q 4:6, Q 4:15). That is, the limitation on grass roots lobbying (essentially, 5 percent of total expenditures, or 25 percent of 20 percent) may be too stringent for an organization that is principally or exclusively engaging in grass roots lobbying. A public charity of this nature is almost certain to find that it is preferential to be under the substantial part test, whereas the test of insubstantiality is likely to be more tolerant and does not differentiate between the two types of lobbying (Q 4:9).

Q 4:21   When should a charitable organization elect the expenditure test?

A public charity should not elect the expenditure test unless and until it is positive that the advantages of the election outweigh the disadvantages of it.

The principal advantage of the expenditure test is that it affords a public charity considerable certainty as to how much lobbying it can engage in without adverse tax consequences. The mechanical nature of the test and the warning nature of the excise tax (Q 4:15) contribute to that advantage. Other advantages include: (1) an array of activities that are specifically exempted from consideration as lobbying activities (Q 4:17), (2) exemption from the excise tax imposed on public charities in cases of excessive lobbying (Q 4:12), and (3) exclusion from the lobbying amount calculation for lobbying done by volunteers. For the latter calculation, the test applies only to expenditures; volunteer time is disregarded.

There are, however, some disadvantages to being under the expenditure test. These include: (1) the stringent limitation on allowable grass roots lobbying activities (25 percent of total allowable lobbying activities), (2) more extensive record-keeping requirements, (3) more extensive reporting requirements (Q 4:36), (4) a significant likelihood of audit exposure if the test is not elected (Q 4:22), and (5) inability to convert to a tax-exempt social welfare organization if lobbying activities become too extensive (Q 4:19).

Q 4:22 Under what circumstances would an organization elect to revoke its election to be under the expenditure test?

Having elected to come under the expenditure test, a public charity would revoke that election only where its direct lobbying or grass roots lobbying expenditures became, or were about to become, too extensive to be tolerated under the test.[37] This could happen where the grass roots lobbying expenditures of a public charity exceeded or were about to exceed the special 25 percent limitation, even though overall lobbying expenditures remained below the 20 percent limitation. Caution should be exercised when canceling an election: it will signal to the IRS that extensive legislative activities are or will be occurring and that they are perhaps too extensive to be allowable under the substantial part test.

Q 4:23 What planning can a charitable organization under the expenditure test engage in to avoid adverse tax consequences because of lobbying?

A public charity should avoid electing the expenditure test until and unless it is certain that the test should be elected. Stated another way, a public charity should elect the test only where all of the advantages and disadvantages involved in making of the election are assessed (Q 4:21). For example, the 20 percent ceiling may initially appear attractive and then prove illusory if a significant amount of grass roots lobbying is to be undertaken. For this assessment, all applicable exceptions should be taken into account (Q 4:17). The election should not be made until sufficient record-keeping and accounting procedures are in place, so that the organization knows with some confidence precisely what its lobbying expenditures are or will be. The organization should prepare, on a test basis, the portion of the annual return required of public charities under the expenditure test. It should examine the results and determine whether it will be able to comply with these reporting requirements in subsequent years. This analysis should take into account the fact that lobbying by affiliated organizations may be attributed to the organization.

Before making the election, a public charity should consider the alternatives of placing the lobbying program in an affiliated tax-exempt social welfare organization (Q 4:26) or converting to such an organization (Q 4:13, Q 4:19).

Once the election is made, adverse consequences may result if the organization revokes it (Q 4:22). If the organization loses its tax exemption because of an inability to stay within the bounds of the expenditure test, it forgoes the opportunity to convert to an exempt social welfare organization (Q 4:19).

SOCIAL WELFARE ORGANIZATIONS

Q 4:24   Are there any restrictions on lobbying by tax-exempt social welfare organizations?

No. Tax-exempt social welfare organizations may engage in legislative activities without limitation. The only significant constraint is that their lobbying must be in advancement of exempt purposes or at least not be a deterrent to the ability of the organization to primarily engage in exempt activities. This ability of an exempt social welfare organization to extensively lobby makes it a useful repository of legislative activities as a subsidiary to a public charity (Q 4:26). The rules pertaining to the deductibility of business expenses (Q 4:27) apply with respect to social welfare organizations; however, dues paid to these entities are generally not deductible as business expenses in any event.

Q 4:25   Why don't all lobbying charities convert to social welfare organizations?

Public charities that engage in lobbying normally do not want to forgo their status as charities and become social welfare organizations. One of the principal reasons for this decision is that contributions to social welfare organizations are not tax-deductible as charitable gifts. Thus, although both charitable and social welfare organizations are tax-exempt entities, only the former can attract deductible gifts. Also, social welfare organizations, particularly those that engage in considerable lobbying, are unlikely candidates for private foundation grants. Therefore, a public charity would convert to a social welfare organization only where it would otherwise be an action organization (Q 4:4), did not or could not elect the expenditure test (Q 4:15), or did not want to use a lobbying subsidiary (Q 4:26).

Q 4:26 How can a public charity utilize a tax-exempt lobbying subsidiary?

There are several instances in the federal tax law pertaining to exempt organizations where the principle of bifurcation is usefully applied. *Bifurcation* means that the functions of what would otherwise be one organization are split, largely or exclusively for tax reasons, and placed in two entities. That is the case with respect to public charities and substantial lobbying.

A public charity that wishes to engage in substantial amounts of lobbying cannot be tax-exempt as a charitable entity. One of its options is to be a tax-exempt social welfare organization (Q 4:25). Another option is to establish a related tax-exempt organization and conduct the lobbying activities through that entity. The principal advantage of this second option is that it preserves the organization's status as a charitable organization with respect to its other programs and it retains its ability to attract tax-deductible contributions.

There are several ways in which the public charity can control its lobbying subsidiary (Q 1:3). The most common mechanism of control in this context is an interlocking (or overlapping) board of directors. With this approach, the board of directors of the social welfare organization is selected, in whole or in part (but at least a majority), by the board of directors of the charitable organization. Other control features include making the subsidiary a membership organization, with the public charity the sole member, or creating it as a stock-based nonprofit organization, with the public charity the sole shareholder. (See Q 1:23.)

TRADE, BUSINESS, AND PROFESSIONAL ASSOCIATIONS

Q 4:27 Are there any restrictions on lobbying by tax-exempt trade and other associations?

In general, no. Tax-exempt trade, business, and professional associations may engage in legislative activities without limitation, albeit with two constraints. First, the lobbying must be in advancement of exempt purposes or at least not be a deterrent to the ability of the organization to primarily engage in exempt activities.

Second, the lobbying activities can trigger some adverse tax consequences to the association's members. Generally, the dues paid by a member to one of these associations is tax-deductible as a business expense. However, with minor exceptions, there is no business expense deduction for amounts expended in attempts to influence legislation.[38] Where an exempt association engages in lobbying, a portion of the dues, deemed allocable to the lobbying activities by operation of a *flow-through rule,* is not deductible.[39] For example, an exempt association that expended 30 percent of its funds for lobbying in a year and has annual dues of $100 would cause its members to have a dues deduction of only $70 for that year.

An association in this circumstance must calculate its expenditures for lobbying. In doing this calculation, it must allocate the appropriate portion of salaries paid to employees with multiple responsibilities, using one of three accounting methods.[40] Certain *in-house expenditures* must also be taken into consideration.

Q 4:28   How does the member know how to calculate the dues deduction?

As a general rule, the association must calculate the various amounts expended for influencing legislation and then report the resulting ratio to its membership.[41] The reporting is to be done at the time of assessment or payment of the dues. This ratio must also be reported to the IRS by means of the association's annual information return.[42]

Q 4:29   What happens if the association makes an error in the calculation of the dues deduction ratio?

The organization may have to pay a 35 percent *proxy tax* on the difference between the amount reported to the membership and the actual lobbying amount.[43] This can occur where the lobbying outlays are higher than anticipated or where the dues receipts are lower than projected.

There is a procedure, however, by which an association in this situation can arrange for a waiver from the IRS and adjust the figures to report the excess lobbying amounts in the subsequent year.[44]

Q 4:30 Are there any exceptions to these rules?

… ith respect to
… the members
… surveys are in-
… are opting for

… rules do not
… an association
… or dues in any
… means at least
… lly available to
… ailable to trade,
… able to demon-
… members cannot
… nt floor on mis-
… dues are paid
… IRS may be re-

… ct to charitable

… -house expendi-
… of these expendi-
… s exception does
… d payments to a

… on are not consid-

… r public charities?

No. The te… espect to the rules
denying the business expense deduction. In this setting, the term em-
braces not only lobbying of nearly all legislative bodies, but also the
President of the United States, the Vice President, the members of the
Cabinet and their executive staff, and the principal White House staff.
The term also includes research that is undertaken and subsequently

used in a lobbying effort, irrespective of the intent of the parties involved for initiating the research effort.[48]

VETERANS' ORGANIZATIONS

Q 4:32   Are there any restrictions on lobbying by tax-exempt veterans' organizations?

No. Tax-exempt veterans' organizations may engage in legislative activities without limitation. The only significant constraint is that the lobbying must be in advancement of exempt purposes or at least not be a deterrent to the ability of the organization to primarily engage in exempt activities. Unlike the situation with respect to exempt social welfare organizations and trade and business associations, however, contributions to most veterans' organizations are tax-deductible as charitable gifts.[49]

Q 4:33   Aren't the tax rules for veterans' organizations unfair in relation to those for charitable organizations?

In both cases, the organizations are tax-exempt and can attract deductible gifts, yet the lobbying by veterans' organizations does not affect their tax exemption or charitable donee status. The U.S. Supreme Court, in rejecting an equal protection doctrine argument on the point, held that Congress may make such distinctions in crafting the tax laws.[50] The favoritism toward veterans' organizations in this regard was characterized as a "subsidy" created by Congress as part of the nation's long-standing policy of compensating veterans for their past contributions by providing them with numerous advantages.

REPORTING REQUIREMENTS

Q 4:34   Are any reporting requirements imposed on tax-exempt organizations that lobby?

A portion of the annual information return that must be filed by public charities is devoted to the reporting of their lobbying activities (Q 4:35 and Q 4:36). The information return filed by private foundations includes a provision concerning any legislative activities.[51] The information return that must be filed by all other tax-exempt organizations inquires as to lobbying efforts.[52] Also, certain reports must be filed pursuant to the Federal Regulation of Lobbying Act (Q 4:8). Some states' laws have similar requirements.

Q 4:35   What are the reporting requirements under the substantial part test?

The annual information return filed by public charities requires that those under the substantial part test include information about the use of volunteers and/or paid staff or management in attempts to influence legislation.[53] The organization must also report the amounts it expended in furthering its lobbying efforts via media advertisements; mailings to members, legislators, or the public; publications or published or broadcast statements; grants to other organizations for lobbying purposes; direct contact with legislators, their staffs, government officials, or a legislative body; rallies, demonstrations, seminars, conventions, speeches, and lectures; and any other means of attempting to influence legislation.

Q 4:36   What are the reporting requirements under the expenditure test?

Public charities under the expenditure test must report total direct lobbying expenditures, total grass roots lobbying expenditures, exempt purpose expenditures, the direct lobbying nontaxable amount (the amount protected by the applicable percentages (Q 4:15)), and the grass roots lobbying nontaxable amount (not to exceed 25 percent of the foregoing amount).[54] These figures must be separately reported for the organization and affiliated organizations.

An organization in this circumstance must also report, for each year in the four-year averaging period (Q 4:15), its direct lobbying nontaxable amount, direct lobbying ceiling amount (not to exceed 150 percent of the four years' total of the preceding amount), total direct lobbying expenditures, grass roots lobbying nontaxable amount, grass roots lobbying ceiling amount (not to exceed 150 percent of the four years' total of the preceding amount), and total grass roots lobbying expenditures.

Any taxable amounts, for either direct lobbying or grass roots lobbying, are to be reported to the IRS on a tax return.[55]

CHAPTER 5

Political Activities

The principal body of federal tax law concerning political activities pertains to public charities. These organizations are prohibited from participating in nearly all political campaigns. Although the official position of the IRS is that this restriction is absolute, the courts tolerate at least a de minimis amount of political campaign involvement by public charities. The IRS administrative practice in this area also is one of considerable tolerance. There is a tax on political campaign activities by public charities.

However, not all political activities are political campaign activities. Tax-exempt organizations that engage in noncampaign political activities may become subject to a political activities tax. Private foundations are subject to other taxes for involvement in political campaign activities.

Political organizations may be exempt, in whole or in part, from income taxation. The business expense deduction is not available for an expenditure for political campaign purposes.

Here are the questions most frequently asked by clients about political activities by nonprofit organizations, the tax rules concerning political campaign and other efforts, and the use of political action committees—and the answers to them.

OVERVIEW

Q 5:1   What are political activities?

Political activities are of two categories, one subsuming the other. The broader of the two categories refers to any activity that is undertaken with a political purpose, that is, to affect the structure or other affairs of government. The narrower definition refers to an activity that is engaged in to assist or prevent an individual's election to a public office; this latter type of political activity is a *political campaign activity*.[1] The narrower range of activities requires participation or intervention in a political campaign (Q 5:3).

For example, the presentation of testimony before the Senate Committee on the Judiciary, regarding a nominee of the President to the Supreme Court, is a political activity.[2] However, this is not a political campaign activity because there is no *campaign* for a public office (Q 5:7). By contrast, a contribution to the campaign organization of an individual, to assist him or her in attempting to win election to the U.S. Senate, the U.S. House of Representatives, or a state legislature, is a political campaign activity.

Q 5:2   What are the rules, for tax-exempt organizations, concerning political activities?

There are several rules, but two are particularly important. One is that a charitable organization is not allowed to participate in or intervene in any political campaign on behalf of or in opposition to any candidate for a public office.[3] This constraint pertains to political campaign activities (Q 5:1); if violated, the organization becomes classified as an *action organization*[4] and must pay a tax and suffer revocation of its tax-exempt status.[5]

The other rule concerns organizations that are political organizations, that is, have political activities as their exempt function (Q 5:16).[6] These organizations frequently engage in political campaign activities; they also undertake political activities that are not political campaign activities.

The business expense deduction is not available for an expenditure for political campaign purposes.[7] If a tax-exempt organization, such as a trade or business association or a labor union, were to make such an expenditure, the extent of deductibility of the organization's dues might be affected (Q 5:20). Because of the federal campaign laws, organizations of this nature should not engage in political campaign activities directly but can do so by means of political action committees (Q 5:21).

Q 5:3   What do participation and intervention mean?

Essentially, the words *participation* and *intervention* mean the same thing: an involvement in some way, by an individual or an organization, in a political campaign. These types of activities include the solicitation or making of political campaign contributions, the use of resources of an organization to benefit or thwart the candidacy of an individual in a political campaign, the volunteering of services for or against a candidate for a public office, and the publication or distribution of literature in support of or in opposition to a candidate for public office.

Traditionally, the IRS broadly defines these terms—sometimes finding violation of the political campaign activity constraint when some elements of the prohibited activity are not present. For example, a charitable organization was denied tax exemption because its purpose was to implement an orderly change of administration of the office of a governor in the most efficient and economical fashion possible by assisting the governor-elect during the period between his election and inauguration.[8] In this instance, while there was to be participation and/or intervention in a government's affairs, there was no *candidate* (Q 5:6) nor *campaign* (Q 5:7). However, the IRS ruled that the organization's "predominant purpose is to effectuate changes in the government's policies and personnel which will make them correspond with the partisan political interests of both the Governor-elect and the political party he represents."

In another illustration of these rules—one that is more in conformity with the language of the prohibition—the IRS ruled that charitable organizations may not evaluate the qualifications of potential candidates in a school board election and support particular slates in a campaign.[9] Today, however, that organization would likely qualify for tax exemption as a charitable entity if its activities were confined to the evaluative function.

In this context, the IRS has historically taken a hard-line position with respect to advocacy organizations that become entangled with political issues; where the objectives of these organizations can only be achieved through political change, they cannot—in the government's view—be charitable. In support of this position, a court held that an organization established with the dominant aim of bringing about world government as rapidly as possible cannot qualify as a tax-exempt charitable organization.[10] This approach is difficult to rationalize under the contemporary law, however, because of the absence of any involvement in a *campaign* for or against a *candidate* for *public office* (Q 5:8).

Q 5:4   Can a charitable organization educate the public about candidates and issues in the setting of a political campaign?

Yes. However, the IRS has been rather grudging in allowing this type of activity. In fact, there can be a fine line between participating in a political campaign and engaging in public education about that campaign. Organizations like the League of Women Voters and the Commission on Presidential Debates, which utilize the resources of organizations such as universities, have moved the law to a point where there is, today, a fuller recognition of *voter education* activities.[11]

The contemporary view is that a charitable organization, as part of an education process, can disseminate the views, voting records, and similar information about candidates in the context of a political campaign where neutrality is, or substantially is, observed. The key factor is that the organization may not indicate partisanship on the issues. Popular practices include the compilation and dissemination of the voting records, or responses to questionnaires elicited by the organization, of members of a legislature on a variety of topics. Also in vogue is the issuance of "report cards"—a listing of votes on selected issues in which a legislator receives a "+" if his or her vote coincided with the organization's position and a "−" if it did not.[12]

Factors the IRS takes into account are: Is there comment on an individual's overall qualifications for public office? Are there statements expressly or impliedly endorsing or rejecting an incumbent as a candidate? Has the organization observed that voters should consider matters other than voting, such as service on committees and constituent services? Is the material distributed to the organization's constituency or the general public? Is the dissemination of publications timed to coincide with an election campaign, particularly during its closing days? In one instance, the IRS position was stated this way: "[I]n the absence of any expressions of endorsement for or in opposition to candidates for public office, an organization may publish a newsletter containing voting records and its opinions on issues of interest to it provided that the voting records are not widely distributed to the general public during an election campaign or aimed, in view of all the facts and circumstances, towards affecting any particular elections."[13]

The expansionist view as to what is participation or intervention in a political campaign is derived from a federal court of appeals opinion authored over 20 years ago.[14] There, a religious ministry organization was denied tax-exempt status, in part because of ostensible interventions in political campaigns. The organization, by means of publications and broadcasts, attacked candidates and incumbents (the President and members of Congress) who were considered too liberal, and endorsed conservative officeholders. The court summarized the offense: "These attempts to elect or defeat certain political leaders reflected . . . [the organization's] objective to change the composition of the federal government." However, open criticism of an elected public official, including one who is eligible for reelection, was held violative of this proscription, even where not done in the context of a political campaign. It is unlikely that this aspect of the opinion would be reiterated by a court today.

There is, therefore, great confusion in the federal tax law as to the reach of the prohibition on political campaign activities by public charities. That is, there is far less guidance in this area than there is in the realm of lobbying activities by public charities, where considerable detail is given in regulations, rulings, and court opinions. (See Chapter 4.) This dichotomy is aggravated by very inconsistent and selective enforcement practices by the IRS, which aggressively pursues transgressions (alleged and otherwise) by the "Christian Right" (such as the activities of televangelists), yet ignores the most blatant of violations by the clergy of innumerable African-American churches.

The federal and state political campaign regulation rules apply to charitable organizations, and thus can operate as an additional set of limitations on their ability to participate in political campaigns. For example, the prohibition on campaign contributions by corporations is applicable to charitable entities.

Q 5:5 Does the law differentiate between the political positions of organizations and those of individuals associated with them?

Yes. An individual does not lose his or her rights to engage in political activity solely by reason of being an employee or other representative of a public charity. The IRS, however, expects that an individual in this position will make it clear in the appropriate context that the political views expressed are his or hers, and not those of the organization. For example, in its tax guide for churches and clergy, the IRS stated that "[m]inisters and others who commonly speak or write on behalf of religious organizations should clearly indicate, at the time they do so, that public comments made by them in connection with political campaigns are strictly personal and are not intended to represent their organization."[15] As a practical matter, this distinction is often difficult to credibly maintain.

Q 5:6   When is an individual a candidate?

For the proscription on political campaign activity to be applicable, the public charity must be a participant in the campaign of an individual who is a *candidate* for a public office.[16] The federal tax regulations define the phrase *candidate for public office* to mean "an individual who offers himself, or is proposed by others, as a contestant for an elective public office, whether such office be national, state, or local."[17] An individual becomes a candidate for a public office on the date he or she announces his or her candidacy for that office. But, the fact that an individual is a prominent political figure does not automatically make him or her a candidate. This is the case notwithstanding speculation in the media and elsewhere as to the individual's plans or where an individual is publicly teasing about running for office. For example, as of late 1995, are Bill Bradley, Newt Gingrich, Colin Powell, or Ross Perot "candidates" in respect to the 1996 campaign for the presidency of the United States? The label "candidate" is often applied with the benefit of hindsight.

The IRS refuses to commit itself to any specific rule in this regard, preferring to leave the matter to a general facts-and-circumstances test; it has been known to assert the candidacy of an individual far before any official announcement. Mere speculation in the media that an individual may campaign for an office can be the basis of an IRS insistence that the individual has become a candidate. By contrast, the federal election law defines the term *candidate* to mean an individual seeking nomination for election or election to federal office; one who has directly or indirectly received contributions or made expenditures for such a purpose in excess of $5,000 is deemed to seek nomination for election or election.[18]

Q 5:7   When does a campaign begin?

The federal tax law lacks any definition of the term *campaign*. For the proscription on political campaign activity to be applicable, the public charity must be a participant in the *campaign* of an individual seeking a public office.[19] This body of law is silent as to when there is a commencement of a political campaign; again, it is the practice of the IRS to apply a facts-and-circumstances test. The IRS has been known to assert the launching of a campaign far in advance of a formal announcement of candidacy.

One court opinion stated that "a campaign for public office in a public election merely and simply means running for office, or candidacy for office, as the word is used in common parlance and as it is understood by the man in the street."[20] The federal election law likewise does not define the term *campaign;* in general, however, under that law, as to a particular individual, a campaign commences once he or she has become a candidate, which entails receiving the requisite level of contributions or making the requisite level of expenditures (Q 5:6).[21]

Q 5:8 What is a public office?

For the proscription on political campaign activity to be applicable, the public charity must be a participant in the campaign of an individual seeking a *public office.*[22] This term is specifically defined in two sets of federal tax regulations to mean a policy-making position in the executive, legislative, or judicial branch of a government; it means more than mere public employment.[23] (These regulations relate to the definition of the phraseology in the rules concerning disqualified persons with respect to private foundations and in defining exempt functions of political organizations.)

On occasion, the IRS will openly decline to follow that definition. For example, an intraparty position, such as a precinct delegate, clearly is not a public office, yet the IRS pursued the revocation of the tax-exempt status of a public charity that influenced the selection of individuals to such delegate positions, on the ground that they are types of "public offices."[24]

CHARITIES AND POLITICAL ACTIVITIES

Q 5:9 Is there a substantiality test for charitable organizations concerning political activities?

For the most part, no. The position of the IRS on this point is that the proscription on political activities by charitable organizations is an absolute one. The statute stating this proscription does not contain a substantiality test, as it does with respect to legislative activities (Q 4:5).

However, the judiciary is reluctant to foreclose the possibility of a de minimis test in any setting. One court observed that "courts recognize that a nonexempt purpose, even 'somewhat beyond a de minimis level,' may be permitted without loss of exemption."[25] Thus, for example, it is unlikely that the inadvertent application of $1.00 of the funds of a public charity to a political campaign activity would be treated as a violation of the constraint, although that would literally be a violation of the language of the statute.

Q 5:10   What happens when a public charity engages in a political campaign activity?

Actual practice is often different from what the applicable statutes mandate. A public charity's participation in a political campaign is a ground for revocation of tax-exempt status, assuming the participation is greater than a very insignificant involvement (Q 5:9). Also, it is the basis for assessment of an initial 10 percent excise tax on the organization and a 2½ percent tax on each of the organization's managers, and additional taxes of 100 percent on the organization and 50 percent on its managers.[26] However, to date, no instance has been made public where the IRS has assessed that tax. Moreover, there have been situations where the organization negotiated a closing agreement with the IRS by admitting the violation, promising to not repeat it, and making the agreement public; in these circumstances, the IRS has refrained from revoking the exemption (see Q 12:21).

The IRS has two other weapons in this regard:

1. It can trigger accelerated tax assessment rules when it finds that the political campaign activities constraint on public charities is being violated.[27] Under these procedures, the IRS need not wait until the close of the organization's tax year to commence an audit; it can prematurely terminate the entity's year and promptly begin the audit process.

2. It has special authority to request a court injunction to stop political campaign activity by a public charity in certain circumstances.[28]

Q 5:11   Do these rules apply to churches and other religious organizations?

As a matter of statutory law, yes. An institution of religious worship—such as a church, synagogue, or mosque—or any other type of religious organization[29] is barred from political campaign activity. These entities are charitable ones for tax purposes, and the federal tax law prohibits charitable organizations from participating or intervening in political campaigns (Q 5:3). Moreover, churches and the like are public charities, where these rules are focused (Q 5:2).

Q 5:12   Are these rules enforced against religious organizations?

Not very often. When it is done, the enforcement is selective. There are a few court cases where these rules have been applied to religious organizations other than churches and the like.[30] However, there have been, and continue to be, many instances where churches are directly involved in political campaigns. Candidates have campaigned in churches as part of the religious services and members of the clergy have endorsed candidates from the pulpit. These are blatant transgressions of the law—routinely engaged in by presidents, members of Congress, governors, mayors, and individuals seeking those and other positions. Even when these practices are reported in the public media, the IRS rarely acts.

Q 5:13   Is the prohibition against political campaigning by religious organizations constitutional?

That issue has yet to be decided by a court, particularly where a church is involved. There is a very good argument that, as long as churches and other religious organizations are treated in this regard no differently than other public charities, there is no unwarranted entanglement of church and state or impingement on the practice of religious beliefs.

The converse argument is that government should not be able to dictate what churches and similar institutions say in the context of propagation of their religious beliefs. This argument is more compelling where the church is speaking out on social issues and, only in that setting, is supporting or criticizing political candidates. It is less attractive when the church involvement is purely political, such as where a member of the clergy endorses a particular candidate from the pulpit during a church service.

This constitutional law issue may be decided by a federal court in the coming months. A lawsuit has been filed in the U.S. District Court for the District of Columbia, contending that the revocation of the tax exemption of a church for political campaign activities is contrary to the First and Fifth Amendments to the U.S. Constitution and the Religious Freedom Restoration Act.[31] Late in the 1992 presidential campaign, the church had paid for newspaper advertisements attacking candidate Bill Clinton's positions on social issues, including abortion and the distribution of condoms. This is the first time the IRS has proceeded against a church on this subject.

Q 5:14 What happens when a private foundation engages in a political campaign activity?

The law involving private foundations includes all of the law pertaining to public charities (Q 5:9, Q 5:10), as well as some special rules. If a private foundation engages in a political campaign activity, it may lose its tax-exempt status[32] and also be subject to excise taxation.[33] An expenditure of funds by a private foundation for a political campaign purpose—termed electioneering—is a *taxable expenditure;* the foundation would be subjected to an excise tax of 10 percent of the amount involved, plus a requirement that the expenditure be timely corrected. Foundation managers who knowingly allowed the foundation to engage in electioneering could be the recipients of a 2½ percent tax. If there is no timely correction, the foundation could be subjected to an additional tax of 100 percent, and the managers, to an additional tax of 50 percent.

Q 5:15 Can a charitable organization utilize a political action committee without adversely affecting its tax exemption?

Yes, but only under very limited circumstances. As a general rule, the function of a political action committee is to assist one or more individuals in becoming elected to political office—a political campaign activity in which a charitable organization is forbidden to engage (Q 5:1, Q 5:16). Because the functions of a political action committee are attributed to the affiliated charitable organization for this purpose, the political activities of the committee generally would cause the charity to forfeit its tax exemption and pay the excise tax on political expenditures.

However, this use of a political action committee is permissible where the political activities engaged in by the committee are other than political campaign activities. These activities must be exempt functions of political organizations (Q 5:16) but not political campaign activities by public charities. For example, a public charitable organization could, without loss of tax-exempt status, utilize a political action committee to work to defeat the nomination by a President of an individual to become a member of the Supreme Court.[34] This use of a political action committee would also preclude the charity from having to pay the political organization tax on expenditures associated with that political activity (Q 5:10).

OTHER EXEMPT ORGANIZATIONS AND POLITICAL ACTIVITIES

Q 5:16   What is a political organization?

A political organization is a type of tax-exempt organization. It is a party, committee, association, fund, or other organization formed and operated primarily for the purpose of directly or indirectly accepting contributions or making expenditures for an *exempt function*.[35] The principal exempt function of a political organization is influencing or attempting to influence the selection, nomination, election, or appointment of any individual to any federal, state, or local public office or office in a political organization. An organization of this nature can also be used to effect the election of presidential or vice-presidential electors. Political organizations include political parties, political action committees, campaign funds for individual candidates, and incumbents' newsletter funds. Other activities may be engaged in, but they must not divert the organization from its principal purpose. An organization that engages wholly in legislative activities cannot qualify as a political organization.

Political organizations are taxable on all income other than exempt function income, which includes contributions, membership dues, proceeds from fund-raising events, and receipts from the sale of political campaign materials.[36] All other income, including investment income, is taxable.

The federal election laws, which do not always parallel the federal tax laws in these respects, term organizations such as political action committees *separate segregated funds*.[37] Political organizations usually are not incorporated because of the strict limitations of the federal election law on political contributing and other political campaign activities by corporations.

Q 5:17   Aren't political action committees affiliated with other tax-exempt organizations?

They often are, but not always. The types of tax-exempt organizations that have political action committees usually are business leagues (such as trade or business associations) and labor organizations (such as labor unions) (Q 5:21). The membership of these organizations is the prospective donor base for the political entity (Q 5:22). A business enterprise can have a political action committee.

The federal election law recognizes the independent political action committee.[38] This is a political committee that is free-standing; that is, it is not affiliated with any sponsoring organization. However, the IRS has yet to rule on the qualifications of a free-standing political action committee as a tax-exempt political organization.

Q 5:18   Is the tax imposed on political organizations confined to those organizations?

No. The tax scheme for political organizations contains a tax that can be imposed on a wide range of other tax-exempt organizations. If an exempt organization expends any amount during a tax year, either directly or through another organization, for what would be an exempt function for a political organization (Q 5:16), it must include in its taxable income for the year an amount equal to the lesser of its net investment income for the year or the aggregate amounts expended for the exempt function.[39] This tax can be applicable where the tax-exempt organization does not keep accurate records that differentiate between soft money and hard money (Q 5:22).[40] This rule is applicable to charitable organizations, without corresponding loss of tax exemption, where the political activities involved are exempt functions that are not political campaign activities (Q 5:15).

Q 5:19   What are the rules concerning political activities by social welfare organizations?

A tax-exempt social welfare organization is not bound by the constraints on political activities that apply to charitable organizations (Q 5:1, Q 5:3). A social welfare organization can engage in political campaign activities as long as it is not thereby prevented from the conduct of its exempt functions.[41] There have not been any rulings or court opinions in amplification of that rule.

However, the political organization tax would be applicable with respect to these political campaign activities (Q 5:18). Also, if the organization has a membership and the members have joined in furtherance of business purposes, the deductibility of their dues may be affected by any political campaign activities of the organization (Q 5:20). Social welfare organizations are further restricted by the federal and state political campaign regulation laws.

Q 5:20   What are the rules concerning political activities by trade and business associations?

From the standpoint of tax-exempt status, the federal tax laws are essentially silent on the matter of political campaign activities by tax-exempt associations. There is no stated limitation in this regard, other than the general one that the political activities cannot be so extensive as to preclude the association from carrying out its exempt functions. Also, tax-exempt associations are subject to the political organizations tax when they engage in political activities (Q 5:18), and they are restricted by the federal and state political campaign regulation laws. Consequently, nearly all political campaign activities of tax-exempt associations are conducted by means of political action committees.

However, there is another body of federal tax law that must be taken into account for these purposes by a tax-exempt association. This law pertains to the deductibility, as a business expense, of the dues paid by the members of the association; as a general rule, these dues are fully deductible as expenditures made for business purposes. However, the deductibility of association dues can be circumscribed where the association engages in political campaign activities; these rules are the same as those pertaining to lobbying activities by business leagues (Q 4:27).

Q 5:21   To what extent can exempt organizations other than charities utilize political action committees?

Nearly all types of tax-exempt organizations can utilize political action committees. In fact, this is often done to avoid the political organization tax (Q 5:18).

If a tax-exempt organization establishes a political organization and operates the political activities through it, rather than through the sponsoring organization, the political exempt functions (Q 5:16) are in the political organization and not the parent entity. As exempt functions of the political organization, they are not taxed. Inasmuch as the political activities are not in the parent exempt organization, there is no political activities tax at that level either.

Q 5:22   What do the terms hard money and soft money signify?

The distinction between *hard money* and *soft money* is critical to avoidance of the political organizations tax; that is, the principal way to avoid this tax is to confine all political activities to the affiliated political organization (Q 5:21). All hard money expenditures are to be made only by the political organization; the affiliated (parent) exempt organization may make soft money expenditures.

Hard money is money that is used for political campaign contributions and similar purposes. Soft money is money that is used to establish and administer a political organization. For example, a business association may have a political action committee. The funds used by the association to create and operate the political action committee are soft funds; the amounts expended by the political action committee to support political candidates are hard funds. To continue with this example, the association would want to avoid making hard money expenditures, so as to not be subject to the political organization tax (Q 5:18) and not violate the federal campaign laws. This dichotomy in turn requires the parent tax-exempt organization (the association, in this example) to keep adequate records to differentiate between the two types of expenditures. In one instance, the IRS imposed the political organizations tax on an exempt organization because its records were inadequate to enable it to distinguish its soft money expenditures from its hard money outlays.[42]

Q 5:23   How do the federal election laws interrelate with the federal tax laws?

Not particularly well. Both bodies of law pertain to many of the same subjects, and the federal election law defines some pertinent terms where the tax laws do not. But, the IRS refuses to follow the interpretations of the Federal Election Commission. For example, the IRS does not follow the commission's rules as to definition of the term *candidate* (Q 5:6).

REPORTING REQUIREMENTS

Q 5:24   What are the reporting requirements for charitable organizations?

A public charity (see Chapter 6) must file an annual information return with the IRS. One of the questions on this form is whether the organization made any political expenditures.[43] Another question is whether the organization filed the income tax return required of political organizations.[44]

The annual information return that private foundations must file requests information about any expenditures the foundation may have made for political activities during the year.[45]

Q 5:25   What are the reporting requirements for other tax-exempt organizations?

The first reporting requirement stated for charitable organizations (Q 5:24) is applicable to all tax-exempt organizations required to file an annual information return.

Tax-exempt social welfare organizations, business leagues (including trade, business, and professional associations), and labor organizations must also report political expenditures that pertain to the rules concerning the nondeductibility of dues (Q 4:27).[46]

CHAPTER 6

Public Charity Status

The federal tax law separates charitable organizations into two categories: public and private. The latter are termed private foundations. Although the law presumes that all charitable organizations are private foundations, nearly all charities are public charities. There are three basic classifications of public charities, but there are many types within each classification. Because the body of federal tax law concerning private foundations is so onerous, it is important for a charitable organization to achieve public charity status if it can.

Here are the questions most frequently asked by clients about the difference between public charities and private foundations, how to acquire and maintain public charity status, the oft-misunderstood supporting organization—and the answers to them.

OVERVIEW

Q 6:1 What is a public charity?

A tax-exempt charitable organization is either a *public charity* or a *private foundation*. Every exempt charitable organization, domestic or foreign, is presumed to be a private foundation; this presumption can be rebutted by demonstrating to the IRS that the organization is a public charity.[1] There are three basic classifications of public charities, but there are many types of them (Q 6:3).

Q 6:2   What is a private foundation?

There is no true definition of a private foundation; there is only a "virtually real" definition of that term. This definition describes charitable organizations that are not private foundations.[2]

A generic private foundation has three characteristics: (1) it is a charitable organization that was initially funded by one source (usually an individual, a family, or a business), (2) its ongoing revenue income comes from investments (in the nature of an endowment fund), and (3) it makes grants to other charitable organizations rather than operate its own program. The nature of its funding and, sometimes, the nature of its governance (such as a closed, family-oriented board of trustees (Q 2:6)), are the characteristics that make this type of charitable organization *private*.

TIP: The federal tax rules applicable to private foundations are onerous and, because of various penalty excise taxes, can be costly.[3] One of the most important services a lawyer for a charitable organization can offer is advice on the organization's basis for avoidance of the private foundation rules.

Q 6:3   What are the categories of public charities?

Basically, there are three categories of public charities: (1) institutions, (2) publicly supported organizations, and (3) supporting organizations.

Institutions are charitable organizations that are clearly not private foundations, simply by virtue of their programs and structure.[4] These entities are churches, associations and conventions of churches, integrated auxiliaries of churches, colleges, universities, schools, hospitals, certain other health care providers, medical research organizations, certain supporting foundations for governmental colleges and universities, and a variety of governmental units.

Because they have a broad base of contributions from the general public, publicly supported charities generally are the antithesis of private foundations. Publicly supported organizations and supporting organizations are discussed below (Q 6:7–Q 6:29).

Q 6:4   How does an organization acquire public charity status?

Most commonly, an organization acquires public charity status at the same time it acquires recognition of tax-exempt status as a charitable organization. As part of the organization's filing of an application for recognition of exemption, it selects the category of public charity that it wants.[5] If the IRS agrees that the organization qualifies as a type of public charity, it includes that classification on the determination letter or ruling that it issues. (This is the process by which a charitable organization rebuts the presumption that it is a private foundation (Q 6:1).) Depending on the category of public charity, the organization will receive either an advance ruling (Q 6:9) or a definitive ruling (Q 6:11).

Q 6:5   How does an organization maintain its public charity status?

The manner in which an organization maintains its public charity status depends in large part on the type of public charity that it is. If it is an institution (Q 6:3) or a supporting organization (Q 6:15–Q 6:29), it remains a public charity as long as it continues to satisfy the programmatic or structural criteria that originally gave rise to the classification. If it is a publicly supported organization (Q 6:7–Q 6:14), it must provide its public support information to the IRS each year. This is done as part of the annual information return; there is a schedule by which both donative publicly supported charitable organizations and service provider publicly supported organizations display support information for a four-year measuring period.[6] An organization must only demonstrate that it qualifies under one of the categories each year, irrespective of the category that is reflected on its ruling.

Q 6:6   Why is it so important to be classified as a public charity and avoid private foundation status?

There are *no disadvantages* to public charity status; all of the disadvantages lie in classification as a private foundation. The disadvantages vary according to the nature of the organization; for some organizations, all of the disadvantages are important.

One of the principal disadvantages to private foundation status is the fact that, as a practical matter, private foundations will not make grants to other private foundations. A private foundation grantor must exercise *expenditure responsibility* as part of this type of grant,[7] and most private foundations do not have the resources to undertake, and do not want the risk of, expenditure responsibility grants. Also, in some instances, this type of grant will not qualify for the mandatory payout.[8] Any charitable organization that is structured as a private foundation has basically denied itself access to funding by private foundation grants.

Another disadvantage to private foundation status is that contributions to private foundations may be less deductible than those to public charities.[9] For example, in a single tax year, an individual may make deductible gifts of money to public charities in amounts up to 50 percent of his or her adjusted gross income, whereas gifts of money to private foundations are subject to a 30 percent limitation. Similarly, gifts of appreciated property to public charities are deductible up to a 30 percent limitation, but the limitation generally is 20 percent in the case of private foundations. (See Q 1:42–Q 1:43.)

Other disadvantages to private foundation status include (1) compliance with the federal tax rules regulating the conduct of private foundations,[10] (2) payment of a 2 percent tax on investment income, including capital gain,[11] (3) the requirement of filing a more complex annual information return,[12] and (4) the need to publish a newspaper advertisement as to the availability of the annual return.[13]

CAUTION: On occasion, a charitable organization—not understanding the rules in this area—will indicate on the application for recognition of exemption (Q 6:4) that it is a private foundation, when in fact it will clearly be qualifying as a publicly supported charity. The IRS is unnecessarily harsh on the point, rarely permitting the organization to amend the application and instead forcing it to formally terminate its private foundation status, including "starting over" with an advance ruling (Q 6:9). This can cause enormous funding problems in the early years when reliance is placed on private foundation grants (Q 6:6). Thus, a charitable organization should be certain, when selecting foundation status, that that is the correct classification.

PUBLICLY SUPPORTED CHARITIES

Q 6:7   What is a donative publicly supported charitable organization?

A *donative* publicly supported charitable organization is an organization that receives a substantial amount of its support in the form of
gifts and grants from the general public or from the U.S. government, a
state, or a political subdivision.[14] In this setting, *substantial* generally
means at least one-third. The denominator of this support ratio includes investment income; fee-for-service revenue is not included in
either the numerator or denominator. These calculations are made on
the basis of a four-year moving average. (Generally, the source of the
balance of the support is irrelevant.)

Support from any one source is public support to the extent that the
amount does not exceed an amount equal to 2 percent of the support
fraction denominator. For example, if an organization received $400,000
over its most recent four years, its public support would be the contributed amounts that did not exceed $8,000 per source (.02 × $400,000).
If the organization is able to show that at least $167,000 of the $400,000
came from public support, it can be considered a donative publicly supported organization for the two years immediately succeeding the four
measuring years. Unusual grants are excluded from the computation.

TIP: If an organization receives a substantial part of its support in
the form of fee-for-service revenue, it cannot qualify as a donative
publicly supported organization, even if it meets the support test for
the small amount of contributions it receives.

Some additional rules apply to the computation of support for donative publicly supported organizations: (1) amounts from other donative publicly supported organizations constitute public support in full
(that is, they are not limited by the 2 percent rule), (2) gifts and grants
that exceed the 2 percent limitation constitute public support to the extent of the 2 percent limitation amount, and (3) there are attribution
rules in determining sources of support (for example, gifts from a husband and wife are considered as coming from one source). To illustrate
the second additional rule, if the organization in the above example

received a $10,000 contribution from one source, $8,000 of it would be public support.

Two other categories of publicly supported organizations can be realized (1) by virtue of the *facts-and-circumstances–test*[15] or (2) because an organization is a community foundation.[16] Organizations in the former category have at least 10 percent of public support and have characteristics that demonstrate public involvement with the organization (such as public use of facilities, public involvement in the programs, or a board of directors reflective of the community). A community foundation is a charitable organization that receives funding from and makes grants within a discrete community.

Q 6:8   What is a service provider publicly supported charitable organization?

A *service provider* publicly supported organization is the other basic type of publicly supported charity.[17] This type of an organization normally receives at least one-third of its support in the form of gifts, grants, and exempt function revenue from the general public. The ratio calculation is made on the basis of a four-year moving average. The denominator of the ratio consists of the various forms of public support, net unrelated business income, investment income, tax revenues levied for the benefit of the organization, and the value of certain services or facilities furnished by a governmental unit.[18] Gift and grant support from any one source is public support to the extent that the amount derived did not come from a *disqualified person*.[19] Unusual grants are excluded from the computation.

The term *disqualified persons* includes an organization's directors, trustees, officers, key employees having responsibilities similar to those of officers, substantial contributors, family members of these individuals, and certain entities related to or affiliated with these persons. A *substantial contributor* is a person who contributed or granted more than $5,000 to the charitable organization, where that amount was more than 2 percent of the gifts and grants to the organization during the period of its existence.[20] In almost all cases, once a person is classified as a substantial contributor, that classification remains irrespective of the growth of the charity.

Public support can include *exempt function revenue*.[21] This is revenue in the form of gross receipts from admissions, sales of merchandise, performance of services, or furnishing of facilities, in an activity that is not an unrelated business. However, revenue of this nature is not public support to the extent that the receipts from any person or from any bureau or similar agency of a governmental unit in any tax year exceed the greater of $5,000 or 1 percent of the organization's support in that year. Also, this type of support from disqualified persons is not public support.

Using the figures of the above example, an organization attempting to qualify as a service provider publicly supported charity would also have to receive at least $167,000 in public support during the four-year measuring period. This support could be in the form of gifts, grants, and/or exempt function revenue. However, none of this support could be from substantial contributors, board members, or other disqualified persons.

A service provider publicly supported organization cannot normally receive more than one-third of its support from gross investment income.[22]

NOTE: A service provider publicly supported organization that utilizes a supporting organization must be cautious: funds transferred from the supporting organization may, in whole or in part, retain their character as investment income.

Q 6:9   What is an advance ruling?

An *advance ruling* is a ruling issued by the IRS to a new charitable organization that is expecting to qualify as a publicly supported organization (in either category, donative or service provider).[23] This ruling is part of the basic ruling recognizing tax-exempt status and charitable donee status. Being new, the organization does not have a financial history on which to base a determination as to whether it is publicly supported. Consequently, the IRS makes this initial determination of the organization's publicly supported charity status on the basis of a budget provided by the organization; where that information appears credible, the IRS will rule that the organization is reasonably expected to constitute a publicly supported organization. The term *advance* is used because the ruling is issued before actual development of the necessary financial data that will indicate whether the organization is in fact publicly supported. In this sense, the ruling is a probationary or tentative ruling as to publicly supported charity status.

NOTE: The concept of an advance ruling does not apply to recognition of tax exemption or charitable donee status. Advance rulings are issued to both putative donative publicly supported organizations and service provider publicly supported organizations.

If a new charitable organization wishes to be regarded by the IRS as a publicly supported charity, it must receive an advance ruling where it is in existence for only one year. (That "year" must be less than eight months.[24]) Where the organization has a financial history that is longer, it is entitled to, but need not pursue, a definitive ruling (Q 6:11).

TIP: This area of the law can be confusing, because of the source of it. The IRS does not follow the existing regulations on the subject. Instead, it uses different rules that can be found only in the instructions accompanying the application for recognition of tax exemption.

The period of time the advance ruling is in effect is the *advance ruling period*—the organization's first five years.

NOTE: The use of the term *year* can be tricky. For purposes of being able to gain a definitive ruling with only one year of existence, the "year" must be a period of at least eight months (Q 6:11). However, when *measuring* an entity's advance ruling period, the first year can be a period of any length—months, weeks, or some number of days. This may mitigate against forming, late in a year, a charitable entity that is intended to be publicly supported.

Once the advance ruling period has expired (at the close of the appropriate year) and if the organization has satisfied one of the public support tests, the advance ruling will ripen into a definitive ruling. The organization is expected to apply for a definitive ruling within 90 days after the close of the advance ruling period. The requisite financial information should be provided on an IRS form.[25]

Q 6:10   At the end of the advance ruling period, will the IRS automatically request more information regarding the organization's public support, or does the organization need to initiate contact with the IRS?

The responsibility to apply to the IRS for a definitive ruling within 90 days following the close of the advance ruling period lies with the organization. The IRS will not initiate contact with the charitable organization on this point at this time, beyond sometimes sending a copy of the requisite form (Q 6:9). Although it is not specifically required, the IRS prefers that the necessary information be tendered on that form.

Once the information is submitted, it is very rare for the IRS to request additional information; that is, the IRS will normally accept the public support information on its face. If the information reflects sufficient public support, the IRS will issue a definitive ruling. If the information shows that the organization did not receive adequate public support during the advance ruling period, the IRS—without inquiry—will classify the organization as a private foundation.

It is important for an organization in this position to accompany the form with a cover letter explaining why the organization meets the public support test (assuming it does) and to include the precise public support ratio. On occasion, if an organization has not met a public support test during the advance ruling period but seems clearly on the way to doing so in the succeeding year, the IRS will issue a favorable definitive ruling.

Q 6:11   What is a definitive ruling?

A *definitive ruling* is a ruling issued by the IRS to a charitable organization that qualifies as a publicly supported organization. This ruling is part of the basic declaration that recognizes tax-exempt status and charitable donee status. Definitive rulings are issued to both donative publicly supported organizations and service provider publicly supported organizations.

An eligible charitable organization is entitled to a definitive ruling if it has completed at least one tax year (consisting of at least eight months) and meets the requirements for one of the categories of publicly supported organization. However, a charitable organization that has been in existence for a period of that duration and has not yet achieved the necessary level of public support to qualify as a publicly supported organization, yet expects to qualify as a publicly supported organization, can obtain an advance ruling that it is reasonably expected to be a publicly supported organization.[26]

Q 6:12   Does it matter which category of publicly supported charity an organization uses?

Once a charitable organization meets the criteria of either type of publicly supported organization (donative or service provider), the IRS does not care which category the organization is in at any point in time. For example, an organization may receive an advance ruling that it is a donative publicly supported organization and subsequently be able to qualify only as a service provider publicly supported organization. Or, once a definitive ruling as to one of the classifications is received, the organization may annually shift from one category of publicly supported charity to the other.

In general, it is preferable, if possible, for a charitable organization to be classified as a donative publicly supported organization. Policy makers and regulators tend to look more favorably on charitable organizations that are supported primarily by gifts and grants. Charitable organizations that receive significant amounts of fee-for-service revenue are far more susceptible to allegations that they are operating in a commercial manner.

Whatever its actual category, a charitable organization may prefer to be regarded as a donative publicly supported organization rather than a service provider publicly supported organization. (There is no advantage to classification as a service provider publicly supported organization instead of a donative publicly supported organization.) Only a donative publicly supported organization is eligible to maintain a pooled income fund.[27] However, this eligibility extends to organizations *described in* the rules pertaining to donative publicly supported organizations.[28] If a charitable organization has received a definitive ruling that it is a service provider publicly supported organization, but it meets the support requirements for a donative publicly supported organization, it may maintain a pooled income fund (see Chapter 8).

TIP: The IRS prefers to classify publicly supported organizations as donative. On occasion, an organization that has applied for service provider status will find that the IRS wants to accord it donative status. Unless it is clear that the organization will not meet the service provider entity rules or there is a specific reason for wanting the service provider category, it is best to go along with the IRS on this point.

Q 6:13 What happens when an organization ceases to be a publicly supported charity?

If a charitable organization ceases to qualify as a publicly supported entity, the technical rule is that it automatically becomes a private foundation. This can happen in one of two ways: (1) the organization may reach the end of its advance ruling period (Q 6:9) and not have the requisite public support or (2) the organization may have a definitive ruling that it has publicly supported charity status (Q 6:11) but, at a point in time, fail to continue to qualify under either category of publicly supported charity.

In either circumstance, the organization will become a private foundation unless some other category of public charity status is available. One possibility is that the organization can (temporarily or otherwise) qualify as a publicly supported organization by reason of the facts-and-circumstances test (Q 2:5, Q 6:7). Another is that the organization can be restructured as a supporting organization (Q 6:15–Q 6:29). Still another is that the organization can become one of the institutions (such as an educational organization structured as a school) (Q 6:3).

If a charitable organization in this circumstance cannot avoid private foundation status, it is hardly the "end of the world" for the entity. It may be possible for the organization to become a hybrid entity (a blend of public charity and private foundation), usually a private operating foundation[29] or an exempt operating foundation.[30] A charitable organization that is classified as a private foundation can at any time demonstrate compliance with one of the bases for public charity status, terminate its private foundation status, and proceed on a definitive ruling or advance ruling basis.

Q 6:14 What should an organization do when it realizes, during the course of its advance ruling period, that it will not qualify as a publicly supported organization as of the close of that period?

There is no law on this point. In practice, a charitable organization that has an advance ruling, and realizes along the course of its advance ruling period that it cannot qualify as a publicly supported organization, can convert to a supporting organization (Q 6:15–Q 6:28) or, as a less likely choice, an institution, such as a school (Q 6:3). If the organization qualifies for the alternative status, the IRS will issue a ruling to that effect and will not attempt to assess tax on the organization's investment income (Q 6:6) for the early years. The fact that the organization did not meet a public support test during the initial months of the advance ruling period is ignored.

One aspect of this matter is clear: the organization should not simply allow the advance ruling period to expire without taking action. Occasionally, where the organization meets a public support test by taking into account the year following the advance ruling period but has not timely filed the support information (Q 6:9), the IRS will still issue a definitive ruling. But this action is wholly within the discretion of the IRS personnel and that outcome should not be assumed.

TIP: A charitable organization that expects to meet a public support test as of the close of its advance ruling period, but then does not, is likely to not have the requisite private foundation provisions in its articles of organization. Unless this matter is remedied by state law, the organization will lose its tax-exempt status. It is imperative to place the private foundation provisions in the governing instrument as a "fall-back" position where the state does not impose the rules as a matter of law. On occasion, the IRS will elongate the advance ruling period where the test is met using the support in the year following the advance ruling period, but that type of administrative relief cannot be assumed.

SUPPORTING ORGANIZATIONS

Q 6:15   What is a supporting organization?

A *supporting organization* is a charitable organization that would be a private foundation but for its structural or operational relationship with one or more charitable organizations that are either public institutions (Q 6:3) or publicly supported organizations (Q 6:7, Q 6:8).[31] This type of organization must be organized, and at all times thereafter operated, exclusively for the benefit of, to perform the functions of, or to carry out the purposes of at least one of these public charities, which are *supported organizations.* Also, it must be operated, supervised, or controlled by or in connection with one or more supported organizations. A supporting organization may not be controlled directly or indirectly by one or more disqualified persons (Q 6:23), other than foundation managers and one or more supported organizations.

The supporting organization must meet an *organizational test,* which basically requires that its articles of organization must limit its purposes to those of a supporting entity and not empower the organization to support or benefit any other organizations.[32] The supported organization(s) must be specified in the articles, although the manner of the specification depends on the nature of the relationship with the supported organization(s) (Q 6:16). Also, the supporting organization must adhere to an *operational test:* it must engage solely in activities that support or benefit one or more supported organizations (Q 6:17).[33]

Q 6:16 What are the requisite relationships between a supporting organization and a supported organization?

There are three of these relationships, defined as (1) *operated, supervised, or controlled by,* (2) *supervised or controlled in connection with,* or (3) *operated in connection with.* Irrespective of the relationship, the supporting organization must always be responsive to the needs or demands of one or more supported organizations and constitute an integral part of or maintain a significant involvement in the operations of one or more supported organizations.[34]

The relationship encompassed by the phrase *operated, supervised, or controlled by* contemplates the presence of a substantial degree of direction by one or more supported organizations over the policies, programs, and activities of the supporting organization.[35] This relationship, which is basically that of parent and subsidiary, is normally established by causing at least a majority of the directors or officers of the supporting organization to be composed of representatives of the supported organization or to be appointed or elected by the governing body, officers, or membership of the supported organization.

TIP: This is the most common relationship of the three. It is the easiest and most direct control relationship to construct, and it assures the supported organization that the benefits it expects from the supporting entity will be received.

The relationship manifested by the phrase *supervised or controlled in connection with* contemplates the presence of common supervision or control by persons supervising or controlling both entities to ensure that the supporting organization will be responsive to the needs and requirements of the supported organization(s).[36] This relationship—one of "brother and sister" entities—requires that the control or management of the supporting organization be vested in the same persons who control or manage the supported organization(s).

The relationship envisioned by the phrase *operated in connection with* contemplates that the supporting organization is responsive to and significantly involved in the operations of the supported organization(s).[37] Generally, the supporting organization must meet both a *responsiveness test* and an *integral part test*.

The responsiveness test is satisfied where the supporting organization is responsive to the needs or demands of one or more supported organizations.[38] The test can be satisfied where the supporting organization and the supported organization(s) are in close operational conjunction. There are several ways to show this. They include: (1) having one or more of the officers or directors of the supporting organization elected or appointed by the officers or directors of the supported organization(s) or (2) demonstrating that the officers or directors of the supporting organization maintain a close and continuous working relationship with the officers and directors of the supported organization(s). The officers and directors of the supported organization(s) must have a significant voice in the investment policies of the supporting organization; the timing of and manner of making grants, and the selection of grant recipients by the supporting organization; and the direction of the use of the income or assets of the supporting organization.

The responsiveness test may also be met where (1) the supporting organization is a charitable trust under state law, (2) each specified supported organization is a named beneficiary under the trust's governing instrument, and (3) each supported organization has the power, under state law, to enforce the trust and compel an accounting.

A supporting organization satisfies the integral part test where it maintains a significant involvement in the operations of one or more supported organizations and the beneficiary organization(s) are dependent on the supporting organization for the type of support it provides.[39] This test is met where the activities engaged in by the supporting organization for or on behalf of the supported organization(s) are activities to perform the functions of, or to carry out the purposes of, the supported

organization(s) and, but for the involvement of the supporting organization, would normally be engaged in by the supported organization(s).

There is a second way to meet the integral part test.

TIP: Although these requirements are considerably complex, these
rules represent the furthest reaches under which a charitable organization can avoid private foundation status.

Under this approach, the supporting organization makes payments of
substantially all of its income to or for the use of one or more supported
organizations, and the amount of support received by one or more of
the supported organizations is sufficient to ensure the attentiveness
of the organization(s) to the operations of the supporting organization.
The phrase *substantially all* means at least 85 percent.[40] A substantial
amount of the total support from the supporting organization must go to
those supported organizations that meet an attentiveness requirement
with respect to the supporting organization.

In general, the amount of support received by a supported organization must represent a sufficient part of its total support so as to ensure
the requisite attentiveness. If the supporting organization makes payments to or for the use of a department or school of a university, hospital,
or church, the total support of the department or school is the measuring
base, rather than the total support of the beneficiary institution.

Even where the amount of support received by a supported organization does not represent a sufficient part of its total support, the amount
of support from a supporting organization may be sufficient to meet the
requirements of the integral part test if it can be demonstrated that, in
order to avoid the interruption of the conduct of a particular function or
activity, the beneficiary organization will be sufficiently attentive to the
operations of the supporting organization. This may be the case where
either the supporting organization or the beneficiary organization ear-
marks the support received from the supporting organization for a particular program or activity, even if the program or activity is not the
beneficiary organization's primary program or activity, so long as the
program or activity is a substantial one.

All pertinent factors—including the number of the supporting organizations (Q 6:19), the length and nature of the relationship between
the beneficiary organization and the supporting organization, and the

purpose to which the funds are put (Q 6:17)—are considered in determining whether the amount of support received by a beneficiary organization is sufficient to ensure its attentiveness to the operations of the supporting organization. Inasmuch as, in the view of the IRS, the attentiveness of a supported organization is motivated by reason of the amount of funds received from the supporting organization, the more substantial the amount involved (in terms of a percentage of the total support of the supported organization), the greater the likelihood that the required degree of attentiveness will be present. However, other evidence of actual attentiveness by the supported organization is of almost equal importance. The mere making of reports to each of the supported organizations does not alone satisfy the attentiveness requirement of the integral part test.

Where none of the supported organizations is dependent on the supporting organization for a sufficient amount of the beneficiary organization's support, the integral part test cannot be satisfied, even though the supported organizations have enforceable rights against the supporting organization under state law.

Q 6:17   What are the functions of a supporting organization?

With the emphasis on *support,* the most common function of a supporting organization is as a funding mechanism for the supported organization(s).[41] In some instances, the supporting organization is the endowment fund for one or more beneficiary organizations. Endowments can be established by a public charity's transfer of some or all of its investment assets to a newly created supporting entity.

TIP: There seems to be a widespread belief that a public charity cannot spawn a supporting organization. This is not the case. For example, in the endowment fund setting, there may be considerable merit in having the fund in a separate entity (1) for liability purposes and (2) to place the assets in the hands of trustees who are more concerned with long-term operations than immediate budgetary pressures.[42] Health care providers and other public charities use the supporting organization vehicle to establish "holding companies" for more effective management.[43]

The law in this area speaks also of providing a *benefit* to a supported organization (Q 6:15). Aside from providing the supported organization with money, an organization can support or benefit another organization by carrying on its own programs or activities to support or benefit a supported organization. For example, a supporting organization supported a medical school at a university by operating teaching, research, and services programs as a faculty practice plan.[44] As another illustration, as part of its relationship with a public charity that provided residential placement services for mentally and physically handicapped adults, a supporting organization established and operated an employment facility for the handicapped and an information center about various handicapping conditions.[45]

A supporting organization may engage in fund-raising activities, such as charitable gift solicitations, special events (such as dinners and theater outings), and unrelated business activities, and give the funds for the supported organization(s) or to other permissible beneficiaries.

Q 6:18 Does the supported organization have to be identified in the organizational document of the supporting organization?

Usually, but not always. Generally, it is expected that the articles of organization of the supporting organization will designate the (or each of the) supported organization(s) by name. The manner of the specification depends on the nature of the relationship between the supported and supporting organizations (Q 6:16).[46]

If the relationship is one of *operated, supervised, or controlled by* or *supervised or controlled in connection with,* designation of a supported organization by name is not required as long as two rules are followed:

1. The articles of organization of the supporting organization must require that it be operated to support or benefit one or more supported organizations that are designated by class or purpose.

2. The class or purpose must include one or more supported organizations to which one of the two relationships pertains, or organizations that are closely related in purpose or function to the supported organizations to which one of the relationships pertains.

If the relationship is one of *operated in connection with,* generally the supporting organization's articles must designate the specified supported organization by name.

TIP: Irrespective of the relationship, it is usually preferable—from the standpoint of all organizations involved—for the supported organization(s) to be designated by name in the supporting organization's articles.

Where the relationship between the organizations is other than *operated in connection with,* the articles of organization of a supporting organization may (1) permit the substitution of an eligible organization within a class for another organization either in the same class or in a different class designated in the articles, (2) permit the supporting organization to operate for the benefit of new or additional organizations in the same class or in a different class designated in the articles, or (3) permit the supporting organization to vary the amount of its support among different eligible organizations within the class or classes of organizations designated by the articles.

An organization that is *operated in connection with* one or more supported organizations can satisfy this specification requirement even if its articles permit an organization that is designated by class or purpose to be substituted for an organization designated in its articles, but only where the substitution is "conditioned upon the occurrence of an event which is beyond the control of the supporting organization." Such an event would be: loss of tax exemption, substantial failure or abandonment of operations, or dissolution of the supported organization(s) designated in the articles. In one instance, a charitable entity failed to qualify as a supporting organization because its articles permitted substitution too freely: whenever, in the discretion of its trustee, the charitable undertakings of the supported organizations become "unnecessary, undesirable, impracticable, impossible or no longer adapted to the needs of the public," substitution was permitted.[47]

Q 6:19   How many supported organizations can a supporting organization support?

The law does not place any specific limitation on the number of supported organizations that can be served by a supporting organization. Whatever the number, there must be a requisite relationship between the supporting organization and each of the supported organizations (Q 6:16). As a practical matter, this relationship requirement serves as somewhat of a limitation on the number of supported organizations that can be clustered around a supporting organization. Yet, there is a supporting organization that serves over 300 public charitable entities.

Q 6:20 Can a supporting organization support or benefit a charitable organization or other person, in addition to one or more specified supported organizations?

Yes, although the opportunities for doing this are limited. The constraint comes from the fact that the law requires that a supporting organization be operated *exclusively* to support or benefit one or more qualified public entities (Q 6:15). The limitation also stems from the requirement of the requisite relationship and the specification rules (Q 6:16, Q 6:18). In general, a supporting organization must engage *solely* in activities that support or benefit one or more supported organizations.

A supporting organization may make payments to or for the use of, or provide services or facilities for, individual members of the charitable class that is benefited by a specified supported organization. Also, a supporting organization may make a payment through another, unrelated organization to a member of a charitable class benefited by a specified supported organization, but only where the payment constitutes a grant to an individual rather than a grant to an organization. At the same time, a supporting organization can support or benefit a charitable organization (other than a private foundation) if it is operated, supervised, or controlled directly by or in connection with a supported organization.[48] However, a supporting organization will lose its status as such if it pursues a purpose other than supporting or benefiting one or more supported organizations.

A supporting organization can carry on an independent activity as part of its support function (Q 6:17). This type of support must be limited to permissible beneficiaries, as described above.

In practice, however, it is quite common for supporting organizations to make payments to noncharitable entities as part of their support activities. For example, a supporting organization can procure and pay for services that are rendered to or for the benefit of a supported organization. The supporting organization can also engage in fund-raising activities, such as special events, for the benefit of a supported organization. In that capacity, the supporting organization can contract with and pay for services such as advertising, catering, decorating, and entertainment.

Q 6:21 Can a supporting organization support another supporting organization?

Although the law is not clear on the point, the answer probably is no. The law requires that a supporting organization operate for the benefit of, to perform the functions of, or to carry out the purposes of one or more public institutions or publicly supported organizations.[49] A superficial reading of this law could lead one to the conclusion that a supporting organization may not be supported in this manner because it is not a public institution or publicly supported organization. However, it is quite possible that, by supporting a supporting organization, a supporting organization could simultaneously benefit or carry out the purposes of a public institution or publicly supported organization. In fact, the regulations state that any charitable organization (other than a private foundation) can be a beneficiary of a supporting organization where the recipient organization is operated or controlled by a qualified supported organization.[50] However, the IRS is of the view that this regulation was not intended to allow one supporting organization to support another—under any circumstances. Thus, it would not be advisable to structure such an arrangement without first obtaining a ruling from the IRS.

NOTE: To date, the IRS has not issued a ruling on the point. This is either because the IRS has not received a ruling request or because any such request was withdrawn in the face of an adverse position by the IRS.

Q 6:22 Can a charitable organization be a supporting organization with respect to a tax-exempt organization that is not a charitable one?

Yes. A charitable organization can support or benefit an exempt organization other than a charitable entity where the supported organization is a tax-exempt social welfare organization, a tax-exempt labor organization, or a tax-exempt association that is a business league.[51] However, for this arrangement to be successful, the supported organization must meet the public support test applied to service provider publicly supported charitable organizations (Q 6:8). This rule is largely designed to establish nonprivate foundation status for "foundations" and other funds that are affiliated with and operated for the benefit of these eligible non-charitable exempt organizations.

Q 6:23 Are any limitations placed on the composition of the board of directors of a supporting organization?

Yes. The general concept is that a supporting organization will be controlled, through a structural or programmatic relationship, by one or more eligible public organizations. Thus, a supporting organization may not be controlled, directly or indirectly, by one or more disqualified persons (Q 6:15)—other than, of course, foundation managers and one or more supported organizations.[52] A supporting organization is controlled by one or more disqualified persons if, by aggregating their votes or positions of authority, they may require the organization to perform any act that significantly affects its operations or may prevent the supporting organization from performing the act. Generally, a supporting organization is considered to be controlled in this manner if the voting power of disqualified persons is 50 percent or more of the total voting power of the organization's governing board or if one or more disqualified persons have the right to exercise veto power over the actions of the organization. All pertinent facts and circumstances are taken into consideration in determining whether a disqualified person indirectly controls an organization.

An individual who is a disqualified person with respect to a supporting organization (such as being a substantial contributor (Q 6:8)) does not lose that status because a supported organization appointed or otherwise designated him or her a foundation manager of the supporting organization as the representative of the supported organization.

In one instance, the IRS concluded that the board of directors of a supporting organization was indirectly controlled by a disqualified person.[53] The organization's board of directors was composed of a substantial contributor to it, two employees of a business corporation of which more than 35 percent of the voting power was owned by the substantial contributor (making the corporation itself a disqualified person (Q 6:8)), and one individual selected by the supported organization. None of the directors had any veto power over the organization's actions. While conceding that the supporting organization was not directly controlled by the disqualified person, the IRS said that "one circumstance to be considered is whether a disqualified person is in a position to influence the decisions of members of the organization's governing body who are not themselves disqualified persons." The IRS concluded that the two individuals who were employees of the disqualified person corporation should be considered disqualified persons for purposes of applying the 50 percent control rule. This led to a ruling that the organization was indirectly controlled by disqualified persons and therefore could not qualify as a supporting organization.

TIP: This matter of indirect control by disqualified persons is very much a facts-and-circumstances test. The IRS is particularly sensitive to the possibility that creative structuring is being used to mask control of a supporting organization by one or more disqualified persons. The IRS tends to be rather strict on this point.

This control element can be the difference between the qualification of an organization as a supporting organization or as a common fund private foundation. The right of the donors to designate the recipients of the organization's grants can constitute control of the organization by them; supporting organization classification is precluded where this control element rests with substantial contributors.[54]

Q 6:24   Should a supporting organization be separately incorporated?

The law does not require that a supporting organization be incorporated. In most instances, however, supporting organizations *are* incorporated, for the same reasons most nonprofit corporations use the corporate form (Q 2:41). One context in which the trust form may be advisable is where it may be needed as a way to satisfy the responsiveness test (Q 6:16).

Q 6:25   Should a supporting organization have bylaws?

The answer depends on the type of organization that the supporting organization is. If it is a corporation (Q 6:24) or an unincorporated association, it should have bylaws. Charitable trusts do not usually have bylaws, although when the trust form is used for a supporting organization, a set of bylaws or a document akin to bylaws is advisable.

NOTE: There is a specific organizational test in this setting (Q 6:15). However, the requisite language must be contained in the articles of organization; inclusion only in the bylaws is inadequate.

Q 6:26 Who elects or appoints the directors of a supporting organization?

Selection of directors depends on the type of supporting organization, that is, on the nature of the relationship between the supporting entity and the supported organization(s) (Q 6:16). If the relationship is that of *operated, supervised, or controlled by,* at least a majority of the board of the supporting organization would be elected or appointed by the supported organization. The entirety of the supporting organization's board can be selected in this manner, or the minority members can be selected by the majority members.

If the relationship is that of *supervised or controlled in connection with,* the boards of directors of the two organizations will be the same. Thus, the organizational documents of the supporting organization would state that its governing board is the same group that comprises the board of the supported entity.

Where the relationship is embraced by the phrase *operated in connection with,* the board of directors of the supporting organization can possibly be wholly independent of the supported organization from the standpoint of its governance. Thus, the board can be structured in any way that is deemed appropriate by the parties involved.

NOTE: The board of directors of the supporting organization cannot be controlled by disqualified persons with respect to it (Q 6:23).

It may be necessary to have one or more of the directors of the supporting organization elected or appointed by the directors of the supported organization, to facilitate compliance with the responsiveness test (Q 6:16).

Q 6:27 Can a supporting organization maintain its own financial affairs (such as by means of a separate bank account and separate investments)?

The supporting organization not only can maintain its own financial affairs but it should. This type of entity is a separate organization, and its legal status (including tax exemption) is predicated on that fact. Thus, separate financial resources are (or should be) always the case. This is particularly true with respect to supporting organizations that support or benefit noncharitable entities (Q 6:22).

One of the overarching requirements often is that the supported organization have a significant involvement in the operations of the supporting organization (Q 6:16). This is likely to mean that the board of the supported organization has direction over the investment policies of the supporting organization. For example, for purposes of meeting the responsiveness test, the officers and directors of the supported organization(s) may have to have a significant voice in the investment policies of the supporting organization, the timing of grants, the manner of making them, and the selection of recipients by the supporting organization, and in otherwise directing the use of the income or assets of the supporting organization (Q 6:16).

Q 6:28   What financial reports and disclosure should a supporting organization make to the supported organization?

The law on this point is next to nonexistent. For the most part, this is a management matter rather than a legal one. State law may apply, particularly if the supporting entity is a charitable trust.

To the extent the federal rules address the point, it is a function of the relationship between the supported organization and the supporting organization. In general, the supporting organization must be responsive to the demands of the supported organization (Q 6:16). Thus, the law generally requires that the supporting organization provide whatever financial information about itself that the board of the supported organization "demands." Where the relationship is one of *operated, supervised, or controlled by* or *supervised or controlled in connection with,* the board of the supported organization is in the position of receiving any information about the supporting organization—financial or otherwise—that it wants.

Financial disclosure to the supported organization becomes most problematic when the relationship is evidenced by the phrase *operated in connection with.* In this situation, the board composition of the supporting organization may be such that financial information is not readily available to the board of the supported organization. A problem may arise in the context of meeting the attentiveness requirement of the integral part test. However, the mere making of reports to a supported organization does not alone enable the supporting organization to meet this requirement (Q 6:16). Thus, where the *operated in connection with* relationship is involved, the sharing of financial information may be largely political, that is, whatever the parties can work out.

Q 6:29   What oversight should the supported organization perform?

No oversight requirement is imposed by law on the supported organization (other than the supervision that may flow out of fiduciary responsibility duties (Q 1:19)). The relationship responsibilities all fall on the supporting organization, as part of its justification for nonprivate foundation status. The supporting organization must always be responsive to the needs or demands of one or more supported organizations and must constitute an integral part of or maintain a significant involvement in the operations of one or more supported organizations (Q 6:16).

Good management practice would dictate that the supported organization be concerned with, and do what it can to conserve, the state and nature of the resources held by the supporting organization. Where the relationship is one of *operated, supervised, or controlled by* or *supervised or controlled in connection with,* any management oversight duties that the supported organization may wish to undertake are readily available (Q 6:28).

CHAPTER 7

Fund-Raising Regulation

The process of raising funds for charitable purposes, despite protection under constitutional law, is heavily regulated by the federal and state governments. The states exercise this authority largely by means of statutory law, reflective of their police powers. Most of these laws are known as charitable solicitation acts. Nearly all of the states have some form of charitable solicitation act; 35 of them have extensive statutes in this area.

Federal regulation is largely through the tax system, although the postal and trade laws are of increasing importance. The IRS has several sets of regulations audit guidelines in this area. Other bodies of federal tax law that amount to fund-raising regulation are contained in the charitable giving rules, the unrelated business rules, and the exemption application and annual reporting requirements.

Here are the questions most frequently asked by clients about federal regulation of charitable fund-raising (including the ever-expanding rules as to gift substantiation and quid pro quo situations), and the contents and enforcement of the many state charitable solicitation acts—and the answers to them.

OVERVIEW

Q 7:1   How does the federal government regulate fund-raising for charitable purposes?

For the most part, federal regulation in this area is through the tax system, principally the income tax laws. The chief subparts of the law in this area are IRS audit guidelines, the charitable gift substantiation requirements, the quid pro quo contribution rules, the procedure for applying for recognition of tax exemption, the unrelated business rules, the annual information return requirements, the public charity rules, and the many intricacies of the law surrounding the income, gift, and estate tax charitable contribution deductions.

There is also some regulation at the hands of the U.S. Postal Service, through its monitoring of use of the special bulk third-class mailing rates, and the Federal Trade Commission, particularly as it regulates telemarketing (see Q 7:19).

Q 7:2   How do the state governments regulate fund-raising for charitable purposes?

All but three of the states have some form of statutory law governing the solicitation of charitable gifts. (The states that lack any such law are Delaware, Montana, and Wyoming.) Thirty-five states have formal, comprehensive *charitable solicitation acts*. The elements of these laws are summarized below (Q 7:10). The attorney general of a state has inherent authority to oversee charities; this authority is derived from the *parens patriae* doctrine.

The states also have laws concerning the availability of tax exemptions, the deductibility of charitable gifts, the offering of securities, the sale of insurance programs, unfair trade practices, misleading advertising, and fraud—each of which can be applied in the realm of charitable fund-raising.

Q 7:3   Are these state laws constitutional?

In general, yes, although the tension in this field is intense. A state, for example, has the police power and can use this authority to protect its citizens against charitable fund-raising fraud and other abuse. However, this type of regulation needs to be more than *reasonable* in scope, as determined by the state. Fund-raising for charitable purposes is one of the highest forms of free speech, and thus governments can regulate it only by the narrowest of means.

Some features of state and local charitable solicitation acts have been struck down as being unconstitutional, in violation of free speech rights. The most infamous legislated features are limitations on the fund-raising costs of charitable entities or on the levels of compensation paid to professional solicitors. Certain forced disclosures are also banned. However, overall, the charitable solicitation acts themselves have been upheld, in the face of claims that they wrongfully hamper free speech or unduly burden interstate commerce.

The police power of the states (and local governments) directly clashes with the free speech rights of charities and their fund-raisers. To date, this tension has been modulated by the courts, with the consensus being that the police power allows for the general application of the charitable solicitation laws, while constitutional law principles force governments to regulate in this area by the narrowest of means.[1]

FEDERAL LAW REQUIREMENTS

Q 7:4   What are the IRS audit practices as applied to fund-raising charitable organizations?

The IRS has specific concerns about charitable organizations that are engaged in charitable solicitation; these concerns are reflected in IRS audit guidelines promulgated for its examining agents. There are two sets of guidelines with which these charitable entities should be particularly familiar.

The first guideline is a "checksheet" that the IRS has developed for use by agents in auditing the fund-raising programs of charitable organizations. This checksheet, containing 82 questions of direct pertinence to a wide variety of fund-raising practices, is termed the "Exempt Organizations Charitable Solicitations Compliance Improvement Program Study Checksheet."[2] This checksheet requires the auditing agent to review, in conjunction with examinations of annual information returns (see Q 9:17), the fund-raising practices of charities, including the solicitation of gifts where the donor is provided a benefit, the use of special events, the conduct of games of chance, travel tours, thrift stores, and the receipt of noncash contributions. A special section inquires about the use of professional fund-raisers.

The second set of guidelines was published for college and university audits in 1994.[3] Although these guidelines technically apply only in the context of higher education, they describe in considerable detail how the agent is to conduct the fund-raising audit in general. There should be no doubt that an audit of any charitable organization, from the standpoint of its fund-raising practices, would be conducted in a manner close to that summarized in these guidelines.

The IRS will want to identify each individual responsible for soliciting and accounting for charitable contributions. Copies of the appropriate job descriptions will be requested. The minutes of any committee involved in fund-raising (such as a development, finance, or budget committee) will be reviewed; board minutes may be examined also, particularly if the board is involved in accepting gifts. Correspondence with donors will be reviewed, along with gift agreements; the IRS will be searching for restrictions, earmarkings, or conditions by which benefits may be provided to contributors. Any private benefit could affect the organization's tax exemption (see Chapter 3); certain benefits could affect the extent of deductibility of contributions (Q 7:7).

NOTE: These guidelines do not expressly describe this practice, but the IRS will read correspondence and agreements, looking for anticipatory assignments of income (where the income can be taxed to the donor) and step transactions (where the capital gain element in a gift of property can be taxed to the donor).

Fund-raisers should be prepared to share with the IRS the organization's lists of contributors by name and category (such as individuals and corporations), lists of restricted gifts, lists of in-kind gifts, and other internal lists and reports relating to contributions.

Q 7:5   How do the charitable giving rules apply?

The charitable giving rules apply in many ways, because they govern the deductibility of charitable gifts for federal tax purposes (Q 1:41–Q 1:44; Chapter 8). The facets of this application include the definitions of the terms *charitable* and *gift,* the percentage limitations as to annual deductibility, the deduction reduction rules, the rules concerning gifts of partial interests, and a variety of rules pertaining to contributions of specific types of property.

There are, however, three bodies of charitable giving law that have particular relevance in the realm of fund-raising regulation: (1) the charitable gift substantiation requirements, (2) the quid pro quo contribution rules, and (3) the appraisal requirements.

Q 7:6   What are the charitable gift substantiation requirements?

The essence of the substantiation requirements is that there is no federal income tax charitable contribution deduction for any charitable gift of $250 or more, unless the donor has contemporaneous written substantiation from the donee charitable organization.[4] In cases where the charity has provided goods or services to the donor in exchange for the contribution, this contemporaneous written acknowledgment must include a good-faith estimate of the value of the goods or services.

TIP: If no goods or services are provided, the substantiation document must state that fact. Some charitable organizations, not realizing this, are providing to their donors documents that technically are not in compliance with these rules—thus jeopardizing the charitable deductions.

These rules are inapplicable to the provision of intangible religious benefits (Q 7:11).

If the contribution is of property, the acknowledgment must describe the property.

NOTE: The donee charitable organization is not required to value the property for the donor—and should not do so. Valuation of the donated property is the responsibility of the donor. The donee organization does have to place a value on the contributed property for purposes of its own financial records.

Separate gifts to a charitable organization are regarded as independent contributions and are not aggregated for purposes of measuring the $250 threshold. Donations made through payroll deductions are considered separate payments from each paycheck. The IRS is authorized to establish antiabuse rules to prevent avoidance of the substantiation requirements—for example, by writing separate smaller checks to the same charitable organization on the same date.

For the substantiation to be *contemporaneous,* it must be obtained no later than the date the donor files a tax return for the year in which the contribution was made. If the return is filed after the due date or on an extended due date, the substantiation must have been obtained by the due date or extended due date.

NOTE: The charitable community has not, to date, evidenced much of an understanding of these rules. Thus, many donors did not have the requisite substantiation documentation when the time came to prepare tax returns for 1994. The IRS provided some relief by allowing the documentation to be provided to contributors by October 16, 1995.[5] However, this was a one-time-only relaxation of this rule.

A charitable organization that knowingly provides false written substantiation to a donor may be subject to the penalties for aiding and abetting an understatement of tax liability.

Q 7:7   Do these rules apply with respect to benefits provided to donors after the gifts were made, where there was no prior notification of the benefit, such as a recognition dinner?

Generally, no. These rules apply to payments made in consideration for some benefit provided by the donee charitable organization. Pending regulations state that the rules are applicable where a good or service is provided in *consideration* for a payment to the charity, meaning that the donor expects the good or service at the time the payment is made.[6] Thus, this type of an after-the-fact benefit generally does not need to be taken into account in determining the amount of the charitable deduction.

NOTE: Some caution must be exercised here. If the charitable organization always provides a recognition dinner for certain donors, at some point, an "expectation" can be presumed, even when there is no express promise of it at the time of the gift. Lines of demarcation in this area will be made on the basis of facts and circumstances.

Q 7:8   How do the substantiation rules apply to gifts made by means of charitable remainder trusts, charitable lead trusts, and pooled income funds?

According to pending regulations,[7] the rules will not apply to gifts made by means of charitable remainder trusts (Q 8:6) and charitable lead trusts (Q 8:8). This is because donors to these trusts are not required to designate a specific charitable organization as the beneficiary at the time money or property is transferred to the trust. Thus, there may not be a charitable organization available to provide the requisite written acknowledgment. Also, even where a specific charitable beneficiary is designated, the designation is often revocable. By contrast, the law requires that one or more charitable organizations must maintain a pooled income fund (Q 8:7), so contributions made by means of these funds must be substantiated.

Q 7:9   What are the quid pro quo contribution rules?

A *quid pro quo contribution* is a payment made partly as a contribution and partly for goods or services provided to the donor by the charitable organization.[8] A charitable organization must provide a written disclosure statement to donors who make a quid pro quo contribution in excess of $75. The required written disclosure must inform the donor that the amount of the contribution that is deductible for federal income tax purposes is limited to the excess of any money, or the excess of the value of any property, the donor contributed over the value of the goods or services provided by the charity. The disclosure must provide the donor with a good faith estimate of the value of the goods or services the donor received.

The charitable organization must furnish the statement in connection with either the solicitation or the receipt of the quid pro quo contribution. The disclosure must be in writing and presented in a manner that is reasonably likely to come to the attention of the donor. A disclosure in small print within a larger document may not satisfy the requirement.

A penalty is imposed on charitable organizations that do not meet these disclosure requirements.[9] For failure to make the required disclosure in connection with a quid pro quo contribution of more than $75, there is a penalty of $10 per contribution, not to exceed $5,000 per fund-raising event or mailing. An organization may be able to avoid this penalty if it can show that the failure to comply was due to reasonable cause.

NOTE: The basic principle that a charitable deduction is allowed only to the extent that the payment exceeds the fair market value of the goods or services received in return is generally applicable to all quid pro quo contributions. The $75 threshold pertains principally to the nature of the obligation to disclose (statutory rather than by IRS rule) and imposition of the penalty; it does not apply to the rules as to the extent of deductibility of the payment.

Q 7:10 What is a good faith estimate?

The statute does not define the phrase *good faith estimate*. Pending regulations state that a good faith estimate of the value of goods or services provided by a charitable organization is an estimate of the fair market value of the goods or services. These regulations add that an organization can use a reasonable methodology in making a good faith estimate, as long as it applies the methodology in good faith.[10] These forms of circular reasoning are not likely to be of much help.

Q 7:11 Are there any exceptions to the quid pro quo contribution rules?

There are seven exceptions. The first three apply where the only goods or services provided to a donor are those having an incidental value.[11] The exceptions are:

1. Where the fair market value of all the benefits received is not more than 2 percent of the contributions or $50, whichever is less.

   NOTE: This $50 threshold is adjusted for inflation. For 1995, the amount is $66.

2. Where the contribution is $25 or more and the only benefits received by the donor in return during the calendar year have a cost, in the aggregate, of not more than a *low-cost article*. A low-cost article is one that does not cost more than $5 to the organization that distributes it or on whose behalf it is distributed.[12]

   NOTE: The $25 contribution, indexed for inflation, is $33 for 1995. The cost of a low-cost article, also adjusted for inflation, is $6.60 for 1995.

3. Where, in connection with a request for a charitable contribution, the charity mails or otherwise distributes free, unordered items to patrons, and the cost of the items (in the aggregate) distributed to any single patron in a calendar year is not more than a low-cost article.

4. Where no donative element is involved in the transaction with the charitable organization. Illustrations of this are payments of tuition to a school, payments for health care services to a hospital, and the purchase of an item from a museum gift shop.

5. Where an *intangible religious benefit* is involved. For the exception to be available, the benefit must be provided by an organization exclusively for religious purposes and must be of a type that generally is not sold in a commercial transaction outside the donative context. An example of a religious benefit is admission to a religious ceremony. This exception also generally applies to de minimis tangible benefits, such as wine provided in connection with a religious ceremony. The intangible religious benefit exception does not apply to items such as payments for tuition for education leading to a recognized degree, travel services, or consumer goods.

6. Annual membership benefits offered for no more than $75 per year that consist of rights or privileges that the individual can exercise frequently during the membership period.[13] These benefits include free admission to the organization's events, free parking, and discounts on the purchase of goods.

7. Annual membership benefits offered for no more than $75 per year that consist of admission to events during the membership period that are open only to members of the charitable organization and for which the organization reasonably projects that the cost per person (excluding any overhead) for each event is within the limits established for low cost articles.[14]

Q 7:12   How does a charitable organization value the involvement of a celebrity for purposes of the quid pro quo contribution rules?

If the celebrity performs at the event, using the talent for which he or she is celebrated (such as singing or stand-up comedy), the fair market value of the performance must be determined in calculating any benefit and thus any charitable deduction. However, if the celebrity does something else, his or her presence can be disregarded. For example, in the case of a tour of a museum by an artist whose works are featured there, the value of the tour can be ignored.[15]

Q 7:13   What are the appraisal requirements?

For most gifts of property (or collections of property) to a charitable organization, where the value is in excess of $5,000, there are certain appraisal requirements.[16] (Gifts of money and publicly traded securities are excepted from these appraisal rules.) Property to which the rules apply is termed *charitable deduction property.*

The donor of charitable deduction property must obtain a *qualified appraisal* of the property and attach an *appraisal summary* to the tax return on which the deduction is claimed. The law details the items of information that must be in a qualified appraisal and an appraisal summary. The appraisal must be conducted by a *qualified appraiser.*

Q 7:14   What does the IRS look for with respect to new charitable organization?

Nearly every organization that wants to be tax-exempt as a charitable entity, and be an organization eligible to receive tax-deductible gifts, must give notice to the IRS to that effect by filing an application for recognition of tax exemption.[17] (The principal exceptions are those for churches and their integrated auxiliaries, and organizations that have gross receipts that normally are not in excess of $5,000.) The application requests certain information about the fund-raising program of the organization.

For example, the organization must describe its actual and planned fund-raising program, summarizing its actual use of, or plans to use, selective mailings, fund-raising committees, professional fund-raisers, and the like. Depending on the progress of its solicitation efforts, the organization can describe a very detailed fund-raising program or it can state that it has yet to develop any specific processes for raising funds. If the organization has developed written material for the solicitation of contributions, it should attach copies.[18]

The application—which is publicly accessible—must contain a disclosure of the organization's fund-raising costs. Depending on the length of time the organization has been in existence, this information will be reflected in the financial statement that is a part of the application or in a proposed budget submitted with the application.[19]

Q 7:15   How do the reporting rules apply?

Nearly every charitable organization must file an annual information return with the IRS.[20] (The most notable exceptions are churches and their integrated auxiliaries, and organizations whose gross receipts normally are not in excess of $25,000.) Certain information pertaining to the organization's fund-raising program must be supplied.

The annual information return requires charitable (and other tax-exempt) organizations to use the *functional method of accounting* to report their expenses.[21] This accounting method allocates expenses by function, including those for fund-raising. Thus, swept into the fund-raising category are not only direct fund-raising costs (such as professional fund-raisers' fees and telemarketing expenses) but outlays that are allocable only in part to fund-raising (such as joint-purpose mailings). The organization must (or should) maintain detailed records as to its fund-raising (and other) expenses.

The IRS defines the term *fund-raising expenses* to mean all expenses, including allocable overhead costs, incurred in publicizing and conducting fund-raising campaigns; soliciting bequests, grants from foundations or other organizations, and government grants; participating in federated fund-raising campaigns; preparing and distributing fund-raising manuals, instructions, and other materials; and conducting special fund-raising events that generate contributions.[22]

TIP: The IRS does not differentiate, when referring to *professional fund-raisers,* between fund-raising counsel and solicitors (Q 7:22 and Q 7:23). Professional fund-raising fees are those paid to "outside fund-raisers for solicitation campaigns they conducted, or for providing consulting services in connection with a solicitation of contributions by the organization itself."

Organizations must report their receipts from and expenses of special fund-raising events and activities, separating the information for each type of event. Typically, these events include dinners, dances, carnivals, raffles, auctions, bingo games, and door-to-door sales of merchandise.

Q 7:16 Do the unrelated business income rules apply in the fund-raising setting?

Yes. Several types of fund-raising events or activities—sometimes known as *special events*—are technically *businesses* for federal income tax purposes (Q 10:6). Thus, were it not for certain other provisions in the federal tax law pertaining to unrelated businesses, some or all of the net income from these events would be taxable.

Some of this revenue is sheltered from taxation on the rationale that the activity is not *regularly carried on* (Q 10:13). This shelter protects activities that are conducted only once each year, such as a dinner dance, a theater outing, or an auction. However, if the event is seasonal, such as the selling of holiday cards, the season (not the full year) is the measuring period.

Some revenue-raising activities are considered related businesses (Q 10:18). These include sales of various items in gift shops maintained by hospitals and museums, as well as in college and university bookstores. Other sales in these shops and stores may be nontaxable by operation of the *convenience doctrine* (Q 10:23).

Still other fund-raising practices are protected against taxation by specific statutory exceptions. Some fund-raising events are run entirely by volunteers; businesses that are conducted substantially by individuals who are unpaid for their services are not taxed.

TIP: It does not take much for a court to conclude, for purposes of this exception, that someone is compensated. In one case, involving a gambling operation conducted weekly by a tax-exempt organization, individuals who were otherwise volunteers were found to be paid because they received tips from patrons.[23]

Another exception is for businesses that sell items that were contributed to the organization.[24] This rule was created for the benefit of thrift stores operated by nonprofit organizations, but it can also be applicable to frequent auctions.

Still another exception can protect *royalties* as fund-raising revenue (Q 10:24, Q 10:25). One organization successfully used this exception to immunize income from an affinity card program from tax.[25] In another instance, revenue from the rental of mailing lists was excepted from taxation as royalties.[26] In these cases, the payments were for the use of the organization's name, logo, and mailing list.

Q 7:17 Are there limitations on the use of the royalty exception in the fund-raising setting?

Yes, but where these limitations are is a matter of intense controversy. The IRS position—and that of conventional wisdom—is that, for an item of revenue to be a tax-free royalty, it had to be passively derived, in the nature of investment income, for example. This view of the law sees active participation by the tax-exempt organization in the revenue-raising process as meaning that some form of joint venture is occurring, thereby defeating the exclusion.

The opposite view is that a royalty is a royalty; that is, the factor of passivity is not required. This rationale, which rests on a careful reading of the legislative history of the unrelated business rules, defines a royalty as payment for the use of valuable intangible property rights.[27]

NOTE: If the second view is the correct one, the revamping of the royalty exception is an opportunity to transform what is or may be a taxable unrelated activity conducted by the exempt organization into a nontaxable stream of income. Basically, this involves transferring the function to another party, giving the party the right to use the necessary intangible property rights previously held by the exempt organization, and crafting the appropriate royalty contract. If the transfer is done properly, the organization can enhance its revenue stream with a new source of revenue or with nontaxation of previously taxed revenue—or both.

TIP: If the exempt organization becomes too heavily involved in the conduct of the royalty activity, there remains a line of law that would treat the relationship between the parties as a partnership, with resulting income to the exempt organization taxed as unrelated fee-for-service income. Also, the contract must be written so that the person running the operation that generates the royalty income is not deemed the agent of the exempt organization. This issue is being hotly contested in the courts.

Q 7:18   Are there fund-raising disclosure requirements for noncharitable organizations?

Yes. Fund-raising disclosure rules apply to exempt organizations other than charitable ones, unless the organization has annual gross receipts that are normally no more than $100,000.[28]

Under these rules, each fund-raising solicitation by or on behalf of an organization must contain an express statement, in a conspicuous and easily recognizable format, that gifts to it are not deductible as charitable contributions for federal income tax purposes. (There is an exclusion for letters or telephone calls that are not part of a coordinated fund-raising campaign soliciting more than 10 persons during a calendar year.)

TIP: Despite the clear reference in the law solely to "contributions and gifts," the IRS insists that the rule requires disclosure when any tax-exempt organization (other than a charity) seeks funds such as dues from members.

Failure to satisfy this disclosure requirement can result in a penalty of $1,000 per day (maximum of $10,000 per year), unless a reasonable cause justifies an exception. For an intentional disregard of these rules, the penalty for the day on which the offense occurred is the greater of $1,000 or 50 percent of the aggregate cost of the solicitations that took place on that day—and the $10,000 limitation does not apply. For penalty purposes, the IRS counts the days on which the solicitation was telecast, broadcast, mailed, telephoned, or otherwise distributed.[29]

Q 7:19   Are there any other federal law requirements as to fund-raising?

There are several. Other applications of the federal income tax rules pertain to publicly supported charitable organizations that have that status by virtue of the facts-and-circumstances test (Q 2:5, Q 6:7). Among the criteria for compliance with this test is the extent to which the charitable organization is attracting public support; the IRS wants to know whether the entity can demonstrate an active and ongoing fund-raising program. An organization can satisfy this aspect of the test (where public support can be as low as 10 percent) if it maintains a continuous and bona fide solicitation effort, seeking contributions from the general public, the community, or the membership group involved, or if it carries on activities designed to attract support from government agencies or publicly supported charitable organizations.

The U.S. Postal Service regulates some aspects of charitable fund-raising by means of the postal laws. Qualified organizations (including charities) that have received specific authorization may mail eligible matter at reduced bulk third-class rates of postage.[30]

TIP: In the parlance of the postal laws, charitable organizations are termed *philanthropic* entities. Other qualified nonprofit organizations include religious, educational, and scientific entities. Ineligible organizations include trade, business, and professional associations; certain citizens' and civic improvement associations; and social and hobby clubs.

Cooperative mailings involving the mailing of any matter on behalf of or produced for an organization not authorized to mail at the special rates must be paid at the applicable regular rates.

Material that advertises, promotes, offers, or, for a fee or other consideration, recommends, describes, or announces the availability of any product or service cannot qualify for mailing at the reduced bulk third-class rates unless the sale of the product or the provision of the service is substantially related to the exercise or performance by the organization of one or more of the purposes constituting the basis for the organization's authorization to mail at those rates. The determination as to whether a product or service is substantially related to an organization's purpose is made in accordance with the analogous federal tax law standards (see Chapter 10).

The Federal Trade Commission (FTC) has a role in the realm of fund-raising for charitable purposes, primarily when the fund-raising is in the form of telemarketing. The FTC has regulations on this subject, in amplification of the Telemarketing and Consumer Fraud and Abuse Prevention Act.[31] These rules do not apply to telemarketing conducted for charitable organizations solely for the purpose of generating charitable gifts.

However, the FTC rules apply to for-profit companies that raise funds or provide similar services to charitable and other tax-exempt organizations.

TIP: Consequently, charitable organizations should be cautious when entering into telemarketing contracts. No charity wants to have its telemarketing program found in violation of these rules. The rules took effect as of December 31, 1995; thus, there is little experience with them to date.

These rules (1) define the term *telemarketing;* (2) require clear and conspicuous disclosures of specified material information, orally or in writing, before a customer pays for goods or services offered; (3) prohibit misrepresenting, directly or by implication, specified material information relating to the goods or services that are the subject of a sales offer, as well as any other material aspects of a telemarketing transaction; (4) require express verifiable authorization before submitting for payment a check, draft, or other form of negotiable paper drawn on a person's account; (5) prohibit false or otherwise misleading statements to induce payment for goods or services; (6) prohibit any person from assisting and facilitating certain deceptive or abusive telemarketing acts or practices; (7) prohibit credit card laundering; (8) prohibit specified abusive acts or practices; (9) impose calling time restrictions; (10) require specified information to be disclosed truthfully, promptly, and in a clear and conspicuous manner, in an outbound telephone call; (11) require that specified records be kept; and (12) specify certain acts or practices that are exempt from the requirements.[32]

NOTE: Although the rules on telemarketing practices do not always apply in the charitable fund-raising setting, they serve as useful guidelines to proper telemarketing practices in that context.

STATE LAW REQUIREMENTS

Q 7:20   What are the elements of a typical state charitable solicitation act?

These laws usually open with a set of definitions. The key terms defined are *charitable, solicitation* (a term very broadly defined to capture every type of fund-raising, whether or not successful), *contribution, professional fund-raiser* (Q 7:22), *professional solicitor* (Q 7:23), and *charitable sales promotion* (Q 7:25). The ambit of these laws—which is far-reaching—is basically set by the scope of the words *charitable* and *solicitation.* Charitable in this setting includes religious, educational, arts promotion, and scientific purposes.

NOTE: Charitable in this context is given a much broader definition than in settings such as the federal tax law. Some state laws are applicable to fund-raising by tax-exempt social welfare organizations, business and professional associations, and other types of nonprofit organizations. State laws can differ on the point (for example, some expressly exclude political fund-raising), so it is necessary to check each one that is applicable (Q 7:31).

A key feature of these laws is *registration.* They almost always require soliciting charitable organizations to register, usually annually. There often is a registration fee. The information required by this process usually is extensive; the states have devised required registration forms. Many of the states also require the registration of professional fund-raisers and/or professional solicitors. Some states mandate a bond for fund-raisers and/or solicitors.

TIP: The registration process frequently requires charitable organizations to identify any fund-raisers or solicitors they have hired. The states use this information to determine whether the fund-raiser or solicitor has registered. Charities are often required to provide a list of other states in which they are registered. The registration form for fund-raisers and solicitors usually requires them to identify the charities they are working with. The states cross-reference this information to see whether all parties are appropriately registered and bonded.

Another feature of these laws is annual *reporting.* Each year, charitable organizations are almost always required to submit extensive financial statements either as part of an annual report or by means of annual registration. (Some states mandate both.) Annual reports may also be required of professional fund-raisers and professional solicitors.

In a few states, the laws require solicitors to submit more frequent reports, for example, following each fund-raising campaign.

Many of the state laws contain an extensive listing of *prohibited acts*. These are rules dictating certain fund-raising practices by charitable organizations—usually in the form of practices in which they may not engage. Some of these prohibited acts go beyond the realm of fund-raising and mandate certain actions (or nonactions) by charities and others generally. It is important for charities and those who assist them in the fund-raising process to review each of the applicable sets of these prohibitions (Q 7:26, Q 7:31).

A growing practice is for these laws to mandate the contents of *contracts* between soliciting charitable organizations and their professional fund-raisers and/or professional solicitors (Q 7:28).

Another burgeoning requirement is the presentation of *legends*. These are notices, required by law, that must prominently appear on fund-raising literature and other appeals. The typical legend must state that information about the charity is available from the charity or the state; a registration number may be needed as part of the legend.

NOTE: This requirement of legends is becoming a problem for those making charitable solicitations by mail in several states. The differences in these legends are forcing the solicitation material to become cluttered, detracting from the purpose of the mailing.

Other components of the state laws include record-keeping requirements, disclosure rules, requirements as to financial accounts and sales of tickets, investigatory and injunctive powers by the state, and a range of civil and criminal sanctions.

Q 7:21   Do these laws apply to all charitable solicitations?

Yes, unless the solicitation is expressly exempted from the statutory requirements (Q 7:27). These laws apply where the solicitation is by means of the mail, telephone (telemarketing), facsimile, television, video, and radio, as well as in-person fund-raising. The medium used to solicit is not significant; the key is whether the activity is a solicitation. The fact that interstate commerce is involved is not per se a bar to state regulation.

NOTE: Technically, the solicitation of charitable contributions on the Internet is embraced by these laws.

Q 7:22   How do these laws apply to professional fund-raisers?

They apply to professional fund-raisers in a variety of ways. However, the basic application of these laws is dependent on the definition of the term *professional fund-raiser*. First, not all states use that term; *professional fund-raising counsel* or *paid fund-raiser* may be used instead. Second, the definition of the term can vary. The most frequent definition is "a person who for compensation plans, manages, advises, consults, or prepares material for, or with respect to, the solicitation in this state of contributions for a charitable organization, but who does not solicit contributions and who does not employ, procure, or engage any compensated person to solicit contributions."

NOTE: The states give this term broad application. Those who work in collateral fields should be cautious: they may inadvertently become regarded as fund-raisers and be subject to penalties for noncompliance with state law. Related fields include consulting in the areas of marketing, management, and public relations.

A bona fide salaried officer, employee, or volunteer of a charitable organization is not a professional fund-raiser, nor are lawyers, investment advisers, or bankers.

It is common for a state charitable solicitation act to impose the following requirements on a professional fund-raiser working for one or more charitable organizations: registration, bonding, annual reports, recordkeeping, and a contract with the charity.

Q 7:23   How do these laws apply to professional solicitors?

They apply to professional solicitors in a variety of ways. However, the basic application of these laws is, like those pertaining to professional fund-raisers (Q 7:22), dependent on the definition of the term *professional solicitor*. First, not all states use that term; the terminology instead may be *paid solicitor* or *fund-raiser*. Second, the definition of the term can vary. The most frequent definition is "a person who for compensation performs for a charitable organization any service in connection with which contributions are, or will be, solicited in this state by such compensated person or by any compensated person he employs, procures, or engages, directly or indirectly, to solicit." There usually is an exclusion from this definition for officers, employees, and volunteers of charitable organizations.

NOTE: The states give this term board application—even broader than for the term professional fund-raiser. Many individuals and firms that consider themselves professional fund-raisers are regarded by the state as professional solicitors because of their (ostensible) direct involvement in the solicitation process. For example, a fund-raiser who assists a charity in placing solicitation material into the mails may, for that reason alone, be regarded as a solicitor. Those who work in collateral fields should be cautious: they may inadvertently become regarded as solicitors and be subject to penalties for noncompliance with state law. Related fields include consulting in the areas of marketing, management, and public relations. Lawyers are usually exempted from the definition by statute.

It is common for a state charitable solicitation act to impose the following requirements on a professional solicitor working for one or more charitable organizations: registration, bonding, annual reports, postcampaign reports, the filing of solicitation notices, recordkeeping, and a contract with the charity.

NOTE: Because of greed and other abusive conduct in their ranks, professional solicitors do not enjoy positive reputations. They are in particular disfavor with state legislators and regulators. That is one of the reasons why fund-raisers are loath to be perceived as solicitors. More importantly, by heaping regulatory requirements on them, the states are endeavoring to drive paid solicitors for charity out of their jurisdictions. The laws of some states are so onerous that one wonders how a solicitor can profitably function in the gift solicitation task. Anyone who can avoid classification as a professional solicitor should do so.

Q 7:24   Do these laws place limitations on the fees paid to professional solicitors?

Yes. From time to time, a state will enact a law placing a percentage limitation on the amount of compensation and other funds that can be paid to a professional solicitor. The most recent example occurred in California, where the state legislature passed a statute that attempted to limit solicitors' fees to a maximum of 50 percent of the contributions collected for a charity. Laws of this type are blatantly unconstitutional; this California law was promptly voided.[33]

In another example, the state of Kentucky enacted a law that placed a 50 percent limit on the amount of fees a charitable organization could pay a professional solicitor. In 1994, this law was struck down as being unconstitutional.[34]

Q 7:25   What is a charitable sales promotion and how do the state laws apply to it?

The phrase *charitable sales promotion* is generally defined as "an advertising or sales campaign, conducted by a commercial co-venturer, which represents that the purchase or use of goods or services offered by the commercial co-venturer will benefit, in whole or in part, a charitable organization or purpose." A business enterprise usually will state to the general public that a portion of the purchase price derived from the sale of goods or services during a particular period will be donated to a charity or charities. A commercial co-venturer is a business entity (other than a professional fund-raiser or professional solicitor) that become involved in a charitable sales promotion.

NOTE: The term *commercial co-venturer,* though understandable as to its derivation, is unfortunate phraseology. It suggests that the charity involved is engaged in a *commercial* undertaking, which is not favorable from the charity's standpoint (Q 10:11). It further conveys the thought that the charity is in a joint venture, which also can have adverse legal consequences (Q 7:17).

For the most part, state law mandates accurate disclosure of the arrangement between the charitable organization and the commercial co-venturer. Some states' laws require a formal accounting by the commercial enterprise; two states mandate annual reporting and bonding.

This is an advantageous way for a charitable organization to receive a substantial gift (some of these promotions result in millions of dollars for charity), for a business enterprise to obtain some positive publicity, and for the public to feel that personal consumption of a product is of benefit to charitable programs. (The purchasers do not receive any charitable contribution deduction, however.)

TIP: It is common for a commercial co-venturer to place a limit on the amount of funds that will be transferred to a charity as the result of a particular promotion. In most states, disclosure of this cap is all that is required. In some activist states, however, the practice is deemed misleading, in that purchases made toward the close of the promotion may not, in actuality, cause any funds to pass from the business to charity.

Q 7:26   What is the significance of the portions of these laws concerning prohibited acts?

This aspect of these laws can be very extensive, with a delineation of over 20 *prohibited acts*. Some of these prohibitions apply specifically in the fund-raising setting. For example, it can be a prohibited act to misrepresent the purpose of a charitable solicitation, solicit contributions for a purpose other than that expressed in the fund-raising material, use a name or statement of another charitable organization where its use would tend to mislead a solicited person, lead anyone to believe that registration constitutes or implies an endorsement by the state, or enter into a contract with a person who is required to register under the state's law but who has failed to do so.

However, these prohibitions can apply more broadly in the realm of charitable operations. For example, it can be a prohibited act to misrepresent the purpose of a charitable organization, expend contributions in a manner inconsistent with a stated charitable purpose, violate any of the applicable provisions of the state's consumer fraud law, or engage in other unlawful acts or practices as the attorney general of the state may determine.

TIP: These prohibited acts rules are applicable with respect to any solicitation in the state. A charitable organization or other person

---

soliciting in more than one state can find that there are tens of pro-hibited acts with which to contend (Q 7:31).

Q 7:27   Are there any exceptions to these laws?

Almost always. The exceptions largely apply with respect to charitable organizations. Some states exempt certain types of charitable organiza-tions from the entirety of these laws; others exempt them from only the registration and reporting requirements.

The most common exception—for religious organizations—rests primarily on constitutional law grounds.

NOTE: Ironically, many of the abuses in the field of charitable fund-raising are committed in the name of religion.

The next most common exception is for schools, colleges, and universi-ties. Other entities that often have some form of exemption are health care providers, membership organizations, libraries, veterans' groups, and small organizations. Some states exempt small solicitations and fund-raising for a named individual.

NOTE: These exemptions are largely predicated on the reasonable premise that the organizations can be excused from the rigors of this regulation because those whom they solicit do not need the protec-tions of the statute, due to their close relationship with and under-standing of the charitable organization. At the same time, this approach leaves the remaining regulated charities unhappy with their burdens of compliance. Exemptions from state charitable solic-itation acts can cause divisiveness in the world of public charities.

TIP: There are some traps in this area.

1. These exemptions are not uniform; a charitable organization can be exempt in its home state, yet not in another state where it is also soliciting gifts.
2. The membership exclusion cannot be utilized simply by making a donor a "member"; the state laws usually forbid that practice.

3. Some universities, health care providers, and similar organizations conduct their fund-raising through related "foundations"; not all of the states that exempt these institutions likewise expressly exempt their affiliated foundations.

4. A "small" solicitation in one state is not necessarily small in another; the thresholds range from $1,500 to $25,000.

Some states exempt charitable organizations by name. These laws are of questionable constitutionality; they may be violations of the equal protection doctrine.

TIP: An exception may not be automatic. In some states, a charitable organization must make application for exemption. In other states, an otherwise applicable exemption is not available where a charitable organization uses a professional fund-raiser or a professional solicitor.

Q 7:28   What provisions are generally required in a contract between a charitable organization and a professional fund-raiser or professional solicitor?

The most common provisions that a state will require, in a contract between a charitable organization and a fund-raiser or solicitor, are a statement of the respective obligations of the parties; a statement of the fees that are to be paid by the charitable organization; the projected beginning and end dates of the solicitation; a statement as to whether the fund-raiser or solicitor will have custody of contributions; a statement of the percentage of gross revenue from which the fund-raiser or solicitor will be compensated; the bank location and the number of the account in which all funds from the solicitation will be deposited; and any other information that the attorney general may prescribe.

Q 7:29   When does a charitable organization have to comply with one of these laws?

Assuming the charitable organization is not exempt from the requirement (Q 7:27), it must comply with a charitable solicitation act in a state when it is soliciting contributions in that state. At a minimum, the applicable law is that of the state in which the soliciting charitable organization is located. It is rare for a charity to solicit contributions only outside of the state in which it is headquartered. A soliciting charitable organization should first endeavor to be in compliance with the fund-raising regulation law in the state in which it is based.

NOTE: An argument that a state's law is inapplicable because the charity is only using the U.S. mail or because the fund-raising involves interstate commerce will fail. The state's police power enables it to regulate in this field as long as the forms of regulation are sufficiently narrow (Q 7:3).

Q 7:30 When does a professional fund-raiser or a professional solicitor have to comply with one of these laws?

The considerations regarding compliance are much the same as those for charitable organizations (Q 7:29). A fund-raiser or solicitor may not be assisting a charitable organization in the state where the fund-raiser or solicitor is based. Although this would be infrequent, the state law may nonetheless apply. Each state's law must be examined to see how it treats this subtlety.

Q 7:31 When does a charitable organization have to comply with more than one of these laws?

This is a subject of some confusion and frustration. Basically, the law is that a charitable organization, unless exempted from the requirement (Q 7:27), must comply with *each* of the charitable solicitation acts in force in the states in which it is soliciting contributions. A charitable organization engaged in fund-raising in all of the states and the District of Columbia may have to comply annually with over 40 of these laws (in addition to nonprofit corporation acts and other state laws that may apply in the fund-raising context).

TIP: Soliciting charitable organizations also are supposed to be in compliance with the hundreds of county, city, and town charitable solicitation ordinances in effect throughout the country. Some charitable organizations comply with some of these local ordinances, but, undoubtedly, few if any organizations are in full compliance in

---

this regard. State law compliance is difficult enough; the staff required to cope with all the local regulations would be extensive.

There is no lawful way to avoid this extent of multistate enforcement. These laws are based on the states' police power (Q 7:3) and have been generally upheld in the face of challenges as to their constitutionality. These is no legitimate authority—based on concepts of interstate commerce or other theory—for the proposition that these laws are inapplicable to charitable organizations raising funds on a multistate basis.

Q 7:32   Are solicitations of merely a few individuals subject to these state laws?

Technically, yes. Although these laws are designed to protect the *public* (see Q 7:35), most of them literally apply irrespective of the number of persons solicited. An argument can be made that these laws do not apply to *private* solicitations, but there is no caselaw supportive of the assertion. Only a few states have addressed the subject, usually by exempting a charitable solicitation from the registration and reporting requirements where the organization does not intend to annually receive contributions from more than 10 persons. Two states exempt a solicitation where no more than 100 persons are solicited. Some states attempt to resolve this dilemma by exempting small (in terms of total funds collected) solicitations; these thresholds range from $1,500 to $25,000.

Q 7:33   When does a professional fund-raiser or professional solicitor have to comply with more than one of these laws?

The considerations here are basically the same as with charitable organizations (Q 7:31). That is, a fund-raiser or solicitor must be in compliance with these laws in every state in which it is working with a charitable organization to assist it in raising funds. However, usually where the charitable organization is exempt from the requirements (Q 7:27), so too is the professional fund-raiser and/or professional solicitor.

Q 7:34   What happens when a charitable organization, professional fund-raiser, or professional solicitor violates one of these laws?

The general practice—although not reflected in any statute—is that, when a state regulatory office discovers a violation of the state's charitable solicitation act, the office will contact the offending party and request compliance. This approach is usually taken, for example, when a person is required to register in the state but has not. Where the violation is more egregious, such as the commission of a fraud, the reaction of the state authorities would likely be sterner.

If the violation is willful or ongoing, and persists despite polite requests to come into compliance, most of the state regulators have the authority to obtain an injunction and enjoin the practice that is contravening the law. For example, if a charitable organization is fund-raising in a state without having first registered there, the state's attorney general could enjoin the solicitation until compliance has been achieved. Likewise, a professional solicitor could find the solicitation enjoined if the solicitor's contract with the charity is not in conformity with the state's requirements.

A host of civil and criminal law penalties can come into play as well. These sanctions are civil fines and imprisonment; both can apply.

NOTE: Despite the enforcement that exists—the intensity of which varies from state to state—many charitable organizations, professional fund-raisers, and professional solicitors are not adhering to state laws or are only in partial compliance. Just as few states have the resources necessary to fully enforce these laws, most charitable organizations lack the capacity to fully comply with them. There are more outlaws in this field of the law than in any other applicable to nonprofit organizations.

Q 7:35   What is the rationale for these state laws?

The state charitable solicitation acts are intended to protect the public from fund-raising in the name of charity that is fraudulent or otherwise misrepresentative as to its purpose. Some of the preambles to this type of legislation grandly resonate with this approach to consumer protection. For example, the preamble to the statute in the California law states that "there exists in the area of solicitations and sales solicitations for charitable purposes a condition which has worked fraud, deceit, and imposition upon the people of the state." The legislature in Colorado concluded that "fraudulent charitable solicitations are a widespread practice in this state which results in millions of dollars of losses to contributors and legitimate charities each year." The latter preamble adds: "Legitimate

charities are harmed by such fraud because the money available for contributions continually is being siphoned off by fraudulent charities, and
the goodwill and confidence of contributors continually is being under-
mined by the practices of unscrupulous solicitors."

Q 7:36 Are these state laws effective?

No. The purpose of these laws is to protect people from fake charities
and unscrupulous fund-raisers by deterring unlawful activity and pun-
ishing the illegalities that do occur (Q 7:35). These laws keep increasing
in number and complexity, but they are having little impact on abusive
practices. The chief imprint these laws are placing on the charitable sector is in the form of administrative burdens (including diversions of
funds from charitable programs) on legitimate charities.

   The story line that describes these laws as being effective is a myth
fostered by the regulatory community. On occasion, the courts will accept the rationale. In the most recent example, a court upheld the constitutionality of a registration fee imposed on fund-raising charitable
organizations on the ground that it is a "user fee." The court wrote that
the charitable solicitation acts enhance "donor confidence" by "eliminating illegitimate charities."[35]

   The states focus intently in this area, yet the "big picture" is often
missed. Episodes such as those affecting the United Way of America and
the New Era for Philanthropy Foundation unfold; state law enforcement
misses them completely.

   The truth is that no one knows the full extent of the ineffective-
ness of these laws. More fundamentally, there are no respectable data
that might reveal the magnitude of the problem these laws are supposed to rectify and prevent. It is astonishing that these laws are evolving so quickly and becoming so intricate, when there are absolutely no
definitions of the reason for their existence. Research in these areas is
long overdue.

Q 7:37 To be in compliance with these laws, what type of management system should a charitable organization have?

A charitable organization that is soliciting contributions in several
states and wishes to be in full compliance with the law of those states
needs to take several steps.

1. The organization should obtain a copy of the charitable solicitation act in effect in each of the states. It should determine, with the assistance of a lawyer if necessary, what its various obligations are, under each of these laws. At a minimum, the organization should ascertain whether any exceptions are available to it, principally with respect to registration and reporting requirements (Q 7:27). Some of these laws are amplified by rules and regulations, and the charitable organization or its lawyer should have these sets of additional law to refer to in interpreting the statutes. Some court opinions may pertain to these laws as well.

2. Once the organization has determined which of these states have registration requirements that are applicable to it (Q 7:30), it should obtain, prepare, and file the necessary registration forms. This should be done in advance of solicitation, and the organization should be certain to pay the requisite registration fee and obtain all required bonds.

3. If the organization is using the services of a professional fund-raiser and/or professional solicitor, it should make a reasonable effort to see to it that each of these persons is adhering to these laws as well (Q 7:22, Q 7:23). Although, technically, the responsibility for compliance is on these persons and not the charity, the charity does not want legal difficulties to thwart a fund-raising effort.

4. If the organization is subject to one or more reporting requirements, it should be certain that its financial records are properly maintained. Particular emphasis should be placed on fund-raising costs, so that the organization knows precisely what its solicitation expenses are. If the entity has costs that are allocated between fund-raising and program, it should obtain the services of an accountant who is knowledgeable as to those rules. The due dates for the state forms will vary. To remain in timely compliance with the filing requirements, the organization should have a system for self-notification as the dates draw near.

5. If the charitable organization is being assisted by a professional fund-raiser or professional solicitor, it should execute a written contract between itself and that person (or persons). Further, the organization should see to it that the contract (or contracts) has all of the provisions that are required by states' laws (Q 7:28). These considerations may also apply to relationships with commercial co-venturers (Q 7:25).

6. The organization should be certain that its solicitation materials contain any and all of the applicable legends (Q 7:20).

7. The organization should review the list of prohibited acts in each of these applicable laws (Q 7:26) and be certain that it is in conformity with them.

8. The organization should endeavor to be in compliance with the applicable record-keeping requirements.

There are other aspects of these laws that the charitable organization should monitor. Among them is the receipt of copies of all materials that affiliated parties file with the states, such as the solicitation notices filed by professional solicitors and reports filed by commercial co-venturers.

Q 7:38 How does state law regulation interrelate with the oversight activities of the watch-dog agencies?

The standards promulgated by the "voluntary" watchdog agencies—such as the Philanthropic Advisory Service of the Better Business Bureaus and the National Charities Information Bureau—are not law.

NOTE: The word *voluntary* is in quotes because, despite what these agencies say, the charities caught up in standards enforcement are not doing so voluntarily. The motive of these charities is fear: The credibility these agencies have with funders and the media is such that levels of gifts and grants can plummet due to the adverse publicity that these agencies can quickly generate if their standards are not adhered to—to the letter.

Thus, since these standards are not rules of law, charities are not obligated to comply with them. As noted, however, compliance is coerced. One of the many flaws of these standards is that they can be inconsistent with legal requirements and contrary to good management practices. Attracted by its simplicity, the standards tend to highlight the subject of fund-raising costs; this seems to be where public charities are the most vulnerable, which contributes to their obsequiousness.[36]

Also, state regulators often look to these agencies' lists to see who is compliant and who is not. Further, state authorities have been known to alert one or more of the watch-dog agencies as to charities who may be transgressing the law. Some argue that this form of regulation is preferable to that by government, but government regulation of fund-raising has hardly been abated by the watchdog groups (or any other force).

CHAPTER 8

Planned Giving

No form of charitable giving presents more mystery or generates more confusion than planned giving. Even though this type of giving yields the largest contributions and the greatest benefits to donors, most charitable organizations avoid planned giving, out of fear of its (perceived) complexities and concern with immediate funding. There are intricacies with this type of giving, to be sure, but none is so overwhelming as to be the basis for a decision to not have a planned giving program. The challenge for many charitable organizations is the prompt establishment of this type of program, in addition to their other fund-raising efforts.

Here are the questions most frequently asked by clients about the mysteries of planned giving, the specific uses of charitable remainder trusts and pooled income funds, and how to start a planned giving program—and the answers to them.

OVERVIEW

Q 8:1　What is planned giving?

Planned giving refers to techniques of charitable giving where the contributions are large in amount, are usually of property, and normally are carefully integrated with the donor's (or donors') financial and estate plans. This giving is termed *planned* giving because of the time and planning devoted, by both the donor and the charitable donee, to designing the gift transaction.

The relationship of this type of gift to a donor's financial needs is a critical factor. The donor often structures the gift so that he, she, or it receives income as the result of the transaction. Usually, this benefit is technically accomplished by creating, in the donated property (or money), *income* and *remainder interests* (Q 8:2).

NOTE: One of the most difficult aspects of obtaining planned gifts is persuading prospective contributors that they will be receiving income as the consequence of a charitable act. This is, to many, such a foreign and seemingly inconsistent concept that they will have great trouble grasping it. More difficulties can ensue when an income return is coupled with a sizable charitable contribution deduction. This hurdle can become more formidable when non-income-producing property is converted to income-producing property and/or the income to be received is greater or more tax-advantaged than that being generated before the contribution. The challenge to the gift planner is to overcome these obstacles. Once that is accomplished, the rewards (financial and psychic) are great for all concerned.

Planned gifts may be of two types: (1) the gift made during the donor's lifetime by means of a trust or other agreement, or (2) a planned gift made by will, so that the contribution comes out of a decedent's estate (a bequest or devise).

Contributions of property to charity are often made as outright gifts of the property in its entirety. That is, the donor transfers all of his, her, or its title to and interest in the property to the charitable donee. By contrast, the donor of a planned gift generally contributes something less than the donor's complete interest in the property. In the law, this is known as a contribution of a *partial interest;* planned giving usually is partial interest giving. These partial interests are either income interests or remainder interests.

NOTE: For a charitable contribution deduction to be available, the gift must be to (or for the use of) a charitable organization. The planned gift vehicles are not themselves charities; they are conduits to charities. Nonetheless, it is common to say that a charitable deduction arises when a gift is made to, for example, a charitable remainder trust or pooled income fund. Technically, the deduction is for the remainder interest contributed to the charity; the giving vehicle is merely the intermediary that facilitates this type of gift.

Q 8:2   What are remainder interests and income interests?

These interests are legal fictions; they are concepts of ownership rights inherent in any item of property. An *income interest* in a property is a function of the income generated by the property. A person may be entitled to all of the income from a property for a period of time or to some portion of the income. This person is said to have an income interest in the property. Two or more persons (such as husband and wife) may have income interests in the same property (or share an income interest in the same property). These interests may be held concurrently or consecutively. The *remainder interest* in an item of property is reflective of the projected value of the property, or property produced by reinvestments, at some future date.

These interests are principally measured by the value of the donated property, the age of the donor(s), the period of time that the income interests will exist, and the frequency of the income payout. The actual computation is made by means of actuarial tables, most often those promulgated by the Department of the Treasury.

For the most part, a planned gift is a gift of an income interest or a remainder interest in a property. Commonly, the contribution is of the remainder interest. By creating an income interest (or, more accurately, retaining the income interest), the donor forms the basis for receiving a flow of income as the result of the contribution. This is known as *partial interest* giving (Q 8:1).

When a gift of a remainder interest in property is made to a charitable organization, the charity cannot acquire the property represented by that interest until the income interests have expired. When a gift is made during lifetime, the contributor receives the charitable deduction for the tax year in which the recipient charity's remainder interest in the property is created. A gift of an income interest in property to a charity enables the donee to receive the income at the outset and to continue to do so as long as the income interest(s) are in existence.

Q 8:3   How are these interests created?

Income and remainder interests in property are usually created by means of a trust. This is the vehicle used to conceptually divide the property into the two component interests. The law terms these trusts *split-interest trusts;* usually, a qualified split-interest trust is required if a charitable contribution deduction is to be available.[1] Split-interest trusts are charitable remainder trusts (Q 8:6), pooled income funds (Q 8:7), and charitable lead trusts (Q 8:8).

There are several exceptions to these general requirements of a split-interest trust in planned giving. The principal exception is the charitable gift annuity, which utilizes a contract rather than a trust (Q 8:9). Other approaches can also generate a charitable contribution deduction (Q 8:10 and Q 8:11).

In the planned giving setting, however, it is not enough to create a remainder interest. It is also critical to create a remainder interest, the gift of which yields a charitable contribution deduction. There are only a few ways in which a remainder interest can be the subject of a charitable contribution deduction. Absent qualification of an eligible partial interest (either a qualifying income interest or qualifying remainder interest), there is no charitable contribution deduction.

Q 8:4   What are the tax advantages for a charitable gift of a remainder interest?

For a lifetime gift of a remainder interest in property to a charitable organization, the federal income tax advantages are manifold. The donor creates an income flow as the result of the gift; this income may be preferentially taxed. The donor receives a charitable contribution deduction for the gift of the remainder interest, which will reduce or perhaps eliminate the tax on the income from the property. The property that is the subject of the gift may have appreciated in value in the hands of the donor *(appreciated property);* if that is the case, the capital gain tax that would have been paid had the property been sold is avoided. The trustee of the split-interest trust may dispose of the gift property and reinvest the proceeds in more productive property. Because the trust is generally tax-exempt, the capital gain from such a transaction is not taxed, nor is the income earned by the trust.

Moreover, the donor can become the beneficiary of professional fund management. All of these benefits can be available while, simultaneously, the donor is satisfying his or her charitable desires—and doing so at a level that, absent these tax incentives, would not be possible.

Q 8:5   It was said that the trust generally is tax-exempt. Why the qualification?

In the case of a charitable remainder trust, the trust is tax-exempt unless it has unrelated business taxable income.[2] (This type of income is the subject of Chapter 10.) In making this determination, the exempt purposes of the remainder interest charitable beneficiary are used to ascertain relatedness.[3]

NOTE: A charitable remainder trust with unrelated business taxable income is taxable on all of its income, not just the unrelated income.[4] A charitable remainder trust with unrelated business income that is not taxable (such as because of offsetting deductions or the specific deduction (Q 10:22) does not have income taxable under this rule.

A pooled income fund is not a tax-exempt organization. However, it receives a deduction for its income distributions and for the amounts destined for charitable purposes.

Q 8:6   What is a charitable remainder trust?

A *charitable remainder trust* is one of the types of split-interest trusts (Q 8:3).[5] As the name indicates, it is a trust that has been used to create a remainder interest (Q 8:2), which is destined for charity. Each charitable remainder trust is written specifically for the particular circumstances of the donor(s). The remainder interest in the gift property is designated for one or more charitable organizations. The donor (or donors) receives a charitable contribution deduction for the transfer of the remainder interest.

A qualified charitable remainder trust must provide for a specified distribution of income, at least annually, to one or more beneficiaries, at least one of which is *not* a charity. The flow of income must be for a life or lives, or for a term not to exceed 20 years. An irrevocable remainder interest must be held for the benefit of the charity or paid over to it. The noncharitable beneficiaries are the holders of the income interest and the charitable organization has the remainder interest. Generally, nearly every type of property can be contributed to a charitable remainder trust (Q 8:14).

The income interests in a charitable remainder trust are ascertained in one of four ways: (1) sum certain, (2) fixed percentage/unitrust amount, and (3) and (4), the two makeup approaches. The approach used depends in large part on whether the trust is a *charitable remainder annuity trust* or a *charitable remainder unitrust.* In the case of the former, the income payments are in the form of a fixed amount—an annuity, or what the law terms a *sum certain*. In the case of the latter, the income payments are in the form of a *unitrust amount,* which is an amount equal to a fixed percentage of the net annual fair market value of the assets in the trust. A unitrust may also have one of two types of makeup feature (Q 8:13).

Both of these trusts must adhere to a 5 percent minimum. With an annuity trust, the annuity amount must be at least 5 percent of the initial net fair market value of all property placed in the trust. With a unitrust, the unitrust amount must be at least 5 percent of the net fair market value of the trust assets, calculated annually.

Conventionally, once the income interest expires, the assets in a charitable remainder trust are distributed to, or for the use of, the charitable organization that is the remainder interest beneficiary. In some instances, the property comprising the remainder interest may be retained by the trust for charitable purposes.

NOTE: If the second option is selected, the trust will have to qualify on its own for tax-exempt status. It is likely to constitute a private foundation (Q 6:2) in this form.

Usually, a bank or similar financial institution serves as the trustee of a charitable remainder trust. This financial institution should have the capacity to administer the trust, make appropriate investments, and timely adhere to all income distribution and reporting requirements. However, the charitable organization that is the remainder interest beneficiary often acts as the trustee.[6]

TIP: This is a subject of state law: in some states, a charitable organization cannot serve as a trustee. State law *must* be checked on this point before these arrangements are finalized.

A donor or related party may be the trustee. However, caution must be exercised to avoid triggering the *grantor trust* rules, which, among other outcomes, cause the gain from the sale of appreciated property (Q 8:4) by the trust to be taxed to the grantor/donor.

Generally, a charitable remainder trust is a tax-exempt organization (Q 8:5).

Q 8:7   What is a pooled income fund?

A *pooled income fund* is a type of split-interest trust (Q 8:3).[7] It is a trust (fund) that has been used to create a remainder interest (Q 8:2) destined for charity.

A donor to a qualified pooled income fund receives a charitable deduction for contributing the remainder interest in the donated property to charity. This use of the fund creates income interests in noncharitable beneficiaries; the remainder interest in the gift property is designated for the charitable organization that maintains the fund.

The pooled income fund's basic instrument (a trust agreement or declaration of trust) is written to facilitate gifts from an unlimited number of donors, so the essential terms of the transaction must be established in advance for all participants.

NOTE: This is an important distinction in relation to the charitable remainder trust. Each remainder trust is designed for the circumstances of the particular donor(s) (Q 8:4). This ability to tailor the gift can be a factor in deciding which planned gift vehicle to use.

The pooled income fund is, literally, a pooling of gifts. It is sometimes characterized as functioning in the nature of a mutual fund for charities. Although there is some truth to this—it *is* an investment vehicle—the funding of a pooled income fund is basically motivated by charitable intents.

Each donor to a pooled income fund contributes an irrevocable remainder interest in the gift property to or for the use of an eligible charity. The donor creates an income interest for the life of one or more beneficiaries, who must be living at the time of the transfer. The properties transferred by the donors must be commingled in the fund (to create the necessary pool).

Contributions to pooled income funds are generally confined to cash and readily marketable securities. The pooled income fund, by its nature, must be kept liquid, to enable reinvestments and transfers of remainder interests to the charitable organization. A pooled income fund cannot invest in tax-exempt bonds and similar instruments.

The present value of an income interest in property transferred to a pooled income fund is computed on the basis of life contingencies prescribed in the estate tax regulations and an interest rate equal to the highest yearly rate of return of the fund for the three tax years immediately preceding the tax year in which the transfer to the fund is made. Special rules apply in the case of new pooled income funds (Q 8:25).

Each income interest beneficiary must receive income at least once each year. The pool amount is generally determined by the rate of return earned by the fund for the year. Income beneficiaries receive their proportionate share of the fund's income. The dollar amount of the income share is based on the number of units owned by the beneficiary; each unit must be based on the fair market value of the assets when transferred.

A pooled income fund must be maintained by one or more charitable organizations. The charity must exercise control over the fund; it does not have to be the trustee of the fund, but it must have the power to remove and replace the trustee.

NOTE: Whether a charitable organization can be the trustee of a pooled income fund is a matter of state law (Q 8:6).

A donor or an income beneficiary of the fund may not be a trustee of the fund. However, a donor may be a trustee or officer of the charitable organization that maintains the fund, as long as he or she does not have the general responsibilities toward the fund that are ordinarily exercised by a trustee.

NOTE: A pooled income fund can accommodate a smaller amount (value) of securities or similar property than a charitable remainder trust. From a fund-raising standpoint, this may appear counterproductive. However, these funds offer opportunities for attracting first-time planned givers, setting the stage for larger gifts (including those to charitable remainder trusts) later.

TIP: No limits are imposed by law as to the number of pooled income funds a charitable organization may maintain. One or more funds may be used for general fund-raising purposes; others may be organized around specific investment approaches or purposes.

Q 8:8   What is a charitable lead trust?

In essence, a *charitable lead trust* is the reverse of a charitable remainder trust (Q 8:6): the income interest is contributed to charity and the remainder interest goes to noncharitable beneficiaries.[8] Thus, the charitable lead trust is a split-interest trust.

Under these arrangements, an income interest in property is contributed to a charitable organization for a term of years or for the life of one or more individuals. The remainder interest in the property is reserved to return, at the expiration of the income interest (the *lead period*), to the donor or other income beneficiary or beneficiaries. Often, the property passes from one generation (the donor's) to another.

The charitable lead trust can be used to accelerate into one year a series of charitable contributions that would otherwise be made annually. In some circumstances, a charitable deduction is available for the transfer of an income interest in property to a charitable organization. There are stringent limitations, however, on the deductible amount of charitable contributions of these income interests. Frequently, there is no charitable deduction; the donor's motive for establishing the trust is estate planning.

Q 8:9   What is a charitable gift annuity?

Unlike most other forms of planned giving, which are based on a type of split-interest trust (Q 8:6–Q 8:8), the *charitable gift annuity* is arranged in an agreement between the donor and donee. The donor agrees to make a payment and the donee agrees, in return, to provide the donor (and/or someone else) with an annuity.

With one payment, the donor actually is engaging in two transactions: (1) the *purchase* of an annuity and (2) the making of a charitable *gift*. The gift component gives rise to the charitable contribution deduction. One sum is transferred; the money in excess of the amount necessary to purchase the annuity is the charitable gift portion. Because of the dual nature of the transaction, the charitable gift annuity transfer constitutes a bargain sale.

The annuity resulting from the creation of a charitable gift annuity arrangement is a fixed amount paid at regular intervals. The exact amount is calculated to reflect the age of the beneficiary, which is determined at the time the contribution is made, and the annuity rate selected.

NOTE: As a matter of law, a charitable organization is free to offer whatever rate of return it wishes. However, most charities follow and utilize the rates periodically set by the American Council on Gift Annuities. These voluntary rates are in place to avoid unseemly philanthropic "price wars." Because the establishment and "enforcement" of these uniform rates is currently the subject of litigation in which the Council is charged with antitrust law violations, some charitable organizations have suspended their gift annuity programs until the dispute is resolved.

A portion of the annuity paid is tax-free because it is a return of capital. Where appreciated property is contributed, there will be capital gain on the appreciation that is attributable to the value of the annuity. If the donor is the annuitant, the capital gain can be reported ratably over the donor's life expectancy. However, the tax savings occasioned by the charitable contribution deduction may shelter the capital gain (resulting from the creation of the annuity) from taxation.

Because the arrangement is by contract between the donor and donee, all of the assets of the charitable organization are subject to liability for the ongoing payment of the annuities. (With most planned giving techniques, the resources for payment of income are confined to those in a split-interest trust.) For this reason, some states impose a requirement that charitable organizations establish a reserve for the payment of gift annuities—and many charitable organizations are reluctant to embark on a gift annuity program. Organizations can eliminate much of the risk surrounding ongoing payment of annuities by reinsuring them.

TIP: In general, an obligation to pay an annuity is a debt. The charitable organization involved would have an acquisition indebtedness for purposes of the unrelated debt-financed income rules, were it not for a special rule.[9] To come within this rule, the value of the annuity must be less than 90 percent of the value of the property in the transaction, there can be no more than two income beneficiaries, there can be no guarantee as to a minimum amount of payments and no specification of a maximum amount of payments, and the annuity contract cannot provide for an adjustment of the amount of the annuity payments by reference to the income received from the transferred property or any other property.

TIP: A charitable organization that provides commercial-type insurance as a substantial activity cannot be tax-exempt; this activity, even when of a lesser magnitude, is an unrelated business. Arguably, a charitable gift annuity is not a form of commercial-type insurance. However, to eliminate uncertainty on the point, there is an exception from these rules for these annuities.[10] To be eligible for this exception, a charitable deduction must be involved and the above exception from the unrelated debt-financed income rules must be available.

Q 8:10   What about gifts of life insurance?

Charitable contributions of life insurance policies are popular forms of giving. A gift of whole life insurance is an excellent way for an individual who has a relatively small amount of resources to make a major contribution to a charitable organization. Gifts of insurance are particularly attractive for younger donors.

If the life insurance policy is fully paid, the donor will receive a charitable deduction for the cash surrender value or the replacement value of the policy. If the premiums are still being paid, the donor receives a deduction for the premium payments made during the tax year. For the deduction to be available, however, the donee charity must be both the beneficiary and the owner of the insurance policy.

TIP: A policy of life insurance is valid (enforceable) only where the owner of the policy has an *insurable interest* in the life of the insured. In essence, this means that the owner and beneficiary of the policy (the same person) must be more economically advantaged with the insured alive. (Examples of relationships where insurable interests exist are healthy marriages and the employment of key individuals.) There is disagreement as to whether a charitable organization is better off with this type of donor dead or alive. In many instances, a charity is advantaged by having a donor of a life insurance policy alive: he or she may be an important volunteer (perhaps a trustee or officer) or a potential contributor of other, larger gifts.

Q 8:11   Are there other ways to make deductible gifts of remainder interests?

Yes. Individuals may give a remainder interest in their personal residence or farm to charity. They then receive a charitable deduction without using a trust (indeed, a trust cannot be used in this context). A trust is not required for a deductible gift of a remainder interest in real property when the gift is made in the form of a *qualified conservation contribution*. A contribution of an undivided portion of one's entire interest in property is not regarded as a contribution of a partial interest in property.[11]

CHARITABLE REMAINDER TRUSTS

Q 8:12   What types of charitable organizations can be remainder interest beneficiaries of remainder trusts?

There are no limitations on the types of charitable organizations that can be beneficiaries of charitable remainder trusts. That is, these organizations can be either public charities or private foundations (see Chapter 6).

TIP: The percentage limitations on deductible charitable giving (Q 1:42 and Q 1:43) need to be taken into account. For example, a contribution of appreciated property to a public charity is subject to the 30 percent limitation, and the same gift to a private foundation is subject to a 20 percent limitation. These percentages apply when a gift is made by means of a charitable remainder trust. If the trust instrument does not expressly confine the charitable beneficiary to a public charity (or public charities), the lower private foundation limitations will be imposed.

Q 8:13   How does the makeup feature work?

Two types of *makeup features* can apply with respect to charitable remainder trusts. (These features are not available in the case of charitable remainder annuity trusts.)

TIP: The makeup feature is used when non-income-producing property is contributed to a remainder trust and there are no immediate prospects that it or any successor property will be income-producing (such as because the property cannot be sold in the foreseeable future). This characteristic of the property is critical because of the obligation to make income payments to one or more income interest beneficiaries.

One makeup feature allows the income payments to begin once a suitable amount of income begins to flow into the trust. That is, the income payments begin at a future point in time and are only prospective.

The other makeup feature has the attributes of the above-described makeup feature, with one significant difference: there is provision for a retroactive makeup of income, as well as prospective income payments.

NOTE: The makeup feature selected will have an impact on the charitable deduction for the gift of the remainder interest. Because the makeup feature that allows for retroactive payments will provide more income to the income beneficiary (or beneficiaries) than the other makeup feature, the income interest is greater and, correspondingly, the remainder interest is that much less. The result: a smaller charitable deduction when the retroactive income makeup provision is used.

Q 8:14   What types of property are suitable for charitable remainder trusts?

For the most part, nearly any type of personal or real property may be contributed to a charitable remainder trust. (Money may also be given.) Commonly, the properties contributed (aside from money) are securities (stocks and bonds) and real estate. However, just about any property can be contributed, particularly if the property is income-producing or can be converted to income production.

There can be some tax difficulties when property is transferred to a remainder trust. Many of these problems arise when an item of tangible personal property is contributed to a charity by means of a charitable remainder trust. There principally are three of these conundrums (Q 8:17). Also, properties encumbered with debt pose some tax problems (Q 8:15).

Q 8:15   What happens if the donated property is encumbered with debt?

If property encumbered with debt is transferred to a charitable remainder trust, the result is likely to be unrelated debt-financed income. This is because the debt is an *acquisition indebtedness*.[12] The receipt of unrelated debt-financed income, if it is unrelated business taxable income, will cause the trust to lose its tax-exempt status for each year in which that income is received (Q 8:5).

Q 8:16   What happens when an option is transferred to a charitable remainder trust?

The answer depends on the type of property that underlies the option. If the underlying property could be transferred directly to the trust, the transfer of the option poses only legal problems associated with the timing of the gift. (There is no charitable gift until the option is exercised.) However, if the property would be inappropriate for transfer directly to the trust, then the transfer of the option would cause the trust to lose its tax-exempt status.

The law underlying charitable remainder trusts is intended to ensure that the amount a charitable organization receives following the close of the income payment period reflects the amount on which the donor's charitable deduction was based. This type of trust must function as a remainder trust in every respect from the date of its creation; that cannot happen unless each transfer to the trust qualifies for a charitable deduction. The IRS will be attuned to situations where the donor may be merely using a charitable remainder trust as a means to take advantage of the tax exemption for capital gain incurred by the trust (Q 8:18).

Encumbered property in a charitable remainder trust can jeopardize the trust's tax-exempt status (Q 8:15). Where an option to purchase this type of property, rather than the property itself, is transferred to a charitable remainder trust, the IRS will assume that the donor is attempting to avoid the consequences attendant to a direct transfer of the property. If the option (or purported option) is used in an attempt to sidestep these tax results, the IRS will disqualify the trust as a charitable remainder trust.[13]

Q 8:17   What happens when an item of tangible personal property is transferred to a charitable remainder trust?

The transfer of an item of tangible personal property to a charitable remainder trust does not cause any problems with respect to qualification of the trust. However, three aspects of the general charitable giving laws are implicated.

A charitable contribution of a future interest in tangible personal property is treated, for federal income tax purposes, as having been made only when all intervening interests in, and rights to, the actual possession or enjoyment of the property have expired or are held by persons other than the donor or those closely related to the donor.[14] By contributing this type of property to the trust, the donor is creating and retaining an income interest in it, thus triggering the future interest rule. However, there would be an income tax charitable contribution when the trustee of the fund sold the property, because there would be an income interest in the proceeds of the sale.

Where there is a charitable contribution of tangible personal property and the donee uses the property in a manner that is unrelated to its exempt purpose, the amount of the deduction must be reduced by the amount of gain that would have been long-term capital gain if the property had been sold for its fair value.[15] Usually, gifts of this nature involve long-term capital assets and it is contemplated that the trust will sell the interest. The sale would be an unrelated use. Therefore, the donor's charitable deduction (already confined to that for a remainder interest and in existence only after the sale) would have to be reduced to the amount of the donor's basis in the property allocable to the remainder interest.

Where there is a charitable contribution of tangible personal property by an individual and the donee is not a public charity (see Chapter 6), the charitable deduction for the gift generally must be confined to an amount equal to 20 percent of the donor's adjusted gross income. Where the recipient is a public charity, the limitation generally is 30 percent. The trust instrument must specifically provide that the donee or donees must be public charities for the higher of these two limitations to apply.

> **TIP:** If the trust is silent on the point, the IRS will be of the view that one or more charitable beneficiaries can be a private foundation and hold that the smaller of the two limitations is applicable.[16] This can happen, for example, where the donor reserves a lifetime power of appointment and a testamentary power to designate the charitable organization that will receive the remainder interest—and fails to confine the potential beneficiary or beneficiaries to public charities.

As noted, however, with tangible personal property, the charitable deduction does not come into being until the property is sold. The gift then is of the sales proceeds—money. In the case of charitable gifts, the percentage limitations generally are 50 percent for public charities and 30 percent for private foundations.[17] However, the same considerations apply, in that the IRS will assume that the lower limitation is applicable unless the document confines the remainder interest beneficiaries to public charities. (See Q 1:42, Q 1:43)

Q 8:18   Can there be adverse consequences where the income payment term is very short?

Yes, where the charitable remainder trust is a charitable remainder unitrust (Q 8:6). The IRS will assume that the trust—known as an *accelerated* remainder trust—is being used to liquidate appreciated property while avoiding a substantial portion of the tax on the gain. The IRS will challenge these arrangements, despite a mechanical and literal adherence to the legal requirements.[18]

A prototype of this arrangement is this: An individual establishes a two-year charitable remainder unitrust (income-only variety, with a makeup feature (Q 8:13)), with himself or herself as the income interest beneficiary. The donor transfers to the trust capital assets having a value of $1 million and a zero basis. The assets do not yield any income. The unitrust amount is set at 80 percent of the fair market value of the trust assets, valued annually.

The unitrust amount required to be paid for the first year is $800,000, but there is no distribution to the income beneficiary for that year (no income). At the beginning of the second year, the assets are sold for $1 million and the $800,000 unitrust amount for the first year is distributed to the income beneficiary. The unitrust amount for the second year is $160,000 (80 percent of the remaining $200,000). At the end of the second year, the trust is terminated and $40,000 is paid to a charitable organization.

If this transaction is treated under technical tax rules, here is the outcome. The $800,000 is a distribution of trust corpus (thus, no taxation). The $160,000 unitrust amount for the second year is capital gain, on which the income beneficiary pays tax in the amount of $44,800 (28 percent of $160,000). The income beneficiary has net cash of $915,200 ($800,000 from year 1 and a net of $115,200 for year 2). If the donor had sold the assets, rather than manipulated their sale by means of the remainder trust, the tax would have been $280,000, with the after-tax amount $720,000—rather than the $915,200.

The IRS can use three legal doctrines to contest these transactions. One is that the form of the transaction—a sale by a tax-exempt remainder trust—will not be respected. Another is that the gain on the sale of the trust assets will be considered gross income to the donor, rather than to the trust. The IRS can question the qualification of the trust as a charitable remainder trust in the first instance.

The IRS could also levy the tax on self-dealing. This action would be based on the argument that the trustee's postponement of the sale of trust assets beyond the first year constitutes a use of the assets for the benefit of the donor—who is a disqualified person with respect to the trust (Q 2:27, Q 6:8). Certain other penalties could also be applied.

Q 8:19   Who can be a donor to a charitable remainder trust?

Any person—an individual or a corporation—can be a donor to a charitable remainder trust. (To date, almost all such donors are individuals.) The income payment period, in the case of an individual, can be for one or more lifetimes or for a term of years (Q 8:6). However, where a corporation is the donor, the income payment period must have a definite time limitation.

Q 8:20   Who can be a trustee of a charitable remainder trust?

Under the federal tax law, any person can be a trustee of a charitable remainder trust. This means that the trustee, or one of the trustees, can be the donor, an income interest beneficiary, the charity that will receive the remainder interest, another individual, or a financial institution or other corporate trustee.

TIP: Caution must be exercised when causing the donor to be the trustee: the grantor trust rules are not to be triggered. The principal consequence of application of these rules is that the capital gain resulting from the sale of trust assets would be taxed to the donor.

State law on this point must be examined, because of various limitations on what entities can be trustees of trusts, charitable or otherwise. For example, in some states, a charitable organization is not permitted to serve as trustee.

Q 8:21 When should a charitable remainder trust be used rather than another planned giving technique?

Because the charitable remainder trust has the broadest range of possibilities of any of the planned giving techniques, one way to answer this question is to say that a remainder trust should be used when none of the other techniques can be. The remainder trust offers the greatest flexibility in terms of the types of property that can be transferred to it (Q 8:14). A donor desirous of an annuity and wishing to avoid the bargain sale rules can only use a charitable remainder annuity trust (inasmuch as these rules would be invoked where a charitable gift annuity is created (Q 8:9)). A donor can make additional contributions to a charitable remainder unitrust; that advantage is found only with that planned giving vehicle. A donor who wants to take advantage of a makeup feature must use a charitable remainder unitrust (Q 8:13). The prohibition with respect to pooled income funds (Q 8:24) does not apply to transfer of tax-exempt securities.

Q 8:22 What are the disadvantages of using a charitable remainder trust in relation to other planned giving techniques?

The greatest disadvantage may be the cost of preparing the trust documents. These are tailored to particular gift situations, so the legal fees involved could be in the thousands of dollars. Also, many charitable organizations have a minimum for the value of the property they will accept by means of a charitable remainder trust; commonly, the starting level is $50,000, although some organizations will accept gifts as low as $25,000. Financial institutions have minimums for the amounts in trusts they will manage. From a legal standpoint, there is greater likelihood of becoming entangled in the *grantor trust* rules than with any other giving technique.

POOLED INCOME FUNDS

Q 8:23   What types of charities can be remainder interest beneficiaries of pooled income funds?

There are stringent limitations on the types of charitable organizations that can be beneficiaries of pooled income funds. These organizations can only be certain types of public charities; private foundations are ineligible to be beneficiaries. (See Chapter 6.)

The charitable organizations that can be remainder interest beneficiaries of pooled income funds are churches, conventions and associations of churches, and integrated auxiliaries of churches; universities, colleges, and schools; hospitals, similar health care providers, and medical research organizations affiliated with hospitals; foundations affiliated with public (government-operated) colleges and universities; governmental units; and donative publicly supported charities (Q 6:3 and Q 6:7).[19] This means that other types of public charities—principally, service provider publicly supported charities (Q 6:8) and supporting organizations (Q 6:15)—generally cannot be remainder interest beneficiaries of pooled income funds.

TIP: The Internal Revenue Code, in defining the categories of eligible pooled income fund remainder interest beneficiaries, provides that they must be *described in* a qualifying provision. For example, a charitable organization may have a determination letter from the IRS classifying it as a service provider publicly supported charity, although it simultaneously meets the criteria for a donative publicly supported charity. That type of charitable organization could maintain a pooled income fund.

Q 8:24   What types of property are suitable for pooled income funds?

Generally, only property that is liquid in nature can be transferred to a pooled income fund as a charitable gift, because of the necessity of maintaining the requisite pool of assets (Q 8:7). Transferable property is generally money and publicly traded securities. However, it appears that other types of property—such as real estate—may be transferable to a pooled income fund, if the trustee of the fund can readily sell the property.

NOTE: No court opinion or public or private IRS ruling has addressed this subject.

Q 8:25   How is the rate of return calculated for a new pooled income fund?

For this purpose, a *new* pooled income fund is one that has been in existence for less than three years immediately prior to the tax year in which a transfer is made to the fund.[20] A *deemed* rate of return must be used for any transfer to a new pooled income fund until it can compute its highest rate of return for the previous three tax years under the general rules (Q 8:7).

If a transfer is made to a new pooled income fund after April 30, 1989, the deemed rate of return is the interest rate (rounded to the nearest $2/10$ of 1 percent) that is 1 percent less than the highest annual average of the applicable federally determined monthly rates[21] for the three calendar years immediately preceding the year in which the transfer to the fund was made. This can be illustrated by the method for determining the deemed rate for 1994.[22] The average rates were 9.4 percent for 1991, 7.8 percent for 1992, and 6.6 percent for 1993. The subtraction of 1 percent produces 8.4 percent for 1991, 6.8 percent for 1992, and 5.6 percent for 1993. The highest rate for the three years immediately preceding 1994 is thus 8.4 percent; that is the deemed rate of return for transfers to new pooled income funds in 1994.

Q 8:26   Who can be a donor to a pooled income fund?

Only individuals can be donors to pooled income funds. The income payment periods are confined to lifetimes; pooled income fund income interests cannot be determined by means of terms. Consequently, a corporation cannot be a donor to a pooled income fund.

Q 8:27   Who can be a trustee of a pooled income fund?

The charitable organization that maintains the pooled income fund is required to exercise control over the fund (Q 8:7). The charity does not have to be the trustee of the fund—although, as a matter of federal tax law, it can be—but it must have the power to remove and replace the trustee. A donor or an income interest beneficiary of the fund may not be a trustee.

NOTE: A donor may be a trustee or officer of the charitable organization that maintains the fund, as long as he or she does not have the general responsibilities with respect to the fund that are ordinarily exercised by a trustee.

However, state law must be examined on this point, because of various limitations on what entities can be trustees of trusts, charitable or otherwise. For example, in some states, a charitable organization is not permitted to serve as trustee.

Q 8:28   What happens when a charitable organization that has a pooled income fund ceases to qualify as a type of public charity that can maintain a pooled income fund?

As of the year the charitable organization ceases to constitute a type of public charity that is eligible to maintain a pooled income fund, the fund would lose its favorable tax statuses. Among other outcomes, contributions to charity by means of the fund would no longer be tax-deductible as charitable gifts. Contributions made while the organization was qualified would not be adversely affected by the change in the fund's status.

NOTE: The tax regulations are silent on this subject. There is no case, nor any public or private IRS ruling, that addresses the point.

Q 8:29   When should a pooled income fund be used rather than another planned giving technique?

The pooled income fund can be used where the donor of liquid property is not interested in receiving the income interest in the form of fixed income (that is, as an annuity). The fund also is useful when the gift property is relatively modest in size (that is, it may be too small to be transferred to a charitable remainder trust). Further, the pooled income fund gift is simple to document and does not entail much cost.

Q 8:30 What are the disadvantages of using a pooled income fund in relation to other planned giving techniques?

The principal disadvantage is that the income interest beneficiaries of a pooled income fund have no guarantees as to the amount of income they will receive. They receive their allocable shares of the fund's annual earnings—whatever that amount may be. Also, tax-exempt securities may not be contributed to a pooled income fund.

STARTING A PROGRAM

Q 8:31 How does a charitable organization start a planned giving program?

First and foremost, the members of the organization's board of directors must be involved. (This does not mean involved as donors—that part comes later.) They must be involved in the launching of the program. One of the important elements of this step is the passing of a resolution stating the creation of the program, who is principally responsible for implementing it, and which planned giving vehicles are going to be used (at least at the outset).

A brief presentation should be made at a board meeting on the basics of planned giving. It is best if this mini-seminar is offered by an outsider: a lawyer, professional development counselor, or bank trust officer, for example. The board members should be given some written material to peruse afterward.

Prototype documents should be prepared, such as prototype charitable remainder trusts and pooled income fund transfer agreements. These are likely to be of great interest to the potential donor's adviser, be it lawyer, accountant, financial planner, or similar individual, particularly if the adviser is unfamiliar with planned giving.

Registration of this fund-raising program should be undertaken in the appropriate states (see Chapter 7). Marketing literature should be prepared. The organization can either write and print these materials itself or purchase them commercially.

TIP: Some organizations make the mistake of starting with every available planned giving technique and discussing them all in one sizeable document, replete with lengthy illustrations. While impressive, few will read this material. It is best to have separate brochures on each of the techniques. They should be reasonably easy to read with examples kept as simple as possible.

The organization should then start the process of building a network or cadre of volunteers who will be planned giving advocates to the outside world. This group will ideally include many members of the board. These individuals will need some special training in planned giving. The purpose is not to make them planned giving experts overnight, but to cause them to become sufficiently familiar with the subject so they can meaningfully talk to prospective donors.

TIP: These individuals should all be contributors to the planned giving program. It is also important that the board members participate. The task of launching a planned giving program is made much more difficult when the organization's own leadership has not made a planned gift (or not even committed to one)—or, worse, will not give.

The next steps are obvious but the toughest: Identify prospective planned givers, communicating with them, and obtaining the gifts ("closing the deal"). For organizations with an emerging planned giving program, the best way to proceed is to have a staff person or a volunteer meet with the prospective contributor and work out a generalized plan. Thereafter, a session with a planned giving professional can be held, where advise will be offered as to the specific giving method that is best for all parties. Thereafter, a lawyer can prepare any specific instruments that may be required.

A gift once unfolded in this way, resulting in the organization's first charitable remainder trust. An individual had been contacted about the planned giving program. Having coincidentally received a large sum of money as the result of a sale of property, he was looking for some tax relief. He had a sincere interest in the organization, so he and a staff person met and worked out these general guidelines: he needed a charitable deduction of X amount and an annual income of Y amount. The parties subsequently met with a lawyer, the numbers were run, the deduction and income amounts for each planned giving method were reviewed, and a specific arrangement (using a charitable remainder unitrust) was developed.

As the gifts come in and the various processes that lead to them are experienced, the parties involved will gain greater confidence and thus will need to rely less on outside counsel. The planned giving professional may be kept on call and used as circumstances warrant.

One of the excuses frequently given for postponing the inauguration of a planned giving program (or ignoring the idea of such a program altogether) is that it is not suitable for a new organization. There is no question that a university with decades of graduations has a much more solid donor base than a community service group incorporated yesterday. But that university's relative advantage is not an authentic reason for doing nothing. Every organization has a support base or it would not exist. It may be that, on day one, there is only one planned gift prospect, yet that is no reason for not asking that prospect. The largest planned giving program in the nation started with one gift.

CHAPTER 9

Fund-Raisers' Inquiries

As the fund-raising profession comes under increasing scrutiny and regulation by the federal and state governments (see Chapter 7), those who raise funds for charity are asking more questions about the laws that are applicable to them. This reaction is evident whether the fund-raisers are employees of a charity or independent professional fund-raising consultants.

Their questions are not solely concerned with the rules for charitable giving or tax exemption; they extend to the administration and management of the fund-raising process. (Some of these questions are better answered by an accountant, management consultant, or appraiser.) Fund-raisers are the newest of the persons, acting for the benefit of charity, who are being regulated, so it is not surprising that they have the freshest crop of questions in the nonprofit field.

Here are the questions most frequently asked by clients or fund-raising executives who consult with them about the deductibility of a multitude of charitable gifts, the law pertaining to auctions, the role of the fund-raisers as to legal matters, and techniques for curbing governmental regulation—and the answers to them.

OVERVIEW

Q 9:1   Is there a charitable contribution deduction for a gift of services?

No. The federal tax law does not allow for a charitable contribution deduction for the value of services provided to a charitable organization as a gift.[1] For example, a lawyer may contribute to a charity, as an item to be bid on at a fund-raising auction, his or her services in the writing of a will; there is no charitable contribution deduction for the value (based on the lawyer's hourly rate) of this type of gift.

NOTE: There is another reason why this type of gift is not deductible: There is no deduction for the gifts of "property" created by the donor.[2]

In its annual information return, a nonprofit organization can indicate the value of donated services received.[3] However, the organization cannot include this value as revenue, or expense the services, or (if it is a charitable organization) include the value as public support.

By contrast, in some instances, the out-of-pocket expenses incurred by volunteers are deductible as charitable contributions. This can occur where the expenses are necessary to the accomplishment of the organization's exempt purposes.

Q 9:2   Is there a charitable contribution deduction for a gift of the right to use materials, equipment, or facilities?

No. The federal tax law does not allow for a charitable contribution deduction for the value of materials, equipment, or facilities provided to a charitable organization as a gift.[4] For example, the owner of an office building may contribute office space in the building to a charity; there is no charitable contribution deduction for this type of gift. Likewise, the owner of a beach house may contribute to a charity, as an item to be bid on at a fund-raising auction, a two-week stay at the house; no contribution deduction is available for this type of gift.

However, in its annual information return, a nonprofit organization can indicate the value of materials, equipment, or facilities received as gifts.[5] The organization cannot include this value as revenue, or expense the services, or (if it is a charitable organization) include the value as public support.

Q 9:3   What are the obligations of a charitable organization regarding a restricted gift or bequest received in a prior year for a program that has since been discontinued?

Assuming that the restriction was imposed by the donor (rather than solely by the charity's board of directors), it is the obligation of the charitable organization to use the restricted money or property in a manner that continues to conform to the restriction. Even though the program has been discontinued, there may be other uses of the property that are within the range of the restriction.

NOTE: This may require some creative reading of the restriction. The ease of compliance with the language of the restriction is in direct correlation with the breadth of the restriction.

If there is no reasonable way to conform to the restriction, the organization has these options: (1) where the donor is still alive, obtain a written waiver of the restriction, perhaps replacing it with another restriction that the organization can currently satisfy, (2) make a grant of the funds or property to another organization that can satisfy the restriction, or (3) take the matter into court in an effort to have the restriction revised or lifted.

The restriction is a contract between donor and donee. Once the charitable organization has accepted the restricted gift, it is bound by its terms. At the same time, the overarching concern is that the gift property will be used for charitable ends. If there is no one living to challenge a deviation from the restriction, the organization should consider use of the restricted property in a manner as close to the bounds of the restriction (but presumably not in literal compliance) as possible. This is a "judgment call," based on the facts and circumstances at the time; above all, the organization should be prudent and act in good faith when making this type of management decision.

Q 9:4   How does a nonprofit organization establish the gift value for a contribution of securities?

If the securities are publicly traded, the value can be ascertained by reference to the value of them as traded on a securities exchange on the appropriate valuation date.[6] If the securities are not publicly traded, their value must be established by someone who is competent to ascertain that value.

The valuation date depends on the manner in which the securities are transferred to the charity. If the securities are delivered to the charity with the stock certificate properly endorsed, the valuation date is the date of delivery. This is also the case where the securities are delivered to an agent of the charitable donee.[7]

If the stock certificate is mailed, the deduction arises as of the date on which the certificate was mailed (the law regards the U.S. Postal Service as the charity's agent). Where the certificate is delivered to the corporation that issued the security or to a broker acting on behalf of the donor, for purposes of arranging for transfer of title to the security to the charitable donee, the charitable deduction will come into being on the date the transfer of the security is formally recorded by the issuing corporation.

NOTE: In applying this rule, it must be shown that the intermediate transferee is, in fact, an agent of the donor. There can be controversy on this point.[8]

TIP: A mere notation on the records of the donee charitable organization of a contribution of securities is not sufficient to cause effective transfer of the title.[9]

AUCTIONS

Q 9:5   Is an auction conducted by a charity considered one of the types of special events?

Yes. In this sense, an auction is the same as a dinner, theater outing, car wash, bake sale, or raffle. It is not an exempt activity of the charitable organization; for example, a private school conducting an auction is not engaging in an educational pursuit. This type of auction is a fund-raising event, albeit replete with benefits of nearly equal value, such as public and community relations and what some in the fund-raising profession call *friend-raising.*[10]

Q 9:6   Why is the revenue from a charity auction not taxed?

A charity auction is not an exempt function (Q 9:5). It is, for tax purposes, a *business* (Q 10:6); an auction is the selling of goods. Consequently, the conduct of a charity auction is the conduct of an unrelated business by the charitable organization involved.

The net income generated by a charity auction would, therefore, be taxable as unrelated business income were it not for as many as three features of the unrelated business rules, two of which are exceptions to those rules. The first of these features relates to the fact that, for an unrelated business to give rise to taxable income, it must be regularly carried on (Q 10:13). An annual auction held by a charitable organization is not an activity that is regularly carried on; thus, the net income is not taxable. However, were a charitable organization to hold an auction every weekend, the net revenue from it would be taxable, unless one or two of the other exceptions applies.

There is an exception, from the definition of an unrelated business, for the sale of merchandise that has been donated to the exempt organization (Q 10:23). This exception was written for nonprofit thrift shops, but it is equally applicable with respect to nonprofit auctions. Even if an auction were held weekly, this exception would likely shield the income from taxation.

There is an exception for businesses in which substantially all of the work is done by volunteers (Q 10:23). If a charity auction is conducted largely by volunteers—as is usually the case—the net income from it would not be taxed.

Most charity auctions are protected from income taxation on all three of these points of federal tax law.

Q 9:7   Do those who donate items to an auction receive a federal income tax charitable contribution deduction for the gift?

It depends on what is contributed. Moreover, any deduction can be much less than might be expected. The difficulty is that most items donated to a charity for subsequent auctioning are items of tangible personal property. In general, the contribution of an item of property to a charitable organization is deductible using its fair market value. However, there are unique rules for gifts of tangible personal property.

If an item of personal property has appreciated in value and is contributed to a charity for the purpose of auction, the charitable deduction is confined to the donor's basis in the property. This is because the gift was made for an unrelated purpose—resale by the charitable organization (Q 1:43).

If the item donated has a value in excess of $5,000, the deduction depends on a bona fide appraisal (Q 7:13). An appraisal summary must be included with the donor's tax return. The charitable organization must report the sale to the IRS, assuming the auction takes place within two years of the gift.[11]

There is no charitable deduction for a gift of the right to use property (Q 9:2). Thus, for example, if an individual contributes the opportunity to use his or her home in the mountains for two weeks, there is no charitable deduction equal to the fair rental value of the property.

TIP: Actually, there is a double tax hit here. The donor must consider the period of time the property is used by the winning bidder as personal time for purposes of the rules regarding the deductibility of business expenses in connection with the rental property.[12]

There is no charitable deduction for a gift of services (Q 9:1). Thus, for example, if a lawyer donates his or her services for a particular project, there is no charitable deduction equal to the hourly rate the lawyer would otherwise charge.

Special rules apply when a business makes a charitable contribution of items from its inventory (Q 1:43). The charitable gift substantiation rules may also apply (Q 7:6, Q 9:9).

Q 9:8   Does an individual who acquires an item at a charity auction receive a charitable contribution deduction as a result of the transaction?

Possibly. The law in this area once was that, for a payment to a charitable organization to be deductible as a gift, the payor had to have a *donative intent*. Were that the law today, almost no payments made at a charity auction would be deductible. However, the law has shifted to a more mechanical computation. In general, deductible payments to a charity are those that exceed the fair market value of anything the donor may receive in return, other than items of insignificant value (Q 7:11).

NOTE: The IRS issued proposed regulations that would allow gifts made in the charity auction setting and other quid pro quo contexts

---

to be deductible only where the patron intended to make a payment in an amount that exceeds fair market value.[13] This proposal does not quite involve donative intent but it is close. The requirement will be harmless in circumstances where the patron knows the charity's good faith estimate figure in advance of the payment and thus cannot help but have this intent. Still, the intent may not be donative: the successful bidder may intensely want the item, or may be motivated by peer pressure or extensive access to an open bar; charity may be the furthest thing from the patron's mind.

There are two schools of thought here. Both are facially quite valid. One is that the auction is the marketplace, so whatever is paid for an item at an auction is its fair market value at that time. In this view, the transaction is always a purchase in its entirety; there is no gift element and, thus, no charitable deduction.

The other line of thought is that an item purchased at a charity auction has a fair market value, irrespective of the amount paid for it at the auction. This approach would allow a charitable deduction for an amount paid at a charity auction that exceeds the value of the property.

In actual practice, most items disposed of at a charity auction are acquired for a value that does not involve a gift element (because the amount paid is approximately equal to the value of the item and often is less), so there is no charitable deduction. If a person wants to claim a charitable deduction, the burden of proof is on the putative donor to prove that what was paid exceeded the fair value of the property.

This burden of proof can be met where it is easy to prove the fair market value of the item, such as an appliance or a piece of furniture. But, where the value of an item is difficult to discern, it will be arduous for a patron of the auction to convince the IRS that some portion of the amount paid was a deductible gift.

Thus, the assumptions should be that the auction is the marketplace and that there is no charitable element when items are acquired. However, where the value can be legitimately ascertained and the purchaser paid more than that value, the difference in amount is deductible as a charitable contribution. This conclusion assumes, of course, that all other elements of the law, required for the deduction to be available, are satisfied. The most important of these other elements is probably the gift substantiation requirement (Q 9:9).

Q 9:9   How do the charitable gift substantiation rules apply in the auction setting?

The charitable gift substantiation rules apply with respect to gifts made in the context of acquiring an item auctioned by a charitable organization, assuming there is a gift element and it is $250 or more (Q 7:6). (If there is no contribution component to the transaction, the substantiation rules are not applicable.)

However, where (1) the patron at a charity auction is of the view that he or she has made a charitable contribution in the course of acquiring an item, (2) the ostensible gift element is at least $250, and (3) a charitable deduction is desired, the substantiation rules come into play. However, the donor must notify the charitable organization that he or she believes a gift was made at the auction, with the intent of receiving the necessary acknowledgment. If the charity agrees that a gift was made, it will issue a written substantiation showing the amount that was contributed (the full amount of the winning bid), and a description and good faith estimate of the value of the item acquired. The difference would be the amount deductible as a charitable gift.

The process would not function as smoothly if the charity believed that no part of the payment was a charitable gift—or if it was uncertain. The organization could refuse to issue the acknowledgment or could decline to commit itself to a good faith estimate of the value of the item auctioned; in such an instance, the charitable deduction would be barred. However, as a practical matter, relations with donors and patrons are of a nature that a charity usually is not that cavalier.

TIP: Remember, a charitable organization that knowingly provides a false written substantiation to a donor may be subject to a penalty for aiding and abetting an understatement of tax liability.[14]

Q 9:10   How do the quid pro quo rules apply in the auction setting?

When a person makes a gift to a charitable organization in excess of $75 and receives something of material value in return, the charitable donee is required to make a good faith estimate of the value of the item and to notify the donor that only the difference between the fair market value of the item and the amount paid for it (if any) is deductible as a charitable contribution (Q 7:7).

The application of this rule in the charity auction context is not clear. Superficially, the quid pro quo rules would seem to apply in this setting where the amount transferred is more than $75 and there is a gift element.

A *quid pro quo contribution* is defined as a payment "made partly as a contribution and partly in consideration for goods or services provided to the payor by the donee organization."[15] Thus, it can be argued that the purchase of an item at an auction, at a price known to be in excess of the fair market value of the item, is both a contribution and a payment made in consideration of something (a purchase).

Q 9:11   Does the sales tax apply to purchases made at an auction?

Presumably, yes. Every transaction at an auction is, in whole or in part, a purchase. Thus, the charity is engaging in sales, which can trigger application of the state's sales tax. This is a state-by-state matter, so it is not possible to generalize on the point. The law of the applicable state should be reviewed.

NOTE: A state will often exempt charitable organizations from having to *pay* the state's sales tax. However, this type of an exemption does not mean that the charity is exempt from the requirement of *collecting* the sales tax.

Q 9:12   How are the proceeds of a charity auction reported to the IRS?

A charity auction is a fund-raising event; in the parlance of the federal tax law, it is a *special event* (Q 9:5). The organization is required to report the proceeds from the conduct of the auction on its annual information return as a *special fund-raising event.*[16] (This reporting requirement is inapplicable where the information return for small organizations is used. Also, churches and certain other religious organizations are exempted from the filing of these returns.)

The gross revenue from the auction is reported in this fashion (other than any amounts the charity is treating as contributions). Direct expenses and resulting net income are also reported.

TIP: This is one of the few areas where the tax law allows organizations to net items on the face of the return. Thus, for purposes of the exemption from filing an annual information return for organizations with annual gross revenues not normally in excess of $25,000, only the amount of net income from an auction is taken into account.

VOLUNTEERS

Q 9:13   Should volunteers be included in the directors' and officers' liability insurance coverage?

As a general rule, those being covered by a directors' and officers' insurance policy obtained by a nonprofit organization are volunteers. However, this type of coverage may be provided irrespective of whether the directors and officers are compensated.

Other types of volunteers may be covered by insurance of this nature. For example, some organizations extend this coverage to chairs of committees and even to all of the members of committees.

Coverage beyond directors, officers, and committee members, however, distorts the nature of this insurance. "D and O" coverage is designed to provide insurance for the leadership of the organization as they go about making decisions with respect to management and direction of the organization. This coverage is not suitable for all volunteers.

If insurance coverage is desired below the leadership level, the preferable approach is to purchase a particular type of protection (such as personal injury insurance) rather than to insure particular types of individuals.

Q 9:14   What is the law regarding the conduct of volunteers representing nonprofit organizations?

A nonprofit organization—like all organizations—is a legal fiction. The entity can only be physically manifested as a collective of individuals. These individuals include volunteers.

A nonprofit organization is guided principally by its board of directors, and secondarily by its officers (Q 1:3). These individuals are often volunteers. Thus, volunteers can lead and commit a nonprofit organization.

When a third person (such as a vendor of goods or services) deals with a nonprofit organization, the vendor is entitled to rely—for law purposes, such as a contract—on the representations of those who claim to officially speak and act for the organization. The persons making these representations can be volunteers. The nonprofit organization will not later have a defense—such as in a case of a breach of contract—where the volunteer was acting *under color of authority* and the vendor was acting in good faith (perhaps not knowing that the individual making the representations lacked the authority to do so).

Q 9:15   Can a volunteer sign a contract for services on behalf of a nonprofit organization?

Yes. However, the organization should be very careful in this area. The leadership of the organization should establish clear lines of responsibility as to who can legally commit the organization to contracts, other financial obligations, and the like.

The organization's bylaws should spell out the duties of the directors, officers, and key staff (Q 2:4, Q 2:9). That document should specifically state the individuals who can execute contracts on behalf of the organization. If the organization has internal guidelines for operating procedures, these policies should be reflected in the bylaws as well. If the organization has a set of guidelines for volunteers, this subject should be addressed in that context also.

The organization does not want a situation where volunteers are signing agreements or otherwise binding, or attempting to bind, the organization to obligations, when those volunteers are not properly authorized to act. If adequate policies and controls are not in place, the nonprofit organization could find itself legally bound in circumstances inimical to its interests.

Q 9:16   Are there any requirements or guidelines on length of service for volunteers serving as board members?

This is a state law issue. The precise answer to the question cannot be determined without reference to applicable state law. Most states allow nonprofit organizations—particularly nonprofit corporations—to do what they want on this subject. It is common for a statute to make provisions that come into play only when an organization's bylaws are silent on the point.

A useful pattern is to have a nine-person board, with each individual serving a three-year term; the terms are staggered so that one-third of the board is reelected or replaced each year. This model provides for fresh perspectives as well as continuity of experience.

Many subtleties arise here. The board may include one or more *ex officio* positions. If so, the bylaws should state whether these individuals have the right to vote (Q 2:1). The bylaws should expressly address the point of whether board members—volunteer or otherwise—can be reelected to office. Most states require a term of office; the law may not specify the length of a term, but a defined term may be required. Usually, state law will not allow an individual to hold office in a nonprofit organization for a lengthy unfettered period of time.

OTHER MATTERS

Q 9:17 What role should the professional fund-raiser have in connection with the charity's annual information return?

Ideally, the fund-raiser should have a substantial role in the preparation of this document. Much information given in this return pertains directly to fund-raising (Q 7:15).

These information items range from how much is recorded as public support and the total of fund-raising costs to allocations of expenses between program and fund-raising and the written explanations of the organization's programs. These returns are often prepared solely by accountants and are sometimes reviewed by lawyers.

That practice is no longer satisfactory. These returns are not *tax* returns—they are *information* returns. Much of the information is not purely financial in nature. What the information is and how it is presented can be of considerable significance to the fund-raiser. (Information returns are accessible to the public.[17])

The ideal way to proceed is to have the fund-raising professional review a draft of the annual information return, which has been prepared and reviewed by others. He or she should be certain that all gift support is properly allocated (such as to public support), the total fund-raising cost is accurate, the information with respect to special events is properly shown, the charitable programs are accurately described, and the fund-raising program is being reported in conformity with the unrelated business income rules (see Chapter 10). If the charity is a publicly supported entity, the support schedule should be reviewed for accuracy and for confirmation that the public support ratio is understood on an ongoing basis (see Chapter 6).

The fund-raising professional may be the only individual looking at the annual information return from the perspective of potential donors—or the media.

Q 9:18   How does a fund-raising charitable organization go about selecting a lawyer?

A charitable organization should select legal counsel in the same way that it should select anyone else who will provide it with services: Find someone who knows what he or she is doing. In most instances, the process is not easy.

Lawyers most often obtain new clients from referrals. When officers of a charitable organization are looking for a lawyer with expertise in fund-raising regulation (or any other field of concern to charity, such as planned giving), they should talk with their colleagues, ask around, and compile a list. The names of suitable lawyers should surface. Other sources (although generally less reliable) are journals and conferences; competent counsel can be found among those who write and speak about legal issues pertaining to charities.

Geography is a factor here. The farther away from a large metropolitan area a charitable organization is, the greater the likelihood it will end up with a lawyer who will conduct the necessary practice via telephone and facsimile.

There is another, and very important, criterion: Find someone the organization can work with. Lawyers are not always at the head of personality parades, but clients should at least have a lawyer with whom there is reciprocal trust and comfortable co-existence.

Some additional thoughts:

1. The days when a client was intimidated by a lawyer are over. A lawyer is a human being who is also a service provider with certain skills—some learned, some innate. Frequently, the organization is purchasing the lawyer's judgment. A lawyer is not some deity or oracle who is infallible and above question. A lawyer is a consultant who works for and on behalf of the charitable organization. The relationship, if turned the other way around, will not endure.

2. The nature of the charitable organization–lawyer relationship should be reduced to writing. (Most lawyers' codes of ethics require this.) The charitable organization should understand the billing arrangements, including hourly rates, frequency of bills (usually referred to as statements), and format and contents of the bills. The organization should not hesitate to ask for some billing feature (such as a detailed explanation of services rendered) if it is not offered.

3. The organization should not be afraid to question items on a lawyer's bill. Nonprofit organizations (and anyone else) do not have to pay for a lawyer's learning experience. Bills should be scrutinized for items such as "research" and "interoffice conferences." There is nothing inherently wrong with these items, but they warrant a close look.

4. The hourly rate trap is to be avoided. (This is the legal profession's own fault; it brought this calamity on itself.) For the most part, the hourly rate is irrelevant. The charitable organization should focus on the total fees for legal services, rather than on the mechanics of computing the fee. The true test is: Is the fee reasonable in relation to the services provided (Q 3:1)? A lawyer charging $300 an hour may be able to answer a question in a brief telephone call; a lawyer holding out for $100 an hour may spend hours in a law library ferreting out the answer (assuming it can be found there).

Regrettably, the legal profession has become more of a law business, and a lawyer is sometimes just one more consultant. Yet, fundraising and the law are now inextricably intertwined. A skilled lawyer can bring a unique perspective, a singular judgment. The challenge is to find a good lawyer and use his or her services properly.

Q 9:19 How will some of the recent scandals involving public charities affect fund-raising?

It is too soon to tell. Some segments of the public have become more skeptical about charitable and other nonprofit organizations. Yet, these scandals do not always implicate donors' favorite charities. Charitable giving was at its highest level in 1994—nearly $130 billion.

Past months have not been great for public charities in the news. Recent history on this subject started with the United Way of America scandal, which culminated with the conviction on fraud charges and imprisonment of its former president. The philanthropic sector was surprised to learn the identity of its largest single member: a trust in Hawaii known as the Bishop Estate, which may have as much as $10 billion in assets. There are pending allegations that, while the trust is engaging in some educational activities, it is spending the bulk of its efforts on its investments. Employees of the Catholic Church have embezzled more than $3.5 million over the past three years. An employee of the Episcopalian Church embezzled over $2 million, forcing her husband to resign from the priesthood. One of the most damaging of these episodes involved the Foundation for New Era Philanthropy. When its Ponzi scheme was uncovered, the entity had to file for bankruptcy, and donors and charities were left short of millions of dollars.

The damage being caused by the collapse of the Foundation, and similar other developments, has many organizations worried about the long-term impact of these machinations on future prospects for regulation of public charities. The United Way and Foundation for New Era Philanthropy cases are so bizarre that they should be regarded as criminal and fraud matters, with little regulatory implication for charities as such. Instances of embezzlement do not need new laws to fix them; they need more internal controls and outside auditing.

The headline cases deliver another warning that the law can only go so far; fraud (by definition) is hard to obliterate by statute, and society must rely instead on prosecutions. Many commentators and others believe these episodes demonstrate that public charities must be regulated more strenuously. However, most of the states have extensive statutes in this area; 35 have very comprehensive charitable solicitation acts (see Chapter 7). The size and extent of these laws are growing; several states have expanded their statutes in recent months. Many of the new laws are accompanied by extensive rules and regulations.

At the federal level, the IRS has ample jurisdiction over charities' affairs (see Chapter 7). Charitable organizations must be reviewed by the IRS to obtain recognition of tax exemption at the outset, and they must file comprehensive annual reports to retain that exemption. There are rules on private inurement and private benefit (see Chapter 3); the tax code has a range of laws pertaining to civil and criminal fraud.

Charities are often moved by compassion and altruism rather than commercial business skepticism. No question that charities' boards of directors are too often inadequate or passive. There is pressure to raise funds in the face of greater demands for services. These circumstances create a climate in which an incident such as the Foundation for New Era Philanthropy debacle can take root.

A close look at the facts, however, shows that many charities that fell into the Foundation's trap did their "due diligence." Legislation and regulations are not going to increase the pursuit of due diligence; this case is about reasonable behavior and the vicissitudes of life.

The IRS itself has put the matter about as well as it can be stated. In the procedure relating to charitable organizations formed to respond to the Oklahoma City bombing, the IRS said: "Donors should exercise care before contributing to [or "investing" in] any organization. With increased public interest in making donations to charitable organizations to assist disaster victims, there is the increased possibility that some organizations (or their fundraisers) may make false or inaccurate claims regarding how contributions will be used or whether these contributions are tax deductible."[18]

Recent scandals are being cast as reminders of philanthropic vulnerability. That is not a true description. They are reminders of human vulnerability.[19]

Q 9:20   What can the professional fund-raising community do to curb the increasing amount of government regulation?

There is much to be done. Government regulation of fund-raising today is burdensome and it is increasing.

This form of combat requires strategic planning. The core focus should be on the associations representing the fund-raising profession. They should have strong departments of government affairs, programs for regularly educating their membership as to developments in government regulation, and consistent, contributory interaction with regulators and legislators regarding the regulatory process.

The task is somewhat easier at the federal level. The fund-raising community needs to interrelate more with Congress, the Department of the Treasury, the IRS, and the U.S. Postal Service, as well as other agencies (such as the Federal Trade Commission) when circumstances warrant. If one of these agencies issues for comment a proposed regulation or rule that is of consequence to fund-raising, the profession should be in the thick of the fray with timely and cogent written comments. If there is a hearing, the profession should be there. There is nothing wrong with initiating action, either; the profession need not be merely reactive. Most federal officials will welcome the information and the perspective that the profession can provide.

Lobbying of Congress is critical. The charitable community as an entirety has a better lobbying system in place than ever before, but there is a long way to go. When issues that are unique to the fund-raising profession are unaddressed, this forfeiture of power allows others to make woefully uninformed decisions that emerge as regulation of the profession.

State regulation is much more difficult to grapple with, because so much is transpiring in so many places. Ideally, the fund-raising profession would have in place, for acting in each of (or most of) the states, a system similar to that sketched out with respect to federal regulation. Somehow, the profession must communicate to state legislatures and regulators the urgent need to cap the present spiraling regulation and initiate repeal of some of the more extreme (sometimes, unconstitutional) forms of regulation now in place.

At the state level, many of the old-line techniques have failed: model laws, model regulations, and model forms have only invited as many different versions as there are states in the union. Surely there are ways to make the state regulatory system more uniform and consistent.

The key to a reasoned outcome is held by the legislatures. The regulators, at the federal and state levels, usually are carrying out the dictates of the legislators. More educating and lobbying of legislators by the fund-raising profession is critical. Champions of charitable fund-raising need to be cultivated and sustained at both levels of government.

One of the ultimate solutions may be a political action committee (PAC) that assists the campaigns of incumbents and challengers who agree to support the charitable and fund-raising communities' policy agenda. Such a PAC could either be affiliated with an association of fund-raising professionals or be free-standing.

The foregoing techniques in the field of government affairs can be used by any profession or other field. Some professions are far better organized for concerted action than others. Unfortunately, most members of the fund-raising profession are unwilling to participate in the work entailed by government relations efforts: lobbying, communicating with regulators, and political activities. Until that mindset is changed, the leaders of the profession will find it extremely difficult to channel more energy and resources into government affairs programs.

CHAPTER 10

Unrelated Business Activities

The taxability of income derived by a tax-exempt organization from the conduct of *unrelated business* is a key feature of the federal tax law relating to nonprofit organizations. This aspect of the law of tax-exempt organizations looms large these days as the federal government searches for ways to generate tax revenues. The concept of the unrelated business rules is crisp and clear; application of it, however, is often very difficult because the specifics of these rules can be vague and varying.

No field of the federal tax law applicable to nonprofit organizations is spawning more issues and controversies than that pertaining to unrelated business activities. This area is a high audit priority for the IRS.

Here are the questions most frequently asked by clients about the unrelated business law (including the availability of exceptions), the tax treatment of royalties, and the impact of the "hot" issues facing hospitals, colleges, and universities—and the answers to them.

OVERVIEW

Q 10:1 A tax-exempt organization often needs more money than it can generate through gifts, grants, and dues. Management of the organization is thinking about raising money by charging fees for some products or services, but it is concerned about taxation. Where does it begin?

Basically, the management of the organization should not lose sight of the fundamental fact that the organization is a nonprofit, tax-exempt entity. Thus, the organization needs to be operated *primarily* for its exempt purposes. If there is to be any taxable income, it will be income that is derived from business activities that are *unrelated* to the organization's tax-exempt purpose. As long as operations are primarily for exempt purposes, the organization need not fear loss of its tax-exempt status. However, the income derived from the other, non-exempt activities may well be subject to the federal income tax.

Q 10:2   How does an organization measure what is primary?

That often is not easy to do; there is no mechanical formula for measuring what is *primary*. The measurement is done on the basis of what the law likes to term the *facts and circumstances*. The IRS heartily rejects the thought of applying any particular percentage in measuring primary activities, and invokes this principle of law on a case-by-case basis. In this stance, the IRS is uniformly supported by the courts.[1]

TIP: Percentages are used in this and comparable contexts all the time, if only as a guide. The term *primary* has been assigned percentages in other settings; for unrelated business income purposes, it can mean at least 65 percent. By comparison, *substantial* is sometimes defined as at least 85 percent; *substantially all* is sometimes set at 90 percent. *Incidental* is sometimes defined as up to 15 percent.

If these percentages have any validity—and, to a limited extent, they do for evaluation purposes—then an organization could have as much as one-third of its activities or income be unrelated. There are IRS private letter rulings upholding unrelated income in excess of 40 percent; however, in these cases, the amount of *time* actually devoted to the unrelated business was considerably less. It seems unlikely that any organization receiving over one-half of its income from unrelated business would be tax-exempt.

A prudent assessment or review would cause a tax-exempt organization to seriously evaluate its situation, if its unrelated income annually exceeds 20 or 25 percent of total revenue. The remedies may include setting up a for-profit subsidiary (see Chapter 11).

The statement that there is no mechanical formula for measuring what is *primary* is not precisely accurate. In the case of tax-exempt title-holding companies, the maximum amount of unrelated business income that they can have in a year without endangering tax exemption is 10 percent.[2] However, this rule does not apply with respect to any other type of tax-exempt organization. For most tax-exempt organizations, 10 percent is too narrow a limitation on permissible unrelated activity.

Q 10:3 How does an exempt organization know whether an activity is a related one or an unrelated one?

This is both one of the easiest and hardest questions in the law of tax-exempt organizations.

The easy answer is that an unrelated activity is one that does not substantially advance the exempt purposes of the organization. That is, it is an activity that the organization engages in for the purpose of earning money, rather than furthering one or more programs. The fact that the money earned is used for exempt purposes does not alone make the activity itself related.

The more complex answer is that the activity must be evaluated against as many as five levels of analysis. These are:

1. Is the activity a *trade or business* (Q 10:6)?
2. Is it *regularly carried on* (Q 10:13)?
3. Is the conduct of the activity *substantially related* to the conduct of exempt functions (Q 10:18)?
4. Is the activity exempted from taxation by one or more statutory exceptions (Q 10:23)?
5. Is the income from the activity exempted from taxation by one or more statutory exceptions (Q 10:24)?

Q 10:4 What is the rationale underlying the unrelated income rules?

The basic structure of these rules was enacted in 1950. The essence of this body of law is to separate the income of a tax-exempt organization into two categories: (1) income from related business and (2) income from unrelated business. The income from unrelated business is taxed as if it was earned by a for-profit, taxable company.

The primary objective of these rules was to eliminate a source of *unfair competition* with the for-profit sector by placing the unrelated business activities of exempt organizations on the same tax basis as those conducted by non-exempt organizations, where the two are in competition.[3] Some courts place considerable emphasis on the factor of competition when assessing whether an undertaking is an unrelated business (Q 10:10). However, the existence or nonexistence of competition is not a statutory requirement for there to be unrelated business.

In actuality, the enactment of these rules has not quelled the cries of "unfair competition" from the business sector, particularly small business owners. More than four decades later, the issue is not so much that unrelated business by nonprofits is competitive; rather, the competition is usually derived from *related* businesses. In part, this is the result of (1) shifts in the definition of related and unrelated activities and (2) the entry of for-profits into fields of endeavor previously confined to nonprofit entities. Some small business advocates want competitive practices prohibited, as a way of "leveling the playing the field." These individuals are of the view that unrelated income taxation is not enough; they fret about the fact that some consumers are attracted to, and thus bring their business to, nonprofits just because they are nonprofit—a situation informally known as the "halo effect."

Thus, the purpose of the unrelated income tax itself is to equalize the economics of a transaction, irrespective of whether the vendor of a good or service is tax-exempt or taxable. If an organization can sell a product and not pay income tax on the sales proceeds, that organization can charge a lower price for that product and have more "profit" remaining than an organization selling the same product and have to pay taxes as a cost of doing business. This ability, and occasional practices of price undercutting, is the foundation for the claim of "unfair competition."

Q 10:5 Are these claims of unfair competition leading to anything, such as law changes?

It doesn't look like it. A few years ago, when the small business lobbying on this subject was at its peak, some thought that Congress would toughen the rules. There was a series of hearings before the Subcommittee on Oversight, of the House Committee on Ways and Means, in 1986–1987. The chairman of the subcommittee pushed hard for legislation but could not build a consensus for change. The nonprofit community lobbied very effectively against various proposals, the small business lobby did a particularly poor job of sustaining its efforts, and the movement for revising these laws atrophied. The individual who was the subcommittee chairman is no longer in Congress, and there is no interest, in either chamber, in law change in this area. Still, efforts to make it more difficult for nonprofits to compete are unfolding in several states.

Q 10:6   What is the trade or business requirement?

A statutory definition of *trade or business* is specifically applicable in the unrelated business setting. The phrase means any activity that is carried on for the production of income from the sale of goods or the performance of services.[4] That definition is, of course, quite broad and encompasses nearly everything that a tax-exempt organization does.

In fact, the law regards a tax-exempt organization as a bundle of activities. They may be related or unrelated, but they are still *businesses.*

Q 10:7   Does this mean that the law considers the programs of exempt organizations as businesses?

Yes. Each of the organization's programs is considered a separate business. In fact, a program may embody several businesses. For example, the bookstore operated by a college is a combination of businesses. These include sales of books, cosmetics, computers, appliances, and clothing. The same is true with respect to hospital and museum gift shops and associations' sales of items to their members. In the case of charitable organizations, many of their fund-raising activities are businesses.

It is very difficult to convince the IRS that a particular activity is not a business. The most likely instances where an exempt organization can prevail on this point is with respect to its investment activities and infrequent sales of assets. Occasionally, a court will be more lenient, as illustrated by an opinion finding that an association's monitoring activities with respect to insurance programs for its membership, where the insurance and claims processing functions were elsewhere, did not rise to the level of a trade or business.[5]

Moreover, an activity does not lose its identity as a trade or business if it is carried on within a larger aggregate of similar activities or within a larger complex of other endeavors that may or may not be related to the exempt purposes of the organization.[6] This means that an activity cannot be hidden from scrutiny, as to whether it is a business, by tucking it in with other activities. The IRS has the authority to review each business of an exempt organization in isolation, in search of unrelated activity. That is, it can—figuratively speaking—fragment an organization into as many businesses as it can define. In the jargon of the field, this is known as the *fragmentation rule.*

Q 10:8 **When the federal tax law regards an exempt organization as a composite of businesses, isn't that different from how nonprofit organizations see themselves?**

No question about that. Unfortunately, the matter gets murkier. Actually, the statutory definition of *business* states that the term *trade or business* "includes" that definition of it. That word has opened the door for the courts and the IRS to add other requirements and possibilities that may cause an activity to be a business. Some courts use other criteria, such as competitive activity or commerciality, and then jump all the way to the conclusion that the activity is an unrelated business.

For example, in a completely different area of the tax law, dealing with whether a gambler gambling only for personal ends is engaged in a business for expense deduction purposes, the Supreme Court held that, for an activity to be considered a trade or business, it must be carried on with a profit motive.[7] The Court specifically wrote that this definition of trade or business was not to be used in other tax settings. But, some lower courts ignored that admonition and engrafted that rule onto the definition of exempt organizations' unrelated income purposes.[8]

Q 10:9 **Why would a tax-exempt organization object to that additional element of the definition, concerning a profit motive? Wouldn't that rule always favor exempt organizations, causing some activities to not be businesses in the first instance?**

Actually, it doesn't always work that way. In some instances, an exempt organization *wants* an activity to be considered an unrelated business. This is because income from unrelated activity and losses from other unrelated activity can be aggregated to produce a single, bottom-line item of net income or net loss.

For example, suppose an exempt organization has two unrelated activities. One produces $100,000 of net income, the other generates $70,000 of net losses. On the unrelated business income tax return, the income and losses from the two businesses are blended, and the organization pays the unrelated income tax on only $30,000. However, this works only when both activities are in fact *businesses.*

Suppose the second of these activities consistently, year-in and year-out, yields losses. The IRS will usually take the position that, because the activity always results in an annual loss, it is not being conducted with the requisite profit motive. If that position is sustained, the activity is not considered a *business,* in which case the $70,000 of loss could not be offset against the $100,000 of gain. Then, the organization would have to pay the unrelated income tax on the full $100,000.

All of this is happening even though the tax regulations state that the fact that a trade or business does not produce a net profit is not sufficient to exclude it from the definition of a trade or business.[9]

Q 10:10 What are some of the other elements being engrafted onto this definition?

Sometimes, a business is found when an exempt organization is in competition with for-profit enterprises.[10] The existence of profits may lead a court to the conclusion that an undertaking is a business (usually an unrelated business).[11] The IRS may assert the presence of unrelated business just because a fee is charged for the product or service. Moreover—and this is becoming a growing practice—courts will jump to the conclusion that an unrelated business exists where the activity is undertaken in a *commercial* manner.[12]

Q 10:11 What is a commercial activity?

The commerciality doctrine has been conceived by the courts, although it is not fully articulated. There is, with one relatively minor exception, no mention of *commerciality* in the Internal Revenue Code (Q 10:12). The same is the case with respect to the tax regulations (Q 10:12).

The doctrine essentially means that a tax-exempt organization is engaged in a nonexempt activity when that activity is conducted in a manner that is considered *commercial.* An activity is a commercial one if it is undertaken in the same manner as it would be if it were being conducted by a for-profit (commercial) business. The most contemporary explication of the commerciality doctrine sets forth these criteria: the tax-exempt organization sells goods or services to the public, the exempt organization is in direct competition with one or more for-profit businesses, the prices set by the organization are based on pricing formulas common in the comparable commercial business setting, the organization utilizes advertising and other promotional materials and techniques to enhance sales, the organization's hours of operation are basically the same as those of for-profit enterprises, the management of the organization is trained in business operations, the organization uses employees rather than volunteers, and there is an absence of charitable giving to the organization.[13]

Q 10:12 What are the statutory and regulatory references to the commerciality doctrine?

In 1986, Congress added to the federal tax law a rule stating that an organization cannot qualify as a tax-exempt charitable entity or a social welfare entity if a substantial part of its activities consists of the provision of commercial-type insurance.[14] While that term is not statutorily defined, it generally means any insurance of a type provided by commercial insurance companies. The reach of this aspect of commerciality is being accorded broad interpretation in the courts.[15]

As far as the regulations are concerned, there is a brief mention of commerciality in the rules pertaining to whether an activity is regularly carried on (Q 10:13).[16] There, it is stated that business activities of an exempt organization will ordinarily deemed to be regularly carried on "if they manifest a frequency and continuity, and are pursued in a manner, generally similar to comparable commercial activities of nonexempt organizations."[17]

Q 10:13 What are the rules as to whether a business activity is regularly carried on?

This test was derived because of the purpose of the unrelated business rules: An activity cannot be competitive with for-profit business if it is not regularly carried on.

Thus, income from an unrelated business cannot be taxed where that business is merely sporadically or infrequently conducted. The frequency and continuity of the activity, the manner in which the activity is pursued, and the continuing purpose of deriving income from the activity largely determine whether the activity is regularly carried on.[18]

Q 10:14 How is regularity measured?

There is no precise means of measurement. An activity that consists of a single, one-time-only transaction or event is certainly irregular. For this reason, a sole sale of an item of property often is not taxable. A lot of fund-raising events, like annual dances and theater outings, are usually not taxed because of this rule.

Beyond that, it is a judgment call. A business occupying only a few days in a year would not be regularly carried on. For example, the tax regulations offer a quaint example of the operation of a sandwich stand by a hospital auxiliary for two weeks at a state fair.[19] That business is said to not be regularly carried on. But it cannot be said with any certainty when too many days of activity cause the line to be crossed. The regulations add that the operation of a commercial parking lot for one day in each week of the year is a regularly carried on business. Operation on 52 days out of 365, or operation on one day each week, obviously reflect an operation that is regularly carried on.

Q 10:15 Are there any other aspects of this level of analysis?

Yes, there are three other aspects of regularity.

One is that, where a business activity is, in the commercial sector, carried on only during a particular season, the duration of this season, rather than a full year, is the measuring period for an exempt organization.[20] For example, an organization selling Christmas trees or Christmas cards would measure regularity against the length of the Christmas season. Likewise, an operation of a horse racing track would be measured in relation to the horse racing season.

Q 10:16 What are the other two aspects of regularity?

One is that the IRS has adopted the view that there is more to the measurement of regularity than just the time expended for the event itself. The IRS takes into consideration the amount of time the organization spends in preparing for the event—*preparatory time*—and the time expended afterward in connection with the event—*winding-down time*.[21] If an exempt organization were to sell a product commercially for a few days each year, in assessing regularity it is—according to the IRS view—supposed to include the preparatory time of lining up the product, creating advertising, soliciting purchasers, and the like, as well as the winding-down time spent assessing the operation and arranging for the return of unsold items.

Q 10:17 Do some operations get converted into regular ones by using that approach?

That can be the case. But, there's more. The law in general recognizes the concept of a *principal* and an *agent.* A principal is a person who hires another person to act in his, her, or its stead, for the principal's benefit; the second person is an agent. Generally, the law considers the acts of an agent to be those of the principal. This means that the acts of an agent are attributed to the principal.

In the unrelated business setting, it is common for an exempt organization to contract with a company to perform a service. If the company is considered an agent of the organization and the company's function is in connection with an unrelated business, the IRS will take the position that the time spent by the company is attributed to the exempt organization in determining whether the unrelated activity was regularly carried on.[22]

For example, in one case, a university contracted with a publisher to produce programs for its home football games. The contract reserved advertising space in the programs for the university, any income generated by sales of that space was retained by the university, and the university retained an advertising agency to sell its space. The IRS determined that the revenues from the sale of the advertisements constituted unrelated business income because the advertising agency was an agent of the university. Because of the agency relationship, the agency's activities were attributable to the university for purposes of determining whether the university regularly carried on the business of selling program advertising. However, a court has rejected this approach to the determination of regularity.[23] At the same time, the IRS has openly disagreed with this holding and is adhering to its position in issuing rulings.[24]

Q 10:18 What about the third level of analysis, concerning the substantially related requirement?

This is where the issue usually is: whether the business that is regularly carried on is *related* or *unrelated.*[25] The general rule is that the income from a regularly conducted trade or business is subject to tax unless the income-producing activity is substantially related to the accomplishment of the organization's tax-exempt purpose.

To determine whether an activity is related, an examination is made of the relationship between the business activity and the accomplishment of the organization's exempt purpose. The fact that the income from the business is used for exempt programs does not make the activity a related one.

A trade or business is *related* to tax-exempt purposes only where the conduct of the business has what the tax law terms a *causal relationship* to the achievement of an exempt purpose. The business is *substantially* related only if the causal relationship is recognizably large or material.[26] Thus, for the conduct of a trade or business from which a particular amount of gross income is derived to be substantially related to an exempt purpose, the production or distribution of the goods or the performance of the services from which the gross income is derived must contribute importantly to the accomplishment of these purposes. Where the production or distribution of goods or the performance of services does not contribute importantly to the accomplishment of the organization's exempt purposes, the income from the sale of the goods or services does not derive from the conduct of a related business.

Q 10:19 How is relatedness determined?

There is no formula in this setting. Judgments as to whether there is a causal relationship and whether there is substantiality are made in the context of the facts and circumstances involved.[27] Unfortunately, however, there is not much "straightforwardness." This aspect of the tax law is very complex and murky.

Q 10:20 What are some examples of these judgments?

There are dozens of IRS rulings and court opinions in this area.

In one instance, a local bar association sold standard legal forms to its member lawyers for their use in the practice of law. These forms were purchased from a state bar association. The IRS ruled that the sale of the forms was an unrelated business because it did not contribute importantly to the accomplishment of the association's exempt functions.[28] (There is a court opinion to the contrary, however.[29] Another court held that the sale of preprinted lease forms and landlords' manuals by an exempt association of apartment owners and managers was a related business.[30])

This IRS ruling illustrates that, just because an association's membership uses a product in their own businesses, the sale of the product does not become a related business for the association. When an association of credit unions published and sold a consumer-oriented magazine to its members, the IRS held that to be an unrelated business because the magazine was distributed to the depositors of the members as a promotional device.[31]

Other instances of unrelated businesses of associations include the sale of equipment to members,[32] the operation of an employment service,[33] the conduct of other registry programs, the selling of endorsements (including the right to use the association's name and logo),[34] and the charging of dues to certain categories of purported associate members.

Over the years, one of the issues that has generated considerable attention for associations is whether the provision of insurance for members is an unrelated business. From the outset of the controversy, the IRS was of the position that it was. Associations prevailed at the beginning, but the tide shifted.[35] Now the courts uniformly uphold the IRS on this subject: compensation to associations for assistance in making insurance available to their members is almost always taxable.

In one instance, the IRS examined seven activities of an exempt association and found each of them to be unrelated businesses.[36] These activities were: (1) the sale of vehicle signs to members, (2) the sale to members of embossed tags for inventory control purposes, (3) the sale to members of supplies and forms, (4) the sale to members of kits to enable them to retain sales tax information, (5) the sale of price guides, (6) the administration of a group insurance program, and (7) the sale of commercial advertising in the association's publications.

The outcome isn't always that the business is unrelated. In one case, the IRS concluded that the sale of television time to governments and nonprofit organizations at a discount by an exempt association of television stations was a related business.[37]

Q 10:21 Are there any other aspects of the substantially related test?

There are four other aspects of this test. One of them is the *size and extent test.*

In determining whether an activity contributes importantly to the accomplishment of an exempt purpose, the size and extent of the activity must be considered in relation to the size and extent of the exempt function it purports to serve.[38] Thus, where income is realized by a tax-exempt organization from an activity that is in part related to the performance of its exempt functions, but that is conducted on a scale larger than is reasonably necessary for performance of the functions, the gross income attributable to that portion of the activities in excess of the needs of exempt functions constitutes gross income from the conduct of an unrelated business.

An example of this test involved an exempt association that had a membership of businesses in a particular state.[39] One of its income-producing activities was to supply member and nonmember businesses with job injury histories on prospective employees. Rejecting the association's contention that this service contributed to accomplishment of exempt purposes, the IRS ruled that the activity was an unrelated business, in that the services went "well beyond" any mere development and promotion of efficient business practices.

As an illustration of the application of this test where the IRS concluded that the business was entirely related, the IRS considered a tax-exempt organization that provided a therapeutic program for emotionally disturbed adolescents.[40] It operated a retail grocery store that was almost completely staffed by adolescents to help secure their emotional rehabilitation. The IRS ruled that the store operation was not an unrelated business because it was operated on a scale no larger than reasonably necessary for its training and rehabilitation program.

Another of these aspects is the *same state test*. As a general rule, the sale of a product that results from the performance of tax-exempt functions does not constitute an unrelated business where the product is sold in substantially the same state it is in upon completion of the exempt functions.[41] This rule is significant for organizations that sell articles made by handicapped individuals as part of their rehabilitation training. By contrast, where a product resulting from an exempt function is exploited in business endeavors beyond what is reasonably appropriate or necessary for disposition in the state it is in upon completion of tax-exempt functions, the activity becomes transformed into an unrelated business.[42] For example, an exempt organization maintaining a dairy herd for scientific purposes may sell milk and cream produced in the ordinary course of operation of the project without unrelated income taxation.

However, if the organization were to utilize the milk and cream in the further manufacture of food items, such as ice cream and pastries, the sale of these products would likely be the conduct of an unrelated business.

Another of these subtests of substantiality is the *dual use test*.[43] This concerns an asset or facility that is necessary to the conduct of exempt functions but is also employed in an unrelated endeavor. Each source of the income must be tested to see whether the activities contribute importantly to the accomplishment of exempt purposes. For example, a museum may have a theater auditorium for the purpose of showing educational films in connection with its program of public education in the arts and sciences; use of that theater for public entertainment in the evenings would be an unrelated business. Likewise, a school may have a ski facility that is used in its physical education program; operation of the facility for the general public would be an unrelated business.

The fourth of these subtests is the *exploitation test*.[44] In certain instances, activities carried on by an exempt organization in the performance of exempt functions generate good will or other intangibles that are capable of being exploited in unrelated endeavors. When this is done, the mere fact that the income depended in part on an exempt function of the organization does not make it income from a related business. This type of income will be taxed as unrelated business income, unless the underlying activities themselves contribute importantly to the accomplishment of an exempt purpose. For example, income from advertising in a publication with exempt function content generally is taxable income resulting from an exploitation of an exempt resource.

Q 10:22 How is the unrelated business income tax calculated?

In general, the tax is determined in the same manner as with for-profit entities. The unrelated income tax rates payable by most tax-exempt organizations are the corporate rates. Some organizations, such as trusts, are subject to the individual income tax rates.[45] There is a specific deduction of $1,000.[46]

This tax falls on *net* unrelated business income. An exempt organization is allowed to subtract its business expenses from gross unrelated income in arriving at taxable net unrelated income. The law generally states that a deductible expense must be *directly connected* with the carrying on of the business;[47] an item of deduction must have a proximate and primary relationship to the carrying on of the business.[48] This standard is more rigorous than the one applied to for-profit and individual taxpayers, where the law allows the deductibility of expenses that are reasonably connected with the taxable endeavor. In practice, however, exempt organizations often follow the standard of reasonableness, particularly when allocating expenses. Because of the looseness of the tax regulations, this approach has been upheld in the courts.[49]

There is one exception to the directly connected test. This exception is for the charitable contribution deduction allowed in computing taxable unrelated income. In general, this deduction cannot exceed 10 percent of the unrelated business taxable income otherwise computed.[50]

These taxes are paid by means of an unrelated business income tax return.[51] Tax-exempt organizations must make quarterly estimated payments of this tax.[52]

EXCEPTIONS

Q 10:23 What types of activities are exempt from unrelated income taxation?

An interesting feature of the federal tax laws is the series of *modifications* that are available in calculating taxable unrelated business income. Although these modifications largely exclude certain types of income from taxation (Q 10:24), they also exclude three types of research activities from the tax. This set of exclusions is somewhat of an oddity, in that research activities generally are exempt functions.

One exclusion is for research for the federal government, or any of its agencies or instrumentalities, or any state or political subdivision of a state. Another exclusion is for research performed for any person; however, the research institution must be a college, university, or hospital. The third exclusion is as broad as the second: the organization must be operated primarily for the purpose of carrying on fundamental research and the results of the research must be freely available to the general public.[53]

The modifications also eliminate from taxation revenue derived from the lending of securities by exempt organizations to brokers.[54]

Eleven other statutory exceptions shelter types of activities from unrelated income taxation. One is for a business in which substantially all of the work in carrying on the business is performed for the tax-exempt organization without compensation.[55] Any unrelated business can be protected from taxation by this exception, including the business of advertising. This exception can be useful in shielding fund-raising functions (special events) from taxation.

TIP: The concept of compensation is broadly applied. In one instance, the revenue from gambling events was held taxable because the workers, all of whom were volunteers, were frequently tipped by the patrons.[56]

Another exception is for a business that is conducted by a tax-exempt charitable organization, or a state college or university, primarily for the convenience of its members, students, patients, officers, or employees.[57] This broad exception—known as the *convenience doctrine*—is relied on heavily by colleges, universities, and hospitals. Much of the income from sales of items in college and university bookstores and hospital gift shops is rendered nontaxable because of this rule.

Another exception is for a business that sells merchandise, substantially all of which was contributed to the exempt organization.[58] This exception is generally utilized by thrift shops that sell donated clothing, books, and the like to the general public.[59]

Still other exceptions are for certain businesses of associations of employees conducted for the convenience of their members,[60] the conduct of entertainment at fairs and expositions by a wide range of exempt organizations,[61] the conduct of trade shows by most exempt organizations,[62] the performance by hospitals of certain services for smaller hospitals,[63] the conduct of certain bingo games by most tax-exempt organizations,[64] qualified pole rentals by exempt mutual or cooperative telephone or electric companies,[65] the distribution of low-cost articles incidental to the solicitation of charitable contributions,[66] and the exchanging or renting of membership or donor mailing lists between tax-exempt charitable organizations.[67]

Q 10:24 What types of income are exempt from unrelated income taxation?

The *modifications* (Q 10:23) shield a wide variety of forms of income from unrelated income taxation. These forms of income generally are

annuities, capital gains, dividends, interest, rents, and royalties.[68] For
the most part, there is little controversy in this area as to the definition
of these income items, inasmuch as the terms are amply defined elsewhere in the federal tax law.

There is, nonetheless, an underlying festering controversy. It is the
view of the IRS that the exclusion is available only where the income is
investment income or is otherwise passively received. This approach to
these modifications rests on the rationale for the unrelated income
rules, which is to bring parity to the economics of competitive activities
involving nonprofit and for-profit organizations (Q 10:10).[69] Passive income, by definition, is not derived from competitive activity and thus
should not be taxed. But, the IRS wishes to tax net income from the active conduct of commercial business activities.

This dichotomy presents itself in connection with the exclusion for
rental income. Where a tax-exempt organization carries on rental activities in the nature of a commercial landlord, the exclusion is not available.[70] The exclusion, however, is not normally voided, simply because
the exempt organization provides normal maintenance services. In practice, this opportunity for taxation is obviated by the use of an independent building management and leasing company.

There can be disputes as to whether an income flow is truly rent or
is a share of the profits from a joint venture; revenue in the latter form is
generally taxable. A contemporary illustration of this distinction is the litigation surrounding crop-share leasing. The IRS has lost all of the cases
brought to date; the courts have held that the funds received by the exempt organization were in the form of excludable rent and not from a
partnership or joint venture.[71]

The contemporary battles in this context are being waged over the
scope of the exclusion for royalties. In part, this is because exempt organizations have more latitude, than with any other type of income, in
structuring transactions to shape the resulting income. In this instance,
the objective is to make the income fit the form of a royalty or at least
dress it up like a royalty. For the most part, the dilemma is presented
because the statute does not define the term *royalty.*

The IRS is persisting with its position that a royalty, to be excludable, must be passively received by the exempt organization. However,
this issue has been reviewed by the Tax Court on three occasions, and
the exempt organization has prevailed each time. The Tax Court ruled
that a royalty is a payment for the use of valuable intangible property

rights; it rejected the passive–active dichotomy, at least in the realm of the royalty exclusion.[72]

One of these cases involved use of the royalty exclusion to shield from taxation funds derived from the use of mailing lists, where the special exception is unavailable.[73] Another concerned use of the royalty exclusion to protect income generated from an affinity card program.[74] The latter case has been appealed.

Q 10:25 How can the royalty exclusion be most effectively utilized?

This is a difficult question to answer at this time, because of the varying interpretations of the scope of the exclusion. An organization can adhere to the IRS's view and treat as excludable royalty income only that which is passive in nature. Or, it can follow the Tax Court's approach (Q 10:24) and risk an audit and a tax assessment.

A third approach is to bifurcate the arrangement: execute two contracts, one reflecting passive income/royalty payments and the other, payments for services rendered.[75] The income paid pursuant to the second contract would presumably be taxable. The organization would endeavor to allocate to the royalty contract as much of the income as reasonably possible. The difficulty with this approach is the form-over-substance rule: two contracts of this nature are easily collapsed and treated as one for tax purposes.

Q 10:26 Are there any exceptions to the rules stating these exclusions?

Yes, there are two exceptions. One pertains to the payment of otherwise excludable income from a controlled organization. The general rule is that payments of annuities, interest, rent, and/or royalties by a controlled corporation to a tax-exempt controlling organization are taxable as unrelated income.[76] This is the case even though these forms of income are otherwise passive in nature. For this purpose, an organization controls another where the parent entity owns at least 80 percent of the voting power of all classes of stock entitled to vote and at least 80 percent of all other stock of the corporate subsidiary.[77] This control element can also be manifested by stock or by an interlocking of directors, trustees, or other representatives of the two organizations.[78]

TIP: This control element can be sidestepped relatively easily, thereby often avoiding the unrelated income tax. One way is to cause the exempt organization parent to own no more than 79 percent of the stock (or like percentage of other control). This approach assumes that the parent entity is comfortable with the other 21 percent shareholder(s). Another technique works nicely where there are two related tax-exempt organizations, such as an association and a related foundation (see Q 1:40). The corporate subsidiary is established with two classes of stock; the association holds 100 percent of the voting stock and the foundation holds 100 percent of the nonvoting stock. The income is not taxable to either organization.

The other exception is found in the rules concerning unrelated debt-financed property.[79] Where income is debt-financed income, the various exclusions referred to above[80] are unavailable.[81]

Q 10:27 Are there any exceptions to these exceptions?

Yes, there are two of them. The rule concerning the taxation of income from a controlled subsidiary (Q 10:26) does not apply where the funds are dividends, because dividends are not deductible by the payor corporation. Thus, where other types of income are deductible by the controlled entity that provides the income, the exempt organization that receives the income must regard it as unrelated business income.

The other exception to the exception pertains to circumstances where the income paid to an exempt organization is not from a controlled subsidiary (a first-tier subsidiary) but is from a subsidiary of the first-tier subsidiary (a second-tier subsidiary). In this situation, the income paid by the second-tier subsidiary to the exempt organization is not taxable income by virtue of the controlled subsidiary rule (although it might be unrelated income under some other rule).[82]

TIP: For this approach to be successful, the two subsidiaries must be bona fide legal entities, rather than a sham arrangement.

SPECIFIC APPLICATIONS

Q 10:28 What are the contemporary unrelated business issues for hospitals and other health care providers?

There are more unrelated business issues in the health care field than in any other involving exempt organizations. Undertakings such as gift shops, coffee shops, and parking lots usually are considered either related businesses or activities protected by the convenience doctrine (Q 10:23).

The principal areas of controversy are laboratory testing for physicians in private practice, the maintenance of medical office buildings, sales of medical equipment to the public, sales of pharmaceuticals to nonpatients, the operation of fitness centers and health clubs, and the conduct of physical rehabilitation programs.

Q 10:29 What are the contemporary unrelated business issues for colleges and universities?

The principal unrelated business issues for colleges and universities are the receipt of revenue in the form of corporate sponsorships (where the issue basically is whether the funds are contributions or payments for advertising), sales of nonexempt items in bookstores, travel tours, and rental of campus facilities to businesses.

Q 10:30 What are the contemporary unrelated business issues for museums?

The principal unrelated business issues for museums are the sales of nonexempt items in the gift shop (particularly where the items have a long-term utility, such as furniture) and sales of items by catalog.

Q 10:31 What are the contemporary unrelated business issues for trade, business, and professional associations?

The principal unrelated business issues for trade, business, and professional associations are sales, to members, of items that they utilize in their business or profession, and the receipt of dues from so-called associate members. As to the latter, it is the IRS's view that the associate members join the organization solely to obtain a service (such as insurance coverage) or access to the regular members for business promotion purposes.

Q 10:32 How do the unrelated business rules apply in the context of charitable fund-raising?

There are instances when an activity is deemed a fund-raising event, although technically it is an unrelated business. There are, however, a host of exceptions that shield the resulting income from taxation (Q 10:23 and Q 10:24). The principal exceptions are for activities that are not regularly carried on (Q 10:3), the volunteer exception, and the exception for donated goods (Q 10:23).

Another area of unrelated income taxation that entails charitable fund-raising is the rental and exchange of mailing lists (those of donors and/or members). Where the parties to the transaction are eligible to receive tax-deductible contributions (chiefly, charitable and veterans' organizations), the resulting revenue is not taxed.[83] Otherwise, the net funds from the transaction are taxable, unless the monies can be cast as royalties. Even in instances where lists are simply exchanged (that is, there is no transfer of money), it is the view of the IRS that a taxable transaction occurs (unless the exception applies), with the amount "received" being the fair market value of the list received; usually, there are no offsetting deductible amounts.[84]

Q 10:33 How is the unrelated business income tax reported?

The return filed by nearly all tax-exempt organizations with the IRS on an annual basis is an *information* return. This type of return is not used to report taxable income.[85] For that purpose, a *tax* return is required. The IRS has devised a tax return for reporting unrelated business taxable income. It must be filed in addition to the annual information return.[86]

CHAPTER 11

Subsidiaries

As the federal laws applicable to tax-exempt organizations have become exceedingly complex, these organizations frequently must respond with more sophisticated planning techniques. Often deployed in this context is bifurcation: the use of two organizations because of legal requirements when otherwise only one entity would be utilized. One of the applications of the technique of bifurcation is the use of subsidiaries.

A tax-exempt organization uses an exempt organization subsidiary to house one or more activities that, if the parent conducted directly, would cause the parent to lose its tax exemption (or be ineligible to be exempt in the first instance). A for-profit subsidiary is used as a repository for unrelated business activities, usually where the activities are too extensive to be conducted in the parent organization without loss or denial of tax exemption.

Clients rarely initially ask about subsidiaries. The prospect of a subsidiary organization almost always arises in the context of solving a problem. But, the subject having been broached, here are the questions most frequently asked by clients about the creation, control, and conduct of subsidiaries (both tax-exempt and for-profit)—and the answers to them.

OVERVIEW

Q 11:1   What is a subsidiary in the nonprofit law context?

A *subsidiary,* in the nonprofit law context, is essentially the same as in the for-profit law context. It is a separate organization that has some special, formal, *control* relationship with another organization; the other organization is the *parent* organization. For these purposes, the parent organization always is a tax-exempt organization. The subsidiary, however, may be a tax-exempt organization or a for-profit organization.

Q 11:2   Why would a tax-exempt organization establish a subsidiary?

Part of the answer to this question depends on whether the subsidiary is a tax-exempt organization or a for-profit organization. In general, the principal reason a tax-exempt organization will establish a subsidiary is to house in another organization one or more activities that the parent organization either does not want, or cannot have, as part of its operations. Thus, a *bifurcation* occurs: what would otherwise be one entity is split into two entities. This type of bifurcation almost always is undertaken because of a requirement of law—often, the federal tax law.

Q 11:3   How does a nonprofit organization control a subsidiary?

It depends on whether the subsidiary is a nonprofit or for-profit entity.

If the subsidiary is a nonprofit, tax-exempt organization, the control is likely to be manifested by an *interlocking directorship* or, as it is more commonly called, *overlapping boards.* There are several models of this control mechanism. In one model, the board of directors of the parent organization selects at least a majority of the board of directors of the subsidiary. The *ex officio* approach is also common: the governing instrument of the subsidiary provides that individuals holding certain positions with the parent organization (such as its president or executive director) are, for that reason, the members of, or at least a majority of, the board of directors of the subsidiary. A third approach is a blend of the foregoing two methods. Whatever the method, it is important for the parent organization to have control of the subsidiary by being able to determine at least a majority of the subsidiary's board of directors. (Without that control element, there is no parent–subsidiary relationship.) It is not enough, for example, for the governing instruments of the "subsidiary" of a membership organization parent to state that the members of the subsidiary's board of directors must be members of the parent organization (unless the membership of the parent entity is exceedingly small).

Where the interlocking directorship method is used, two other features are recommended. First, the articles of organization of the subsidiary should provide that its governing instruments cannot be amended, or that any such amendment may not become effective, without the prior approval of the board of the parent organization. The purpose of this provision is to prevent a board of the subsidiary from changing the documents to eliminate the interlocking directorate. Second, the governing instruments should make it clear, where directors of the subsidiary are appointed by the parent (rather than installed through use of the *ex officio* approach), that the board of the parent organization has the right to remove these directors as well.

A tax-exempt organization can also control another tax-exempt organization by utilizing the *membership feature.* The subsidiary entity is structured as a membership organization; the parent entity is thereafter made the sole member of the subsidiary organization. Prudence dictates that the governing instruments of the subsidiary state that the prior approval of the members is required to make amendments to those documents, and that the members have the right to remove directors of the subsidiary. *Ex officio* positions can also be used in combination with the membership approach.

Finally, one tax-exempt organization can control another exempt organization by means of stock. This approach is the most infrequent of the three available methods, probably because it is not widely realized that some states allow stock-based nonprofit organizations. With this approach, the subsidiary is formed as a nonprofit corporation in a state that allows this type of entity to issue stock; the parent organization then becomes the sole stockholder. Other persons are allowed to hold stock as well, but the "parent" organization must own at least 51 percent of the subsidiary's stock.

Where the subsidiary is a for-profit organization, it is almost certainly a corporation. The control mechanism will therefore be stock ownership. The *ex officio* feature can be used in conjunction with the stock approach. Other persons are allowed to hold stock as well, but the "parent" organization must own at least 51 percent of the subsidiary's stock.

Q 11:4   What body can act as the incorporator or corporate member to establish a subsidiary?

Almost always, the board of directors of a parent organization makes the decision to create and use a subsidiary. The board, usually assisted by legal counsel, also decides the form of the subsidiary and the nature of the control mechanism (Q 11:3). The board might decide that the membership feature is to be used; if so, it would make the parent entity a member—most likely, the sole member. If the corporate form is used, along with some other control feature, the board of the parent would decide which individuals would serve as incorporators of the subsidiary (Q 1:7).

Q 11:5   Is there a minimum number of board members required for a subsidiary?

There is no rule of federal law on the point. State law is likely to dictate a minimum number of board members for the subsidiary, particularly if the subsidiary is a corporation. Most states require at least three board members for a corporation (Q 2:2).

The number of board members of the subsidiary is far more likely to be determined by management or political factors. If the control mechanism is the membership feature or the issuance of stock (Q 11:3), the number of board members is irrelevant (unless there is a state-law minimum). If the control mechanism is an interlocking directorate, the parent entity will want to be able to appoint or elect at least a majority of the members of the subsidiary's board. This factor would result in an odd-numbered board of the directors of the subsidiary.

Q 11:6   What legal requirements should be followed in maintaining the parent–subsidiary relationship?

The most basic requirement is that, at all times, the parent organization must be able to show that it "owns" (or, in many instances, controls) at least 51 percent of the subsidiary—whether by stock, membership, or board positions (Q 11:3).

It is essential that all of the legal "niceties" of bona fide organizations be respected. The board of directors of the subsidiary—irrespective of the manner in which it is constituted—must have its own meetings (that is, its meetings should not be a subset or a continuation of the meetings of the parent organization) and maintain minutes of those meetings, and the subsidiary should have its own bank account(s). The law will treat this aspect of bifurcation as a sham if each organization does not have the characteristics of a bona fide separate entity. If regarded as a sham, the arrangement is ignored and the two organizations are treated as one. When this happens, the purposes for creating the subsidiary are almost always nullified: the activities of the subsidiary are attributed to the parent.

Q 11:7   What are the powers and oversight requirements of the parent organization?

The boards of directors of the two organizations—parent and subsidiary—have their own fiduciary or similar requirements (Q 1:19). In general, the oversight function is accomplished through the control mechanism (Q 11:3); whatever means is selected should afford the parent ample oversight opportunities. The law does not impose any particular standard in this context, other than the standard arising from the fact that the resources (income and assets) are indirectly resources of the parent, so that the parent should treat that bundle of resources as an asset and in accordance with the prudent person rule (Q 1:19).

The power of the parent organization with respect to the subsidiary should be complete; the parent controls and sometimes owns the subsidiary (Q 11:3). The subsidiary exists solely to do the bidding of the parent. The principal concern is that the power in the parent should not be exercised in such a way as to cause the arrangement to be perceived as a sham (Q 11:6).

Q 11:8   How is revenue from a for-profit subsidiary taxed?

In general, revenue that flows from a for-profit subsidiary to a tax-exempt parent is deemed to be unrelated business income (see Chapter 10).[1] This occurs where the parent organization owns at least 80 percent of the voting power of all classes of stock entitled to vote and at least 80 percent of all other stock of the corporate subsidiary (see Q 10:26).[2] For example, if the subsidiary rents property from the parent, the rental income would be unrelated income to the parent. Likewise, if the subsidiary borrows money from the parent organization, the interest paid to the parent is unrelated business income to the parent.

There are three exceptions to this general rule. One is that income in the form of dividends from a for-profit subsidiary to an exempt parent is not unrelated income (Q 10:27).

NOTE: This is the only type of income that is accorded this exempt treatment. Dividends are not taxable to the parent because the payment of them is not deductible by the subsidiary.

Another exception pertains to exempt functions in the subsidiary. The income resulting from exempt functions is not taxable. If the income flowing to the parent from the subsidiary is partially from an exempt function and partially from nonexempt activities, only the income from the latter source is regarded as unrelated business income.[3]

The third exception derives from the distinction between *first-tier* subsidiaries and *second-tier* subsidiaries. The subsidiaries discussed in this chapter are first-tier; they are subsidiaries of a tax-exempt organization. A second-tier subsidiary is a subsidiary of a first-tier subsidiary. Revenue paid by a second-tier subsidiary to the parent of the first-tier subsidiary is not unrelated business income to the parent, assuming it is exempt function revenue, passive investment income, or other income sheltered from the unrelated business income tax by statute (Q 10:27).

Q 11:9   What are the tax consequences of liquidation of a subsidiary into its parent organization?

The answer depends on a variety of factors. For example, have the assets in the subsidiary appreciated in value? If they have, there may be a capital gains tax when the assets of the subsidiary are transferred to the parent. The IRS has ruled that this type of capital gain is not taxable by reason of the tax law provision sheltering nearly all capital gains of tax-exempt organizations from taxation (Q 10:24).[4]

However, in all likelihood, this ruling[5] is erroneous. A federal tax law rule is specifically directed at the tax consequences of liquidation of a subsidiary into a tax-exempt parent organization.[6] Under this rule, where the assets in the subsidiary were used in an unrelated business, are transferred to the parent, and are used in a related business, the capital gains tax becomes applicable and remains applicable whenever the assets become employed in a related business, no matter how many years later.

However, there is no tax where the parent organization continues to use the assets in an unrelated business. The flaw in this ruling is that the IRS ignored the fact that the assets in a for-profit subsidiary were, after the transfer of them to the parent, used in a related business. The ruling is silent on the point, but presumably the assets were used by the subsidiary in an unrelated business—otherwise, why were they placed in a for-profit subsidiary at all?

Q 11:10 What are the federal tax reporting requirements with respect to subsidiaries?

If a subsidiary is a for-profit organization, it must file a tax return every year with the IRS.[7] In this return, the corporation must indicate whether any entity owns, directly or indirectly, 50 percent or more of the corporation's voting stock or whether the corporation is a subsidiary in an affiliated group.[8]

If the subsidiary is a tax-exempt organization, it (with some unlikely exceptions) must file an annual information return with the IRS.[9]

NOTE: It is possible to have a subsidiary that is a nonprofit, but not tax-exempt, organization. This type of entity would file a tax return, the same as would a for-profit organization.

The existence of the parent–subsidiary relationship must be reflected on the tax-exempt subsidiary's return. The subsidiary must identify the parent by name and state that it is a tax-exempt organization.[10] If the tax-exempt subsidiary has unrelated business activity, it must file a tax return to report the income so derived (Q 10:33).[11]

The parent organization, being a tax-exempt entity, files an annual information return with the IRS. If the subsidiary is owned by the parent by means of stock, that holding would be reflected on the balance sheet of the annual information return, presumably as an asset.[12] If a director, officer, or key employee of the parent, who is compensated by the parent, is also compensated by a subsidiary, that aggregate compensation may have to be reported on the annual information return (Q 3:8).[13] The existence of the parent–subsidiary relationship must be reflected on the parent's return. The parent must identify the subsidiary by name and state whether it is a tax-exempt or nonexempt organization.[14]

If the subsidiary is a taxable corporation, the tax-exempt parent must complete a special part of the annual information return, stating the name, address, and employer identification number of the subsidiary, the percentage of ownership interest in the subsidiary, the nature of the business activities of the subsidiary, and the total income and end-of-year assets of the subsidiary.[15]

If the parent organization is a tax-exempt charitable entity and the subsidiary is a tax-exempt entity other than a charitable one, the parent must prepare another special part of its annual information return, stating whether it, during the reporting year, transferred cash or other assets to the subsidiary, sold assets to or purchased them from the subsidiary, rented equipment or facilities to the subsidiary, reimbursed the subsidiary for expenses, loaned funds to the subsidiary or guaranteed a loan obligation of the subsidiary, performed any services for the subsidiary, or shared facilities, equipment, mailing lists, other assets, or paid employees with the subsidiary.[16] The parent organization must identify the subsidiary by name, state the type of organization that the subsidiary is, and give a description of the relationship.

If the subsidiary organization is a tax-exempt charitable entity and the parent entity is a tax-exempt organization other than a charitable one, the subsidiary must prepare the special part of its annual information return as identified in the preceding paragraph.

Both organizations are subject to other federal tax reporting requirements, such as those relating to compensation of employees and to profit-sharing and pension plans.

Q 11:11 What are the state law reporting requirements with respect to subsidiaries?

As a separate entity, each organization has its own state law reporting responsibilities. For example, if each entity is a corporation, both are likely to have to file annual reports with the secretary of state. Trusts probably must file annually with the state attorney general. If either organization engages in fund-raising, there must be compliance with the state's law concerning charitable solicitations (see Chapter 7).

Each state's law should be reviewed to determine specific requirements.

TAX-EXEMPT SUBSIDIARIES

Q 11:12 Why would a tax-exempt organization establish a tax-exempt subsidiary?

The principal reason a tax-exempt organization establishes a tax-exempt subsidiary is because the parent entity wants to engage in an activity (or series of activities) that its tax status precludes but that is, under the law, an exempt function for another type of tax-exempt organization. Thus, the function that is nonexempt for the parent is housed in the subsidiary.

On occasion, an activity is placed in a tax-exempt subsidiary in an attempt to shield the parent organization from liability. This reason for creating a subsidiary is also warranted because of legal considerations.

However, management or similar considerations may warrant the conduct of a function in a tax-exempt subsidiary even though the function could be conducted by the exempt parent without jeopardizing its tax exemption.

Q 11:13 What are some of the common uses of tax-exempt subsidiaries?

There are several of these uses, all built around the concept of bifurcation (Q 11:1). The most common combinations occasioned by the permissible-activity reason for creating an exempt subsidiary (Q 11:12) are:

1. A tax-exempt charitable organization with a tax-exempt social welfare organization subsidiary that engages in substantial lobbying activities (Q 4:26).
2. A tax-exempt charitable organization subsidiary of a charitable organization in another country, where the subsidiary is fund-raising in the United States.

NOTE: In general, only charitable gifts made to U.S. charities are deductible. Foreign charities seeking deductible contributions from U.S. donors need to establish a U.S.-based fund-raising organization, and it cannot be merely a conduit of the funds.

---

3. A tax-exempt membership organization (such as a business association or labor organization) with a tax-exempt supporting organization (Q 6:22).

4. A tax-exempt organization with a subsidiary that is a political organization (Q 5:17).

5. A tax-exempt charitable organization with a tax-exempt business league subsidiary that engages in certification activities.

NOTE: It is the view of the IRS that programs of certification of organizations' memberships are not charitable activities, because of the benefits flowing to the members. Since certification is an appropriate function for a business league, a separate organization of that nature is required.

The most common combination occasioned by the liability-shield reason for creating an exempt subsidiary (Q 11:12) is the use by a tax-exempt organization of a tax-exempt title-holding organization.

The most common combinations occasioned by the management reasons for creating an exempt subsidiary (Q 11:12) are: the use by a tax-exempt, noncharitable organization of a charitable supporting organization (Q 6:22) and the use by a tax-exempt charitable organization of a separate charitable organization for fund-raising purposes.

NOTE: Some public charities, such as universities and hospitals, find it more effective to solicit contributions by means of related "foundations." This approach facilitates concentration of the fund-raising function in a single organization and creates a board of directors that is solely focused on charitable solicitations.

Q 11:14 Is it necessary for a tax-exempt subsidiary to obtain separate recognition of tax-exempt status?

It depends on the type of tax-exempt subsidiary. If the subsidiary is a charitable one, recognition of tax-exempt status must be obtained from the IRS (exceptions are unlikely). If the subsidiary is any other type of tax-exempt organization, recognition of exempt status may be acquired, but it is not mandatory.

TIP: Even where recognition of tax exemption is not required, prudence dictates that the determination should be obtained. The

---

subsidiary then has the comfort of knowing that the IRS agrees with its exempt status, and subsequent questions as to its tax status (assuming no changes in material facts) are precluded.

State law should be reviewed to determine whether the subsidiary must or can obtain one or more tax exemptions (most likely, those with respect to income, sales, use, and/or property taxes).

Q 11:15 Should the tax-exempt status of the subsidiary be as a charitable entity or as a supporting organization?

This question presumes that the subsidiary is to be a tax-exempt charitable (including educational, religious, and/or scientific) organization. The question also reflects common misunderstanding of the two tax statuses. If it is appropriate to cause the subsidiary to be a supporting organization—whether in relation to a public charity (Q 6:15) or another type of tax-exempt entity (Q 6:22)—the organization must have *both* tax classifications. This is because all supporting organizations are charitable ones.

The federal tax status of an organization as a charitable entity pertains to its tax-exempt status (and its ability to receive tax-deductible contributions). The tax status of an organization as a supporting organization pertains to its ability to avoid private foundation status (Q 6:1, Q 6:15).

Q 11:16 What are the reporting requirements between the parent and subsidiary organizations?

For the most part, the law does not impose any such requirements. This communication is left largely to the realm of suitable management. Some formal reporting requirements may be appropriate for certain supporting organizations (Q 6:28).

Q 11:17 If a tax-exempt subsidiary can raise money in its own name, what disclosure requirements should it observe with respect to the parent organization?

This is largely a matter of state law. The state's charitable solicitation act—if any (see Chapter 7)—will likely contain some disclosure requirement. It is common practice, however, for this type of subsidiary to reflect the existence of the parent on its stationery and fund-raising literature. For example, if the subsidiary is a fund-raising foundation that is supportive of a hospital, these materials should—and almost certainly will—state that fact.

As to the federal tax law, the charitable subsidiary must adhere to the charitable gift substantiation rules (Q 7:6), the quid pro quo contribution rules (Q 7:9), and the annual return reporting rules (Q 11:10). If the subsidiary is a noncharitable, tax-exempt organization, there are disclosure requirements to which it must adhere concerning the nondeductibility of gifts[17] and the availability of information or services from the federal government.[18]

Q 11:18 What formal action is required to transfer funds between a tax-exempt parent and a tax-exempt subsidiary?

Usually, a transfer of funds of this nature requires a formal action of the board of directors of the transferring organization—a board resolution, for example. This is particularly the case where the transfer is in the form of a contribution of capital or a loan from the parent to the subsidiary, or a rental arrangement or purchase of goods or services between the organizations. Other relationships, such as the sharing of employees, need not be the subject of formal board approval. Whatever the nature of the interorganization funding, it may have to be reported to the IRS (Q 11:10).

Q 11:19 Can a tax-exempt subsidiary raise funds for an endowment and hold these funds separate from the parent?

Yes. This type of subsidiary is likely to be a supporting organization; the maintenance of an endowment fund is a classic activity for this type of organization (Q 6:17). It is possible for the endowment function to be in a publicly supported charitable organization—most likely, a donative publicly supported entity (Q 6:7)—but as the endowment grows, the extent of investment income may cause the organization to receive an inadequate amount of public support (Q 6:14).

The supporting organization would be able to transfer income from the endowment fund to the supported organization (assuming that is the nature of the endowment structure). If the supported organization is not a charitable one, the funds transferred to the parent should be clearly restricted to charitable uses.

TIP: If the supported organization is a service provider publicly supported organization (Q 6:8), caution must be exercised. Investment income in the supporting organization will retain its character as such when transferred to the parent. This can adversely impact the ability of the parent entity to qualify as this type of public charity, because of the limitation on investment income in computing public support.

FOR-PROFIT SUBSIDIARIES

Q 11:20 Why would a tax-exempt organization establish a for-profit subsidiary?

Usually, a tax-exempt organization establishes a for-profit subsidiary because of the existence, or planned existence, of an unrelated business, or set of unrelated businesses, that is too extensive to be conducted in the parent without jeopardizing the parent's tax-exempt status (Q 10:2). Some exempt organizations incubate unrelated businesses within themselves and then transfer them *(spin them off)* to a for-profit subsidiary. Others create a subsidiary at the outset.

The approach to take may be a matter of management's judgment. If it is known at the beginning that the unrelated activity will be extensive, the for-profit subsidiary is basically dictated. However, if the scope of the unrelated business is unknown at the outset and its prospects are dubious, the organization may want to commence with the business within itself and then spin it off when and if it becomes larger.

TIP: If the unrelated business is in the exempt organization, the only deductions that may be taken in calculating unrelated business taxable income are those that are directly related to the unrelated activity.[19] When the unrelated business is in a for-profit subsidiary, all expenses are deductible as long as they are reasonable and necessary to the conduct of the business.

TIP: A tax-exempt organization may wish to go slowly in establishing a tax-exempt subsidiary. If the subsidiary is created and, later, it turns out that it is not needed and the parent decides to liquidate it, there may be adverse tax consequences to the parent (Q 11:9).

The decision as to whether to create a for-profit subsidiary can be a difficult one. At a minimum, it requires a determination as to whether the activity involved is related or unrelated (Q 10:3). The subsidiary may also be needed if the activity (or activities) is to be conducted in a commercial manner (Q 10:11).

Q 11:21 What are some of the common uses of for-profit subsidiaries?

The principal use of a for-profit subsidiary is to *house an unrelated business.* For example, as an offshoot of its membership services, an association may have developed an activity that appeals to the general public, such as a journal or a database. Placement of the activity in a for-profit subsidiary would enable the association to commercially develop and market the service. A research institution may have commercial testing functions or other similar functions that are best furthered by means of a for-profit subsidiary. A hospital may find it appropriate to develop and operate a medical office building in a subsidiary.

There is no limit in the law as to the type of business activity that can be operated out of a for-profit subsidiary; the tax-exempt organization can devise any type of business activity it wants as a means to generate revenue (which, however, is likely to be taxed (Q 11:8)). There is also no limit in the law as to the size of subsidiaries, either absolutely or in relation to the parent, or the number of for-profit subsidiaries a tax-exempt organization may have.

NOTE: To be tax-exempt, the parent entity must function primarily in furtherance of exempt functions. The use of one or more subsidiaries should not cause the organization to deviate from that standard.

Some tax-exempt organizations will place an unrelated business in a for-profit subsidiary even where the tax laws do not require it (that is, where the business is relatively small). This is done for reasons of *politics* and *perception,* particularly where the business is competitive with commercial businesses in the community. As an illustration, a college began using its printing facilities, used primarily for its exempt functions, for occasional jobs for outside purchasers; as the business grew, some of the commercial printers in the community complained about the competition. To appease its critics, the college transferred its commercial printing operation to a for-profit subsidiary. The competition was still present, but the commercial printers were mollified when it came from a for-profit entity.

NOTE: *Competition* can be synonymous with controversy and sensitivity, particularly among small businesses. When a tax-exempt organization is in competition with a commercial business, the latter sees the competition as being *unfair,* in that the exempt organization does not have to pay taxes; with taxes not a cost of doing business, the exempt organization is (at least in theory) able to underprice the commercial business. Nonetheless, despite plaintiffs' attempts, the courts have been unwilling to hold that for-profit businesses have standing to merit ruling in favor of their competitors' challenge to their tax-exempt status.

The third use of a for-profit subsidiary by a tax-exempt organization is as a *partner in a partnership,* in lieu of the exempt organization's direct participation. The exempt parent may fear the potential of liability, or participation in the partnership (usually, as a general partner) might adversely affect the parent's tax-exempt status.

TIP: This is another area where it is critical that the bona fides of the subsidiary be adhered to (Q 11:6). This approach works only when the legal form of the subsidiary is respected. In one instance, the IRS ignored a tax-exempt organization's use of a for-profit subsidiary as the general partner in a partnership, and reviewed the facts as though the exempt organization was directly involved in the partnership.[20]

If a for-profit organization that is a subsidiary of a tax-exempt organization is used in a partnership, *tax-exempt entity leasing rules* may come into play.[21] These rules make the property involved depreciable over a longer recovery period, thereby reducing the annual depreciation deduction.

TIP: These rules can be avoided where a corporate for-profit subsidiary is used as a partner in a partnership in lieu of a tax-exempt organization, if an election is made to treat any gain on disposition of the subsidiary (and certain other accrued amounts) as unrelated business income.[22]

Q 11:22 Are there limits on the use of tax-exempt assets to capitalize a for-profit subsidiary?

There are no specific limits. Basically, the rules are those that generally pertain to the requirement that the governing board of a tax-exempt organization act in conformity with basic fiduciary responsibilities (Q 1:19).

IRS private letter rulings suggest that only very small percentages of an organization's resources ought to be transferred to subsidiaries, particularly where the parent entity is a public charity.[23] However, the percentages approved by the IRS are usually unduly low and, in any event, probably pertain only to cash. In some instances, a specific asset may—indeed, perhaps *must*—be best utilized in an unrelated activity, even though its value represents a meaningful portion of the organization's total resources.

Q 11:23 Can a supporting organization have a for-profit subsidiary?

A supporting organization (Q 6:15) probably cannot have a for-profit subsidiary. This type of public charity is required to be operated *exclusively* to support or benefit one or more eligible public charities.[24] There is a school of thought that holds that a supporting organization cannot have a for-profit subsidiary because to do so would be a violation of the exclusivity requirement. There is merit to this position; the term *exclusively* means *solely*.[25] Contentions to the contrary include the view that, where the reason for organizing and utilizing the subsidiary is to assist in the supporting or benefiting of one or more eligible public charities, there should not be a prohibition on the use of for-profit subsidiaries in this manner. This issue is under consideration at the IRS.

NOTE: The IRS has ruled that, as long as a supporting organization does not actively participate in the day-to-day management of a for-profit subsidiary and both entities have legitimate business purposes (Q 11:6), the supporting entity can utilize a for-profit subsidiary without jeopardizing its tax-exempt status.[26] This ruling, however, is silent on the impact of the use of the subsidiary on the parent's supporting organization status.

Q 11:24 Can a private foundation have a for-profit subsidiary?

In general, no. The excess business holdings rules applicable to private foundations basically limit to 20 percent the permitted holdings in a business enterprise that may be held by a private foundation and its disqualified persons.[27] If effective control is elsewhere, the aggregate limit is 35 percent. These percentages generally preclude the extent of control required for the parent–subsidiary relationship (Q 11:3).

Nonetheless, there are some exceptions. There is no holdings limit on a business at least 95 percent of the gross income of which is derived from passive sources (such as dividends, interest, and certain rents).[28] The limits do not apply with respect to holdings in a *functionally related business,* which usually is a business the conduct of which is substantially related to the exercise by the foundation of its charitable purposes.[29] A functionally related business can also be (1) a business in which substantially all of the work is performed without compensation (Q 10:23), (2) a business carried on by the private foundation primarily for the convenience of its employees (Q 10:23), or (3) a business that consists of the selling of merchandise, substantially all of which has been received by the foundation as contributions (Q 10:23).

CHAPTER 12

IRS Audits of Nonprofit Organizations

Nonprofit, tax-exempt organizations do not escape IRS audits. At the same time, an audit of an exempt organization is not likely to yield a large sum of money, and the IRS audit resources are in decline. These facts force the IRS to conserve its audit abilities and focus them on entities where the revenue potential is the greatest: health care institutions, colleges and universities, and associations.

Other types of tax-exempt organizations are audited; a few (relatively speaking) are audited on a regular basis. Today, however, it is common for an exempt organization to go for years—perhaps decades—without experiencing an IRS audit. Still, the issues raised by these audits and the resolution of those issues contribute to the body of federal tax law applicable in the exempt organizations context in general.

Here are the questions most frequently asked by clients about IRS audits (including why they start and how they are administered), the issues that can arise on audit, and (inevitably) the likelihood of audit—and the answers to them.

OVERVIEW

Q 12:1 How is the IRS organized from the standpoint of its audit function?

The IRS, a bureau of the Department of the Treasury, is administered at the federal level by its office in Washington, D.C.[1] This office is headed by a Commissioner of Internal Revenue, who generally superintends the assessment and collection of all taxes imposed by any law providing for federal (internal) revenue.[2] There are seven Assistant Commissioners, one of whom is the Assistant Commissioner (Employee Plans and Exempt Organizations).[3] The function of this Assistant Commissioner is to set policy for the IRS in the fields of tax-exempt organizations and employee plans.

Within this Assistant Commissioner's structure is the Exempt Organizations Division, the function of which is to develop policy and administer the law in the realm of tax-exempt organizations. This Division includes four rulings branches and one projects branch.

Another component of the IRS at the national level is the Office of the IRS Chief Counsel, which is part of the Legal Division of the Treasury Department. The Chief Counsel is the principal legal adviser on federal tax matters to the Commissioner. There are eight Associate Chief Counsels, one of whom is the Associate Chief Counsel (Employee Benefits and Exempt Organizations). The principal function of this Associate Chief Counsel's office, which includes eight branches, is to develop legal policy and strategy in the fields of tax-exempt organizations and employee benefits. The Assistant Commissioner (Examination) coordinates the IRS audit programs.

There are seven regions for IRS coverage of the entire United States. Each region is headed by a Regional Commissioner and has a Regional Counsel.

There are 63 IRS internal revenue districts throughout the nation, each of which is administered by a District Director of Internal Revenue. Of these, eight are *key* districts—the districts to which most requests for determination letters on tax-exempt organization issues are sent.

The IRS began one of its reorganizations in 1995. One of the outcomes, expected to be effective in 1996 or 1997, is that all applications for recognition of tax exemption are to be sent to the key district in Cincinnati, Ohio.

Q 12:2   Where does the IRS derive its audit authority?

The IRS is empowered to audit the activities and records of all persons in the United States, including tax-exempt organizations.[4] This examination activity is designed to ensure that exempt organizations and other persons are in compliance with all pertinent requirements of the federal tax law.

Q 12:3   What issues are addressed in an exempt organization's audit?

An IRS audit of this type of organization may address matters such as continuation of tax-exempt status, ongoing non-private-foundation status, susceptibility to the tax on unrelated business income, deferred compensation and retirement programs, tax-exempt bond financing, and employment tax issues.

IRS audits, in the exempt organizations field today, are largely focused on health care organizations (Q 12:12–Q 12:21) and colleges and universities (Q 12:22–Q 12:29).

Q 12:4   How is an IRS audit initiated?

An IRS audit is usually initiated in the field, under the auspices of the appropriate key district office. Each district office has an Examinations Division (Q 12:7). The examiners involved are specialists in tax-exempt organization matters and function under the direction of a supervisor in the district office.

NOTE: The IRS has prepared material to guide national headquarters and field personnel who have responsibilities for the examination of tax-exempt organizations.[5] This material, which is publicly available, is known as the *Exempt Organizations Examination Guidelines Handbook.*

The Exempt Organizations Division of the Office of Employee Plans and Exempt Organizations at the National Office of the IRS has the responsibility for establishing the procedures and policy for the conduct of exempt organization audit programs.

Q 12:5   Why is an IRS audit initiated?

Although the IRS, from time to time, initiates audits of particular types of tax-exempt organizations (such as health care organizations, associations, churches, colleges and universities, and private foundations) as a matter of national policy, audits are typically commenced based on the size of the entity and the length of time that has elapsed since any prior audit. Often, an audit is commenced as the result of an examination of an information or tax return; one of the functions of the IRS is to ascertain the correctness of returns. Other reasons for the development of an audit include media or third-party reports of alleged wrongdoing by a taxpayer, selection based on a person's claim for a refund of taxes, or selection as part of an IRS program to focus on a particular problem area (often termed an *industry* by the IRS).

NOTE: Of direct importance in relation to the IRS audit programs for tax-exempt organizations is the IRS industry specialization program for exempt organizations. This program was established to ensure uniform and consistent treatment of issues nationwide and to provide better identification and development of issues. The IRS studies an industry as a whole by analyzing news media, national business-oriented publications, trade journals, market reports, and the like.[6]

NOTE: The IRS audit programs are a matter of considerable controversy. The IRS has what it terms a *routine* audit program, where organizations are periodically reviewed on a regular basis. But, the timing of these audits can make them appear to be *political.* For example, an audit of the National Rifle Association (NRA) was commenced in 1995 immediately following some NRA direct-mail fund-raising that criticized a federal government agency. The IRS said the audit was coincidental and routine; the NRA contended it was a response to the direct-mail appeal.

Q 12:6   What items of a tax-exempt organization will the IRS review on audit?

The IRS is authorized to examine any books, papers, records, or other data that may be relevant or material to an inquiry.[7] The records that must be produced during audit of a tax-exempt organization will include all organizational documents (such as articles of organization, bylaws, resolutions, and minutes of meetings), documents relating to tax status (such as any application for recognition of tax exemption and IRS determinations as to exempt and private status), financial statements (including underlying books and records), recent annual information returns, and newsletters, journals, and other publications. Other items that must be produced will depend on the type of audit being conducted; the audit may or may not encompass payroll records, pension and retirement plans, returns of affiliated organizations, and the like.[8] In some instances, an organization may find it appropriate to produce information only upon the presentation of a summons.

Q 12:7   Are there different types of IRS audits?

Yes. Some examinations are *office examinations,* where contact between the IRS and a taxpayer is by IRS office interview. A *correspondence audit* involves an IRS request for additional information from a taxpayer by letter correspondence. Other examinations are *field examinations,* in which one or more IRS agents review the books and records of the taxpayer on the taxpayer's premises. IRS audits of tax-exempt organizations of any consequence are field examinations.

One of the problems with IRS audit practices in the past was that a typical audit focused on a single organization, ignoring affiliates. This deficiency (from the government's viewpoint) has been remedied with the development of the *coordinated examination program:* complex issues are now addressed and managed using a team audit approach.[9] The objectives of the coordinated examination program are to (1) perform effectively planned and managed coordinated examinations, (2) secure support for district assistance where appropriate, and (3) accumulate and disseminate novel examination techniques, issues unique to specific organizations, tax avoidance and evasion schemes, and other useful examination information.

A coordinated examination case focuses on a domestic or foreign organization, along with effectively controlled entities (regardless of percentage of ownership), whose organizational structure, geographic dispersion, or other examination problems warrant application of the coordinated case procedures. These examinations are susceptible to interdistrict coordination, team audit techniques, and case manager participation. Corporations, trusts, and other forms of entities effectively controlled by the primary organization or otherwise related to the primary organization are components of the case.

Another relatively contemporary IRS examination technique is the *package audit.*[10] This type of audit arises out of the review of one or more annual information returns and/or unrelated business income tax returns. It entails ascertaining whether the exempt organization is filing or has filed all other required federal tax returns, such as the employment tax returns, other information returns, employee benefit plan returns, and the returns of related entities.

Q 12:8   How does the IRS determine whether to use the coordinated examination procedure?

The factors used in determining whether a case qualifies for the coordinated examination procedure include the total assets of the organization (usually more than $50 million), the gross receipts of the organization (usually more than $50 million), the number of controlled or otherwise related entities, the national impact of the case, and the team members, specialists (including industry specialists), support agents, and total direct examination staff-days involved.

Q 12:9   How does an exempt organization cope with IRS personnel during an audit?

Carefully and courteously. The techniques for coping with IRS personnel on the occasion of an audit are easily summarized, but their deployment and success are likely to depend heavily on the personalities involved. The key staff personnel, accountants, and legal counsel of the audited organization should be involved in the process from the beginning, and it is advisable to select one individual who will serve as liaison with the IRS during the audit. The projected duration of the audit and the procedures that are to be followed by the parties involved should be ascertained at the outset, and records should be carefully maintained as information and documents are examined or copied by the revenue agents. All interviews of those associated with the audited organization should be monitored by the liaison individual, with appropriate records made of each interview. At least some of the questioning should occur only in the presence of legal counsel.

Where issues arise, one or both sides may decide to pursue the technical advice procedure.[11]

Q 12:10 What does the IRS do after the audit has been completed?

Upon completion of an audit, the IRS will take one of the following actions:

1. If the IRS determines that there are no inaccuracies with the taxpayer's return, the taxpayer will be issued a *no change letter,* which indicates that no change is being made to the taxpayer's tax liability as reported.

2. If the IRS determines that the taxpayer has overpaid tax, the IRS will issue an overadjustment entitling the taxpayer to a tax refund.

3. If the IRS determines that there is a deficiency in the amount of tax paid or reported by the taxpayer, or some other taxpayer error (such as a failure to file a required tax form), the IRS agent will present the taxpayer with findings that assert a deficiency in tax. If the taxpayer agrees with the alleged deficiency, a form can be executed and the taxpayer is sent a statement for the additional tax owed. If the taxpayer disagrees with the IRS on the point, the collections process will commence.[12]

Q 12:11 What is the likelihood that a tax-exempt organization will be audited by the IRS?

Overall, the likelihood that an exempt organization will be audited by the IRS is remote. The IRS has limited (and, relatively speaking, declining) audit resources, and the number of tax-exempt organizations is increasing. The IRS simply does not have the personnel to audit all exempt organizations on a regular basis. Consequently, the IRS audit focus is confined to the larger organizations, particularly those within a targeted industry or field (Q 12:5).

IRS AUDITS OF HEALTH CARE ORGANIZATIONS

Q 12:12 What is the IRS audit program for hospitals and other health care organizations?

The IRS, in recent years, has been making the audit of tax-exempt hospitals and other health care entities a matter of special priority. In 1992, the IRS developed audit guidelines specific to these types of tax-exempt organizations (although many of the guidelines are equally applicable to other types of exempt entities).[13]

The guidelines emphasize nearly all aspects of qualification for tax-exempt status by hospitals, with emphasis on private inurement and private benefit situations (see Chapter 3). They also focus on joint venture arrangements and unrelated business income circumstances (see Chapter 10).

Q 12:13 What is the focus of the IRS concerning the tax-exempt status of nonprofit hospitals?

The tax exemption of nonprofit hospitals today rests on the *community benefit* standard: the hospital must function to promote health in a particular community. In determining whether a hospital meets this standard, IRS agents are expected to consider the following factors:

1. Is the hospital's governing board composed of "prominent civic leaders" rather than hospital administrators, physicians, and the like? (The agents are requested to review the minutes of the board meeting to determine how active the members are.)

2. Is the organization part of a multientity hospital system, and do the minutes reflect "corporate separateness?" (The minutes should show that the board members understand the purposes and activities of the various entities (Q 2:42, Q 11:6).)

3. Is admission to the medical staff open to all qualified physicians in the area, consistent with the size and nature of the facilities?

4. Does the hospital operate a full-time emergency room open to everyone, regardless of ability to pay?

5. Does the hospital provide nonemergency care to everyone in the community who is able to pay either privately or through third parties (such as Medicare and Medicaid)?[14]

The guidelines contain criteria for assessing whether an "open staff policy" exists at a hospital. The auditing agent is to identify qualification requirements for admission to staff (by referring to the medical staff bylaws), review application procedures and methods of staff selection, review minutes of medical staff meetings, determine whether staff admission fees are charged on a preferential basis, ascertain whether new physicians in the geographic area are admitted to the staff (the absence of new members could indicate a closed staff), consider the number of physicians in each membership category (such as active, associate, and courtesy), interview knowledgeable officials to determine whether physicians have been denied admission to the staff for other than reasonable cause, review the minutes of the credentials committee, and review the hospital's daily consensus report to determine the percentage of use of hospital facilities by various physicians (the names of the patients and the physicians providing services for these patients are listed in the consensus report).

The guidelines also contain criteria for determining whether use of an emergency room is restricted. The agent is to (1) review the manual of operations, brochures, posted signs, and the like, (2) interview ambulance drivers to determine whether they are instructed to take indigent patients to another hospital, (3) interview emergency room staff to determine admission procedures, (4) interview social workers in the community, who are familiar with delivery of emergency health care services, to determine whether the services are known to be available at the hospital, and (5) ascertain when and how determinations of financial responsibility are made and whether a deposit is required of any patient before care is rendered. Examining agents are expected to ascertain whether a hospital engages in the practice known as patient "dumping."

An examining agent is admonished to determine whether nonemergency services are available to everyone in the community who has the ability to pay. To this end, the agent is to review the hospital admission policy, determine whether the hospital admits and treats Medicare and Medicaid patients in a nondiscriminatory manner, review files on denied admissions to ascertain the reasons for denial, determine whether members of the professional staff also serve in administrative capacities and restrict admissions to only patients of staff members, review the accountants' reports for a statement of the hospital's charity care policy and expenditures, and compare the proportion of services provided to Medicaid patients to the proportion of Medicaid beneficiaries living in the area served by the hospital (the latter data are available either from the institution or from the state Medicaid agency).

The examining agent is to obtain copies of any private letter rulings issued to the hospital by the IRS, and to determine whether the hospital is involved in projects and programs that improve the health of the community (such as by reviewing newsletters, press releases, and calendars of events).

Q 12:14 What is the emphasis by the IRS in this area on private inurement and private benefit?

The guidelines contain a discussion of private inurement and private benefit, and the difference between the two doctrines (see Chapter 3).[15] The IRS recognizes two key distinctions between these two concepts.

First, the IRS has reiterated its position that even a "minimal amount" of private inurement will result in loss of tax-exempt status (Q 3:1), and private benefit is tested against an "insubstantiality" threshold (Q 3:4). Second, private inurement applies only with respect to "insiders," but private benefit can accrue to anyone (Q 3:5). (The IRS considers a physician an insider in relation to a hospital in which he or she practices and/or is a member of the hospital's governing body.)

The following guidelines are to be followed in determining private inurement or private benefit:

1. Identify the members of the board of directors or trustees and key staff members of the administrative and medical staff. Examine any business relationships or dealings with the hospital. Note transactions where supplies or services are provided at prices exceeding competitive market prices or at preferred terms. Be alert for any loan agreement at less than prevailing interest rates. Scrutinize any business arrangements under which hospitals finance the construction of medical buildings owned by staff physicians on favorable financial terms.

2. Review contracts and leases. Scrutinize any contracts under which the hospital requires physicians to conduct private practices on hospital premises.

3. Review the minutes of the board of directors' executive committee and finance committee for indications of transactions with physicians, administrators, and board members.

4. Review the articles of incorporation, bylaws, minutes, filings with regulatory authorities, correspondence, brochures, newspaper articles, and the like to determine the existence of related parties.

5. Determine whether the hospital is engaged in commercial or industrial research or testing that would benefit private individuals or firms, rather than scientific or medical research that would benefit the general public.

6. Review third-party reports (such as accountants' audit reports, management letters, and annual reports) to determine whether the hospital's activities further an exempt purpose or serve private interests.

7. Review any conflict-of-interest statements (Q 2:30) to determine whether medical staff or board members have an economic interest in, or significant dealings with, the hospital.

These guidelines focus on the matter of unreasonable compensation and require examining agents to inquire as to recruiting incentives, incentive compensation arrangements, below-market loans, below-market leases, and hospital purchases of a physician's practice. The guidelines also contain an extensive list of "common compensation arrangements" between hospitals and physicians.

Q 12:15 What is the interest of the IRS in this area with respect to joint ventures?

The guidelines focus on joint ventures, pointing out that a variety of forms may be involved, such as a cooperative agreement or the creation of a separate legal entity.[16] Examples of the items or services involved in these joint ventures are said to include clinical diagnostic laboratory services, medical equipment leasing, durable medical equipment, and other out-patient medical or diagnostic services.

Agents are advised to carefully examine joint ventures between taxable and tax-exempt parties in search of private inurement or private benefit (see Chapter 3). The facts must be reviewed to determine whether the partnership involved serves a charitable purpose, whether and how participation by the exempt entity furthers an exempt purpose, and whether the arrangement permits the exempt entity to act exclusively in furtherance of its exempt purposes. Examples of private inurement issues in this setting include participation in a venture that imposes obligations on the tax-exempt health care organization that conflict with its exempt purposes, a disproportionate allocation of profits and losses to the nonexempt partners (particularly if they are physicians), loans made by the exempt partner to the joint venture on a commercially unreasonable basis (such as a low interest rate or inadequate security), provision by the exempt partner of property or services to the joint venture at less than fair market value, and receipt by a nonexempt partner of more than reasonable compensation for the sale of property or services to the joint venture.

Q 12:16 How do the private inurement rules interrelate with the federal antikickback laws?

A variety of private inurement issues involving possible violations of the federal antikickback law are explored in the IRS guidelines.[17] They note that the Office of the Inspector General in the Department of Health and

Human Services (HHS) has a program to reduce fraud in the Medicare and Medicaid programs.[18] This office administers an antikickback statute that penalizes anyone who solicits, receives, offers, or pays anything of value to induce or reimburse for:

1. Referring an individual to any person for the furnishing of, or for arranging for the furnishing of, any item or service payable under Medicare or Medicaid.

2. Purchasing, leasing, or ordering, or arranging for or recommending purchasing, leasing, or ordering, any good, facility, service, or item payable under Medicare or Medicaid.

HHS has published a list of "questionable features which, separately or together, could indicate that a joint venture is suspect" under the anti-kickback law. Physician-investors are given special scrutiny because they are in a position to make referrals. Among the potentially objectionable arrangements are physicians who are expected to make a large number of referrals are offered a greater investment opportunity in the joint venture than those anticipated to make fewer referrals; physician-investors are actively encouraged to make referrals to the joint venture, or are encouraged to divest their ownership interest if they fail to sustain an "acceptable" level of referrals; the joint venture tracks its sources of referrals and distributes this information to the investors; investors are required to divest their ownership interest if they cease to practice in the service area (such as by moving or retiring); investment interests are nontransferable; the amount of capital invested by the physician is disproportionately small and the returns on investment are disproportionately large when compared to a typical investment in a new business enterprise; physician-investors invest only a nominal amount (such as $500–$1,500); physician-investors are permitted to "borrow" the amount of the "investment" from the entity and pay it back through deductions from profit distributions, thus eliminating the need to contribute cash to the partnership; investors are paid extraordinary returns on the investment in comparison with the risk involved (such as over 50 percent to 100 percent per year); or the structure of a joint venture is particularly suspect (for example, one of the parties is an ongoing entity already providing a particular service) and might best be characterized as a "shell" that merely allows referring physicians to share in the income derived from their referrals.

The auditing agent is advised to "[b]e alert for joint ventures involving the sale by a hospital of the gross or net revenue stream from an existing hospital service for a defined period of time to private interests." Alertness is also advised with respect to "arrangements with physician group practices or clinics where the hospital transfers something of value in return for an agreement to refer patients to the hospital for inpatient, surgical, or diagnostic services."

Q 12:17 What types of financial analyses is the IRS likely to make in these audits?

Sixteen types of "financial analyses" by examining agents are requested.[19] These include:

1. Review income and expenditures of affiliated entities to determine whether nonexempt purposes, private inurement, serving of private interests, or unrelated business income may be present (see Chapters 3 and 10).

2. Look for lobbying or political activities or expenditures; determine whether the hospital has elected the expenditure test as to lobbying expenditures (see Chapters 4 and 5).

3. Reconcile the hospital's books with the figures on its annual information return. Reconcile the working trial balance to the general ledger, accountants' report, and the return.

4. Review the accountants' report and management letter for indications of unrelated business income.

5. Review Medicare cost reports for indications of insider (related party) transactions or unrelated activities.

6. Review the correspondence files on large gifts and grants; look for unusual transactions that may prohibit the "donor" from receiving a charitable deduction.

7. Check the value shown on the books for donated property against any appraisals in the file; if any property was sold, note the difference between the book value and the selling price (see Q 9:7).

8. Review the travel ledger accounts of the administrative department and the board of directors; be alert for personal items

such as spouse's travel and ensure that there has been "proper accounting" (Q 2:21).

9. Where private individuals or outside entities operate the hospital cafeteria, gift shop, pharmacy, parking lot, and the like, determine whether the agreements with these individuals or firms provide for reasonable payments to the hospital.

10. Reconcile expenses on the tax return used to report unrelated business income. If specific cost centers are maintained, review them for possible account analysis. If specific cost centers are not maintained, request a copy of the allocation method used and determine whether it is reasonable in accordance with the federal tax requirements.

Q 12:18 What are the rules for analyzing a hospital's balance sheet?

The guidelines contain the following rules for analyzing a hospital's balance sheet:

1. Review the general ledger control account for receivables from officers, trustees, and members of the medical staff, and analyze for private benefit and additional compensation; review loan or other agreements underlying these transactions.

2. Check notes receivable for interest-free loans to insiders (for example, a mortgage loan to an administrator given as an inducement to accept or continue employment at the hospital); these arrangements are to be scrutinized for inurement, proper reporting, and the like.

3. Review property records to determine whether any assets are being used for personal purposes that should be taxable income to the user (such as vehicles and residential property held for future expansion).

4. Review trust funds to see whether the trusts should be filing separate returns.

5. Review investment portfolios and check for controlled entities.

6. Review the ledger accounts and check for notes and mortgages payable that could lead to unrelated debt-financed income (Q 8:15) issues.

7. Analyze any self-insurance trust or fund set up by the hospital to provide liability insurance.

8. Refer to the appropriate IRS guidelines when there is evidence that the hospital has purchased or sold health care facilities utilizing tax-exempt bonds.[20]

Q 12:19 Are there any special rules for hospitals in connection with package audits?

Yes. In the context of discussing package audit items (Q 12:7), the guidelines also contain rules for determining whether physicians are employees of the hospital (rather than independent contractors).[21] According to these guidelines, if the following factors are present, the physician is "most likely" an employee (even if the contract describes the position as an independent contractor): the physician does not have a private practice, the hospital pays wages to the physician, the hospital provides supplies and professional support staff, the hospital bills for physician services, there is a percentage division of physician fees with the hospital (or vice versa), there is hospital regulation of or a right to control the physician, the physician is on duty at the hospital during specified hours, and/or the physician's uniform bears the hospital name or insignia.

One aspect of the package audit accorded prominence in these audit guidelines is an arrangement where a tax-exempt hospital pays certain personal or business expenses of affiliated physicians and the taxable compensation is not properly reflected as wages or other form of compensation in the annual information returns, employment tax returns, or compensation information returns. The example is provided of college and university medical school faculty physicians who often have employment contracts with medical schools that limit their compensation to low levels compared to compensation obtainable in private practice. These physicians may enter into employment contracts as consultants with several hospitals or clinics unrelated to the medical schools where they teach. The written employment contract with these hospitals or clinics may be supplemented by a verbal agreement that provides for the hospital or a third party to pay associated business or personal expenses (such as lease of luxury automobiles, house improvements, and country club memberships) as part of the total annual employment contract amount. Examining agents are cautioned that the compensation information return may reflect the cash amount paid by the hospital or clinic directly to the physician but exclude amounts paid to other parties on the physician's behalf.

The other package audit issues outlined in these procedures cause the examining agent(s) to undertake the following:[22]

1. Review contracts with hospital-based specialists, such as anesthesiologists, radiologists, and pathologists. These physicians may be employees for federal employment tax purposes, including income tax withholding. The agent is to interview these physicians "when necessary to clarify and verify contract items."

2. Review professional service contracts, which usually specify who will carry the malpractice insurance. If the hospital pays for the insurance, that may be an indication that the physician is an employee (rather than an independent contractor) or may constitute private inurement. The agent is to be alert to efforts on the part of physicians to be treated as employees for some purposes (such as deferred compensation benefits) but as independent contractors for compensation purposes.

3. Review fellowships, stipends, or other payments to interns, residents, medical students, and nursing students, to determine whether these arrangements represent taxable income subject to tax and social security withholding if paid in connection with services rendered.

4. Determine how private duty nurses are compensated if the hospital has a responsibility to file a compensation information return.

5. Determine whether the hospital contracts to purchase services that are outside the ambit of those that may be performed by cooperative hospital service organizations. Are these services purchased from one of these organizations or from unrelated tax-exempt organizations? Determine whether the nature and extent of the services purchased indicate that the exempt organization providing the services should be considered for examination.

6. Review employment contracts of medical personnel who have tax-deferred annuity contracts, to ensure that only common-law employees are receiving the benefits of these annuities. Check to determine whether reduction agreements are on file and whether the exclusion allowances are within the federal tax limits.

7. Determine what types of retirement plans, insurance plans, and nonqualified deferred compensation arrangements are in place. Obtain background information by inspecting the brochures provided to employees, interview hospital officials in regard to transactions between the hospital and the plan, identify deferred compensation arrangements and determine the correct tax consequences, and, if the hospital has a profit-sharing plan, determine the effect on the tax-exempt status of the institution and whether an examination of the plan is necessary.

8. Prepare an information report on significant amounts of excess indemnification (patient refunds) received under medical insurance policies where the indemnification is attributable to an employer's contribution, inasmuch as these refunds are includable in the gross income of the patient.

9. Determine whether the hospital has filed or is liable for 11 IRS forms.[23]

Q 12:20 What unrelated business income issues involving health care institutions arise on audit?

Concerning the unrelated business aspects of audits of health care institutions, IRS agents are provided a comprehensive listing of issues and authorities and are advised to be particularly inquisitive about these "[s]pecific examples common in [the] health care field": laboratory testing; pharmacy sales; cafeterias, coffee shops, and gift shops; parking facilities; medical research; laundry services; leasing of medical buildings; supply departments; and services to other hospitals (Q 10:23).[24]

Q 12:21 How is the IRS using closing agreements in the health care context?

Increasingly, the IRS is employing the device of the closing agreement to resolve tax disputes in the tax-exempt organizations context. Although use of the closing agreement is not new, the approach is receiving a new emphasis at the IRS and is being used with increasing frequency to resolve a variety of exempt organization matters. With this technique, the organization obtains both certainty that the matter is permanently concluded and guidance as to future conduct, while the IRS resolves a compliance problem that otherwise would consume time and resources (through the revocation or assessment process) and obtains a commitment as to future compliance. By use of a closing agreement, a tax-exempt organization can avoid revocation of its tax exemption.

The closing agreement procedure is authorized by statute.[25] It is a final agreement between the IRS and a taxpayer on a specific issue or liability. The IRS can negotiate a written closing agreement with any taxpayer to make a final resolution of any of the taxpayer's tax liabilities for any period. After the IRS approves an agreement, it is final and conclusive, and—unless there is a showing of fraud, malfeasance, or misrepresentation of one or more material facts—it cannot be reopened on the basis of the matters agreed on or modified by the IRS, nor may it (or any legal action in accordance with it) be annulled, modified, set aside, or disregarded in any lawsuit, other action, or proceeding.[26] Simple unintentional errors are not treated as fraud, malfeasance, or misrepresentation that would allow reopening of a closing agreement.

The existence of any disqualifying elements is subject to review by a court—a review that may entail examination of an organization's books and records. The burden of proof in establishing the disqualifying factor or factors is on the party seeking to set the agreement aside.

The key determinants governing the election of closing agreements are (1) an apparent benefit in having the case permanently and conclusively closed, (2) good and sufficient reasons on the part of the taxpayer for desiring the arrangement, and (3) evidence that the fulfillment of the agreement will not be detrimental to the federal government.

NOTE: There is no requirement of a showing that the resulting closing agreement will confer any advantage to the federal government.

A closing agreement can cover the entire tax liability for one or more years, be limited to a specific tax item, and/or cover future periods. This type of agreement can be made a condition to the issuance of a letter ruling. Agreements for subsequent periods are subject to changes in or modifications of the law enacted subsequent to the date of the agreement.[27]

There is no revenue procedure specifically applicable to closing agreements concerning tax-exempt organizations. However, the general procedures for the execution of closing agreements can be adapted to exempt organization cases. These general procedures discuss formulation and drafting of agreements, format, step-by-step instructions, identification of parties and issues, and special circumstances.

A tax-exempt health care organization may negotiate and execute with the IRS a closing agreement with assurance that it will conclusively determine tax liability, tax-exempt status, and/or public charity/private foundation status.

In general, favorable occasions for the execution of closing agreements between the IRS and tax-exempt organizations would be situations in which revocation of exemption is supported by the facts but is harsh or excessive—for example, where revocation of exemption for narrow technical infractions would jeopardize a charitable organization's ability to continue its programs. From the viewpoint of the IRS, if technical flaws such as these can be eliminated definitively by means of agreed-on changes in an exempt organization's operations or procedures, it will be receptive to a closing agreement. By contrast, the IRS is not likely to be interested in the closing agreement procedure where an organization has engaged in flagrant and continuous acts compelling revocation and has not been operating in good faith.

COLLEGES AND UNIVERSITIES

Q 12:22 What is the focus of the IRS as to the tax-exempt status of colleges and universities?

The IRS has developed examination guidelines for its agents to use during the audits of colleges and universities.[28] These guidelines provide factors to be considered in determining how a college or university is structured. Focus is also placed on its accounting methods, financial information, compensation arrangements, fringe benefit issues, joint ventures, scholarships and fellowships, unrelated business issues (see Chapter 10), and fund-raising practices (see Chapter 7). While formally confined to institutions of higher education, the guidelines contain much information of use by nearly all tax-exempt organizations, and their managers and advisers.

Q 12:23 How does the IRS approach an audit of a college or university?

Recognizing that there is no typical structure of a college or university, the guidelines require the auditing agent to engage in a pre-examination analysis of the institution, to ascertain the particular structure. This is to be done by reviewing financial reports filed by the institution with other federal departments and agencies in documenting reimbursable direct costs incurred in the performance of sponsored research. These documents are expected to "provide insight into an institution's accounting system and practices and internal controls." The agent also is to review audit reports relating to private research contracts, derive information from the institution's internal auditors, determine whether the institution has adopted and operates in accordance with a racially nondiscriminatory policy as to students, and see whether there are problems related to withholding for and payments to nonresident aliens.

Only then is the agent ready to make the initial contact with the institution, by acquiring "internal items" that provide an overview of its size, structure, and activities.

Q 12:24 What internal items of a college or university will the auditing agent review?

From a large institution, the agent is to request a contact individual who can provide information about each component of the institution. The agent is to peruse bulletins and course catalogs, telephone directories, minutes of the governing board, minutes of committees (including the faculty senate or assembly), student newspapers (which may provide a "different perspective"), alumni bulletins and magazines, catalogs or lists of institution publications, a description of the institution's accounting system, requisition and purchase order files, reports of coaches disclosing outside income, sponsored-research financial reports, descriptions of computer hardware and software, and formats of files and records maintained on computer.

Q 12:25 What other information is the agent likely to evaluate?

The agent is expected to evaluate "outside documentation," which includes audited financial statements, auditors' letters to management, accreditation and reaccreditation reports, and state and local real property tax exemption documents. Also to be studied is information required by the Office of Management and Budget (OMB), including indirect cost proposal data.[29] The instructions guide the agent in making an income analysis, expense analysis, and balance sheet analysis, as well as in examining the institution's statement of cash flows and accountants' statements as to related-party transactions.

Q 12:26 What issues are likely to be reviewed during this type of audit?

The agent is likely to examine employee (rather than independent contractor) status, compliance with the employment tax rules, cafeteria plans, fringe benefits (including tuition remission plans), retirement and pension plans, other deferred compensation arrangements, and the institution's debt structure. In addition, compliance with the bond rules is to be ascertained, where governmental bonds have been issued to state colleges and universities or where "qualified private activity bonds" (or 501(c)(3) bonds) have been issued.

Large charitable contributions are to be reviewed "to identify any conditional contributions that may have questionable terms." In this setting, the agent is to be alert for forms of private inurement or private benefit (see Chapter 3). The process by which the institution values gift properties is to be explored. Where the appraisal rules apply (Q 7:13), the agent is to determine whether the institution completed its portion of the appraisal summary and whether the institution filed the information return reporting sales of gift properties within two years of the contribution (Q 9:7). Compliance with the quid pro quo contribution rules is to be looked into (Q 7:9).

If property was accepted by the institution subject to a mortgage, the agent is to consider potential unrelated debt-financed income implications. Contracts with financial institutions for fund-management services are to be looked at for possible private inurement or impermissible private benefit. The special rules pertaining to contributions that give rise to the right to purchase tickets to athletic events[30] are to be applied. The agent is to examine the possibility of gifts that are in actuality contributions to a fraternity or sorority, with the institution as a mere conduit. Contributions of items of inventory (such as books) are to be evaluated to see whether there has been compliance with the special tax rules applicable to them.[31]

The agent is to devote a significant portion of the audit time to the matter of sponsored research funded by industry or government. Attention is drawn to the subject of technology transfer; the guidelines caution that the "relationship between institutions and these [commercial] licensees is growing more complex." Looking for private inurement, private benefit, and/or unrelated business income (see Chapters 3 and 10), the agent is to probe research contracts, joint ventures, venture capital funds, industry liaison programs, spin-off companies, consortia, jointly owned research facilities, material transfers, commercial licenses, and consultations and clinical trial agreements. The examination is to include a determination as to whether true "research" is being undertaken, rather than testing, sampling, or certification.

The agent is to review the institution's safeguards for managing and reporting conflicts of interest (Q 2:8). Also to be scrutinized is the institution's policy regarding ownership of intellectual property, such as inventions or computer software, and the payment of royalties to faculty inventors. Patent licensing arrangements are to be looked at, as are sample closed research projects and payments to individuals as fellowships or stipends for research activities.

All scholarship and fellowship programs are to be examined for the presence of any gross income items (as opposed to excludable ones), proper withholding and reporting, and the applicability of the social security and unemployment taxes. The agent is to be alert to situations where the "grants" are really payments for services rendered. An examination is to be made of scholarship restrictions on the basis of race, from the perspective of potential violation of the public policy doctrine. The qualified tuition reductions[32] are to be reviewed.

Q 12:27 Do the rules pertaining to lobbying and political campaign activity get reviewed in these audits?

Yes. The agent is to review the activities of the college or university in relation to the proscriptions on substantial legislative and any political campaign activities (see Chapters 4 and 5). Any written policies in this regard are to be examined, as are student newspapers, minutes of committee meetings, and the activities of the institution's department for "political or legislative relationships." Lobbying offices in Washington D.C., and/or state capitals are to be looked into.

Q 12:28 What unrelated business income issues involving colleges and universities arise on audit?

The guidelines place considerable emphasis on bookstore operations, including application of the convenience exception (Q 10:23). Note is made of the fact that the convenience exception does not shelter sales to alumni. Sales of computers are discussed. Other topics are public use of facilities, operation of hotels and motels, operation of parking lots, and travel tours (Q 10:29).

Q 12:29 What other issues can arise in these audits?

The examining agent is to identify related tax-exempt and taxable entities (see Chapter 11). Situations where an individual is being compensated by more than one entity (including the institution) are to be scrutinized in pursuit of unreasonable compensation (Q 3:8, Q 3:12). Arrangements involving shared facilities are to be examined, including the methods of allocating expenses among related entities (Q 10:22). Payments from athletic booster clubs to coaches, other staff, and athletes are to be reviewed for any reporting noncompliance. Separate endowment and similar funds, and joint ventures with charitable remainder unitrusts, research foundations, and fund-raising foundations are all subject to examination.

Endnotes

CHAPTER 1

1 The concept of a *nonprofit* organization, and the legal and political philosophy underpinning it, is summarized at greater length in Chapter 1 of Hopkins, *The Law of Tax-Exempt Organizations,* 6th ed. (1992; New York: John Wiley & Sons, Inc.).

2 Internal Revenue Code of 1986, as amended, section 183. Throughout, "IRC §" is used to designate sections of the Code.

3 The process of starting a nonprofit organization is summarized at greater length in Chapter 2 of Hopkins, *A Legal Guide to Starting and Managing a Nonprofit Organization,* 2d ed. (1993; New York: John Wiley & Sons, Inc.).

4 Exemption from the federal income tax is authorized in IRC § 501(a). Nearly all of these types of tax-exempt organizations are listed in IRC § 501(c). The various types of exempt organizations are summarized in Hopkins, *supra,* endnote 1.

5 IRC § 501(m).

6 IRC § 501(c)(1).

7 The Internal Revenue Service (IRS) is the component agency of the Department of the Treasury that administers the federal tax laws. One of the principal functions of the IRS is application and interpretation of these laws as they apply to nonprofit organizations.

8 The tax exemption recognition process for charitable organizations is authorized by IRC § 508(a). For the most part, the reference to *charitable* organizations throughout is to tax-exempt entities described in IRC § 501(c)(3).

9 IRC § 508(c).

10 Social welfare organizations are IRC § 501(c)(4) entities (see Q 1:38); labor organizations are IRC § 501(c)(5) entities; associations are mostly

IRC § 501(c)(6) entities (see Q 1:39); social clubs are IRC § 501(c)(7) enti-ties; fraternal organizations are IRC § 501(c)(8) and (10) entities; and vet-erans' organizations are IRC § 501(c)(19) entities.

11 IRS Revenue Ruling (Rev. Rul.) 80-108, 1980-1 C.B. 119.

12 Political organizations are IRC § 527 entities (see Q 5:16) and homeown-ers' organizations are IRC § 528 entities.

13 IRC § 102.

14 IRC § 277.

15 See Chapter 8, Q 8:23–Q 8:30. The basic rules as to pooled income funds are in IRC § 642(c)(5).

16 IRC § 170(c).

17 IRC § 501(c)(3) (see *supra* endnote 8).

18 IRC § 170(b)(1)(A). These and the other laws concerning deductible chari-table giving are detailed in Hopkins, *The Tax Law of Charitable Giving* (1993; New York: John Wiley & Sons, Inc.).

19 IRC § 170(b)(1)(B).

20 IRC §§ 170(d)(1), 170(b)(1)(B), respectively.

21 IRC § 68.

22 IRC § 170(b)(2).

23 IRC § 170(d)(2).

24 IRC § 170(b)(1)(C)(i).

25 IRC § 170(b)(1)(D)(i).

26 IRC §§ 170(b)(1)(C)(ii), 170(b)(1)(D)(ii), respectively.

27 Income Tax Regulations (Reg.) § 1.170A-1(c)(1).

28 Capital assets are the subject of IRC § 1221. Long-term and short-term capital gains are the subject of IRC § 1222.

29 IRC § 170(e)(1)(A).

30 IRC § 170(e)(1)(B)(i).

31 IRC § 170(e)(1)(B)(ii).

32 IRC § 170(e)(5).

33 IRC § 170(b)(2).

34 IRC § 170(d)(2).

35 IRC § 170(e)(3).

36 IRC § 170(e)(4).

CHAPTER 2

1 IRS General Counsel Memorandum (Gen. Couns. Mem.) 39498.

2 *E.g.,* IRS Private Letter Ruling (Priv. Ltr. Rul.) 9438030.

3 Closing agreement between the Hermann Hospital and the IRS (Sep. 20, 1994). This viewpoint was not reflected in the more formal guidelines issued as IRS Announcement (Ann.) 95-25, 1995-14 I.R.B. 11.

4 The function of the board of directors is more expansively discussed in Hopkins, *supra* Chapter 1, endnote 3, particularly Chapter 2.

5 Reg. § 1.170A-9(e)(3)(v).

6 IRS Technical Advice Memorandum (Tech. Adv. Mem.) 9451001.

7 *E.g., The Nationalist Movement* v. *Commissioner,* 37 F.3d 216 (5th Cir. 1994).

8 Rev. Rul. 64-182, 1964-1 C.B. (Part 1) 186.

9 *United Cancer Council, Inc.* v. *Commissioner* (U.S. Tax Court, Docket No. 2008-91X; undecided).

10 The settlement (technically, an assurance of discontinuance) is dated Dec. 28, 1994; a summary of it is in XII *The Nonprofit Counsel* (No. 2) 1 (Feb. 1995).

11 In general, see Glaser, *An Insider's Account of the United Way Scandal: What Went Wrong and Why* (1994, New York: John Wiley & Sons, Inc.).

12 IRC § 274(m)(3).

13 IRC § 274(e)(2).

14 IRC § 4941 (rules prohibiting self-dealing).

15 IRC § 4946.

16 A checklist of items to consider in following these guidelines appears in Hopkins, *supra,* Chapter 1, endnote 3, 244–249.

CHAPTER 3

1 IRC § 501(c)(3).

2 IRS Gen. Couns. Mem. 38459.

3 IRS Gen. Couns. Mem. 39862.

4 *E.g., Living Faith, Inc.* v. *Commissioner,* 950 F.2d 365, 370 (7th Cir. 1991).

5 IRC § 4946.

6 IRS Gen. Couns. Mem. 39862, 39670, and 39498.

7 See *supra* Chapter 1, endnote 10.

8 Reg. § 1.501(c)(3)-1(c)(1).

9 Form 990.

10 See Chapter 2, endnote 3.

11 IRS Tech. Adv. Mem. 9451001; *LAC Facilities, Inc.* v. *United States* (No. 94-604T).

12 IRS Gen. Couns. Mem. 39862.

13 Form 990, Schedule A, Part I.

14 There have been, over recent years, many versions of intermediate sanctions. The most recent iteration from the Department of the Treasury is summarized at XII *The Nonprofit Counsel* (No. 10) 1 (Oct. 1995). Legislation containing intermediate sanctions is moving through Congress; a summary of this proposal (which would introduce IRC § 4958) is at VII *The Nonprofit Counsel* (No. 11) 1 (Nov. 1995).

15 IRC § 4962.

16 As to involvements in partnerships and joint ventures, see Hopkins, *supra,* Chapter 1, endnote 1, particularly Chapter 46. Also Sanders, *Partnerships and Joint Ventures Involving Tax-Exempt Organizations* (1994; New York: John Wiley & Sons, Inc.).

17 IRC § 4941.

18 IRS Private Letter Ruling 9530032.

19 *American Campaign Academy* v. *Commissioner,* 92 T.C. 1053 (1989).

CHAPTER 4

1 *United States* v. *Cruikshank,* 92 U.S. 542, 552 (1976).

2 2 U.S.C. § 267(a).

3 IRC § 4911(d)(1).

4 Reg. § 1.501(c)(3)-1(c)(3).

5 IRC § 4945(e).

6 IRC § 162(e)(1)(A) and (C), (4)(A).

7 IRC § 162(e)(1)(D), (6).

8 In general, see Hopkins, *Charity, Advocacy and the Law* (1992; New York: John Wiley & Sons, Inc.).

9 IRC § 4911(e)(2).

10 Reg. § 1.501(c)(3)-1(c)(3).

11 *Regan* v. *Taxation With Representation of Washington,* 461 U.S. 540 (1983).

12 IRC § 501(c)(3).

13 Reg. § 1.501(c)(3)-1(c)(3)(ii).

14 *E.g., The Nationalist Movement* v. *Commissioner, supra,* Chapter 2, endnote 6.

15 Reg. § 56.4911-2(b)(1)(ii).

16 IRC § 162(e)(1)(D).

17 Reg. § 56.4911-2(b)(2)(ii).

18 2 U.S.C. § 267(a).

19 31 U.S.C. § 1352(a)(1)(A).

20 Circular A-122, "Cost Principles for Nonprofit Organizations—'Lobbying' Revision," 49 *Fed. Reg.* 83 (1984).

21 IRC § 501(c)(3).

22 IRC § 4945(d)(1).

23 IRC § 4945(a), (b).

24 IRC § 4945(e).

25 Rev. Rul. 70-449, 1970-2 C.B. 111.

26 IRC § 4912.

27 These agreements are authorized by IRC § 7121 (see Chapter 12).

28 Reg. § 1.501(c)(3)-1(c)(3)(v).

29 IRC § 4911.

30 IRC § 501(h).

31 Form 5768.

32 IRC § 501(h)(4)(F), (5).

33 IRC § 4911(d)(2).

34 IRC § 4911(a).

35 IRC § 501(h)(1).

36 IRC § 504.

37 Revocation of the election is made on Form 5768 (see *supra* endnote 31).

38 IRC § 162(e)(1)(A), (C).

39 IRC § 162(e)(3).

40 Reg. § 1.162-28.

41 IRC § 162(e)(3).

42 IRC § 6033(e)(1)(A).

43 IRC § 6033(e)(2).

44 IRC § 6033(e)(2)(B).

45 IRC § 6033(e)(3).

46 IRS Revenue Procedure (Rev. Proc.) 95-35, 1995-32 I.R.B. 51, as modified by Rev. Proc. 95-35A, 1995-40 I.R.B. 38.

47 IRC § 162(e)(5)(B).

48 IRC § 162(e)(4)(A).

49 IRC § 170(c)(3).

50 *Regan* v. *Taxation With Representation of Washington,* 461 U.S. 540, 550 (1983).

51 Form 990PF, Part VII, line 1.

52 Form 990, Part VI, line 85.

53 Form 990, Schedule A, Part VI-B.

54 Form 990, Schedule A, Part VI-A.

55 Form 4720.

CHAPTER 5

1 IRC § 501(c)(3). In general, see Hopkins, *Charity, Advocacy and the Law,* *supra,* Chapter 4, endnote 8.

2 IRC § 527(e)(2).

3 IRC § 501(c)(3).

4 Reg. § 1.501(c)(3)-1(c)(3)(iii), (iv).

5 IRC § 4955.

6 IRC § 527.

7 IRC § 162(e)(1)(B).

8 Rev. Rul. 74-117, 1974-1 C.B. 128.

9 Rev. Rul. 67-71, 1967-1 C.B. 125.

10 *Estate of Blaine* v. *Commissioner,* 22 T.C. 1195 (1954).

11 Rev. Rul. 78-248, 1978-1 C.B. 154.

12 Rev. Rul. 80-282, 1980-2 C.B. 178.

13 IRS Gen. Couns. Mem. 38444.

14 *Christian Echoes National Ministry, Inc.* v. *United States,* 470 F.2d 849, 856 (10th Cir. 1972), *cert. denied,* 414 U.S. 864 (1973).

15 "Tax Guide for Churches and Other Religious Organizations," IRS Pub. 1828 (1994).

16 IRC §§ 501(c)(3), 4955(d)(1).

17 Reg. § 53.4946-1(g)(2)(i).

18 2 U.S.C. § 431(2); 11 C.F.R. § 100.3.

19 IRC §§ 501(c)(3), 4955(d)(1).

20 *Norris* v. *United States,* 86 F.2d 379, 382 (8th Cir. 1936), *rev'd on other grounds,* 300 U.S. 564 (1937).

21 For these purposes, the term *expenditure* is very broad, generally meaning any purchase, payment, distribution, loan, advance, deposit, or gift of money or anything of value made by a person for the purpose of influencing an election for public office or an agreement to make such an expenditure (2 U.S.C. § 431(9); 11 C.F.R. § 100.8).

22 IRC §§ 501(c)(3), 4955(d)(1)

23 Reg. §§ 53.4946-1(g)(2)(i), 1.527-2(d).

24 IRS Gen. Couns. Mem. 39811.

25 *Living Faith, Inc.* v. *Commissioner, supra,* Chapter 3, endnote 4.

26 IRC § 4955(a), (b).

27 IRC § 6842.

28 IRC § 7409.

29 IRC §§ 170(b)(1)(A)(i) and 501(c)(3).

30 *E.g., Christian Echoes National Ministry, Inc.* v. *United States,* 470 F.2d 849 (10th Cir. 1972), *cert. den.,* 414 U.S. 864 (1973).

31 *Branch Ministries* v. *United States* (D.D.C.) (No. 1: 95CV00724).

32 IRC § 501(c)(3).

33 IRC §§ 4945(d)(2), 4945(a), (b).

34 IRS Priv. Ltr. Rul. 9244003.

35 IRC § 527(e).

36 IRC § 527(f).

37 2 U.S.C. § 441b(b); 11 C.F.R. § 114.5(b).

38 Federal Election Commission Advisory Opinion 1984-12.

39 IRC § 527(f)(1).

40 IRS Private Letter Ruling 9433001.

41 Rev. Rul. 81-95, 1981-1 C.B. 332.

42 IRS Private Letter Ruling 9433001.

43 Form 990, Part VI, question 81a and b.

44 Form 1120-POL.

45 Form 990PF, Part VII, line 1.

46 Form 990, Part VI, question 85.

CHAPTER 6

1 IRC § 509(a).

2 IRC § 509(a)(1)–(4).

3 IRC §§ 4940–4948.

4 IRC §§ 170(b)(1)(A)(i)–(v), 509(a)(1).

5 Form 1023, Part III, questions 7–13.

6 Form 990, Part IV.

7 IRC § 4945(d)(4)(B), (h).

8 IRC § 4945.

9 IRC § 170(b).

10 IRC §§ 4941–4948.

11 IRC § 4940.

12 Form 990-PF; IRS § 6033(c).

13 IRC § 6104(d).

14 IRC §§ 170(b)(1)(A)(vi), 509(a)(1); Reg. § 1.170A-9(e).

15 Reg. § 1.170A-9(e)(3).

16 Reg. § 1.170A-9(e)(10)-(14).

17 IRC § 509(a)(2); Reg. § 1.509(a)-3.

18 IRC § 509(d).

19 IRC § 4946.

20 IRC § 507(d)(2).

21 IRC § 509(a)(2)(B); Reg. § 1.509(a)-3(a)(3).

22 IRC § 509(a)(2)(B).

23 Reg. §§ 1.170A-9(e)(5) (donative organizations), 1.509(a)-3(e)(1) (service provider organizations).

24 Form 1023, instructions as to line 11.

25 Form 8734.

26 Form 1023, instructions as to line 11.

27 IRC § 642(c)(5)(A).

28 Reg. § 1.642(c)(5)-5(a)(5)(iv).

29 IRC § 4942(j)(3).

30 IRC § 4940(d).

31 IRC § 509(a)(3); Reg. § 1.509(a)-4.

32 Reg. § 1.509(a)-4(c).

33 Reg. § 1.509(a)-4(e).

34 Reg. § 1.509(a)-4(f)(2).

35 Reg. § 1.509(a)-4(g).

36 Reg. § 1.509(a)-4(h).

37 Reg. § 1.509(a)-4(i).

38 Reg. § 1.509(a)-4(i)(2).

39 Reg. § 1.509(a)-4(i)(3).

40 Reg. § 1.509(a)-4(1)(3)(iii); Rev. Rul. 76-208, 1976-1 C.B. 161.

41 Reg. § 1.509(a)-4(e)(2).

42 *E.g.,* IRS Priv. Ltr. Rul. 8825116.

43 There are tens of IRS private letter rulings on this point. The practice has become so widespread that Congress is likely to create a separate category of public charity status just for them (new IRC § 509(a)(4)).

44 IRS Priv. Ltr. Rul. 9442025.

45 IRS Priv. Ltr. Rul. 9438013.

46 Reg. § 1.509(a)-4(d).

47 *William F., Mable E., and Margaret K. Quarrie Charitable Fund* v. *Commissioner,* 70 T.C. 182, 187 (1978), *aff'd,* 603 F.2d 1274 (7th Cir. 1979).

48 Reg. § 1.509(a)-4(e)(1).

49 IRC § 509(a)(3)(A).

50 See *supra,* endnote 48.

51 IRC § 509(a), last sentence; Reg. § 1.509(a)-4(k).

52 IRC § 509(a)(3)(C); Reg. § 1.509(a)-4(j).

53 Rev. Rul. 80-207, 1980-2 C.B. 193.

54 Rev. Rul. 80-305, 1980-2 C.B. 71.

CHAPTER 7

1 *Village of Schaumburg* v. *Citizens for a Better Environment,* 444 U.S. 620 (1980); *Secretary of State of Maryland* v. *Joseph H. Munson Co., Inc.,* 467 U.S. 947 (1984); *Riley* v. *National Federation of the Blind of North Carolina, Inc.,* 487 U.S. 781 (1988). In general, Chapter 5 of Hopkins, *The Law of Fund-Raising,* 2d. ed. (1995; New York: John Wiley & Sons, Inc.).

2 Form 9215.

3 Internal Revenue Manual, Exempt Organizations Handbook 7(10)(69), availability noted Ann. 94-112, 1994-37 I.R.B. 36.

4 IRC § 170(f)(8). These rules are the subject of § 21.1(b) of Hopkins, *The Tax Law of Charitable Giving*, Chapter 1, endnote 11.

5 IRS Notice 95-15, 1995-15 I.R.B. 22.

6 Prop. Reg. § 1.170A-13(f)(6).

7 Prop. Reg. § 1.170A-13(f)(13).

8 IRC § 6115. These rules are the subject of § 22.1(b) of Hopkins, *supra* endnote 4.

9 IRC § 6701.

10 Prop. Reg. § 1.6115-1(a).

11 Rev. Proc. 92-49, 1992-1 C.B. 987; Rev. Proc. 90-12, 1990-1 C.B. 471; Prop. Reg. § 1.170A-13(f)(8)(i)(A).

12 IRC § 513(h)(2).

13 Prop. Reg. §§ 1.6115-1(b), 1.170A-13(f)(8)(i)(B)(1).

14 Prop. Reg. §§ 1.6115-1(b), 1.170A-13(f)(8)(i)(B)(2).

15 Prop. Reg. § 1.6115-1(a)(3).

16 Reg. § 1.170A-13(c).

17 IRC § 508(a).

18 Form 1023, Part II, question 3.

19 Form 1023, Part IV, question 14.

20 IRC § 6033(b).

21 Form 990, Part II, line 30.

22 Form 990, Part I, line 9, and accompanying instructions.

23 *Executive Network Club, Inc.* v. *Commissioner,* 69 T.C.M. 1680 (1995).

24 IRC § 512(b)(2).

25 *Sierra Club, Inc.* v. *Commissioner,* 103 T.C. 307 (1994), on appeal to the 9th Cir.

26 *Sierra Club, Inc.* v. *Commissioner,* 65 T.C.M. 2582 (1993).

27 *Sierra Club, Inc.* v. *Commissioner* (1994), *supra* note 25; *Sierra Club, Inc.* v. *Commissioner* (1993) *supra,* note 26; *Disabled American Veterans* v. *Commissioner,* 94 T.C. 60 (1990), *rev'd on other grounds,* 942 F.2d 309 (6th Cir. 1991).

28 IRC § 6113.

29 IRC § 6710.

30 Domestic Mail Manual § E370, Issue 48 (Jan. 1, 1995).

31 15 U.S.C. § 6101 *et seq.*

32 FTC Rule § 310.3.

33 *National Federation of Nonprofits* v. *Lungren* (N.D. Cal., order issued Mar. 29, 1995).

34 *Kentucky State Police Professional Association* v. *Gorman,* 870 F. Supp. 166 (E.D. Ky. 1994).

35 *Center for Auto Safety* v. *Athey,* 37 F.3d 139, 144, n. 9 (4th Cir. 1994).

36 In general, see § 9.8 of Hopkins, *The Law of Fund-Raising, supra,* n. 1.

CHAPTER 8

1 IRC § 170(f)(2)(A) and (B).

2 IRC § 664(c).

3 Reg. § 1.664-1(c).

4 *Lelia G. Newhall Charitable Trust* v. *Commissioner,* 104 T.C. 236 (1995).

5 IRC § 664.

6 Reg. §§ 20.2031-7(d)(6) and 1.642(c)-6(e)(2).

7 IRC § 642(c)(5).

8 IRC § 170(f)(2)(A).

9 IRC § 514(c)(5).

10 IRC § 501(m)(3)(E), (5).

11 IRC § 170(f)(3)(B)(i), (ii), and (iii).

12 IRC § 514(c).

13 IRS Priv. Ltr. Rul. 9501004.

14 IRC § 170(a)(3).

15 IRC § 170(e)(1)(B)(i).

16 *E.g.,* IRS Priv. Ltr. Rul. 9452026.

17 IRC § 170(b)(1)(C)(i) and (D)(i); the limitations on gifts of money are in IRC § 170(b)(1)(A) and (B).

18 IRS Notice 94-78, 1994-32 I.R.B. 15.

19 IRC § 642(c)(5)(A).

20 Reg. § 1.642(c)-6(e)(2)(ii).

21 IRC § 7520.

22 Rev. Rul. 94-41, 1994-1 C.B. 181.

CHAPTER 9

1 Reg. § 1.170A-1(g); *Grant* v. *Commissioner,* 69 T.C.M. 1716 (1985).

2 IRC § 170(e)(1)(A).

3 Form 990, Part VI, question 82.

4 Reg. § 1.170A-7(a)(1).

5 Form 990, Part VI, question 82.

6 Reg. § 1.170A-1(b).

7 *Morrison* v. *Commissioner,* 53 T.C.M. 251 (1987).

8 *Estate of Sawade* v. *Commissioner,* 795 F.2d 45 (8th Cir. 1986); *Greer* v. *Commissioner,* 70 T.C. 294 (1978), *aff'd on another issue,* 634 F.2d 1044 (6th Cir. 1980); *Londen* v. *Commissioner,* 45 T.C. 106 (1965).

9 *McCall* v. *United States,* 72-1 U.S.T.C. ¶ 9263 (D.S.C. 1972).

10 See Greenfield, *Fund-Raising: Evaluating and Managing the Fund Development Process* 79-83 (1991; New York: John Wiley & Sons, Inc.).

11 IRC § 6050L.

12 Rev. Rul. 89-51, 1989-1 C.B. 89.

13 Prop. Reg. § 1.170A-1(h)(1).

14 IRC § 6701.

15 IRC § 6115.

16 Form 990, Part I, line 9.

17 IRC § 6104(e)(1). Applications for recognition of tax exemption are also publicly accessible (IRC § 6104(e)(2)).

18 IRS Notice 95-33, 1995-23 I.R.B. 10.

19 Reflecting a different view, an article stated that the Foundation for New Era Philanthropy and United Way of America scandals "have increased the scrutiny of nonprofits"; the analysis found nonprofit organizations "flouting government regulations, fat salaries for executives, [and] cozy deal making with for-profit companies through private contracting arrangements" ("Tax Exempt!," U.S. News & World Report, Oct. 2, 1995, 36, 39, 51).

CHAPTER 10

1 *E.g., The Nationalist Movement* v. *Commissioner, supra,* Chapter 2, endnote 6.

2 IRC §§ 501(c)(2) (last sentence), 501(c)(25)(G).

3 Reg. § 1.513-1(b).

4 IRC § 513(c).

5 *American Academy of Family Physicians* v. *United States,* 95-1 U.S.T.C. ¶ 50,240 (W.D. Mo. 1995).

6 IRC § 513(c).

7 *Commissioner* v. *Groetzinger,* 480 U.S. 23 (1987).

8 *E.g., National Water Well Association, Inc.* v. *Commissioner,* 92 T.C. 75 (1989); *West Virginia State Medical Association* v. *Commissioner,* 91 T.C. 651 (1988), *aff'd,* 882 F.2d 123 (4th Cir. 1989).

9 Reg. § 1.513-1(b).

10 *E.g., Clarence LaBelle Post No. 217* v. *United States,* 580 F.2d 270 (8th Cir. 1978).

11 *E.g., Carolinas Farm & Power Equipment Dealers Ass'n, Inc.* v. *United States,* 699 F.2d 167 (4th Cir. 1983).

12 Cf. *Consumer Credit Counseling Service of Alabama, Inc.* v. *United States,* 78-2 U.S.T.C. ¶ 9660 (D.D.C. 1978), where this position was rejected.

13 *Living Faith, Inc.* v. *Commissioner, supra,* Chapter 3, endnote 4.

14 IRC § 501(m).

15 *Paratransit Insurance Corporation* v. *Commissioner,* 102 T.C. 745 (1994); *Florida Hospital Trust Fund et al.* v. *Commissioner,* 103 T.C. 140 (1994); *Non-profits' Insurance Alliance of California,* 94-2 U.S.T.C. ¶ 50,593 (U.S. Ct. Fed. Cl. (1994)).

16 Reg. § 1.513-1(c)(1).

17 Reg. § 1.513-1(c).

18 Rev. Rul. 60-228, 1960-1 C.B. 200.

19 Reg. § 1.513-1(c)(2).

20 Reg. § 1.513-1(c)(2)(i).

21 IRS Tech. Adv. Mem. 9147007; IRS Priv. Ltr. Rul. 9137002.

22 IRS Gen. Couns. Mem. 39860.

23 *National Collegiate Athletic Association* v. *Commissioner,* 914 F.2d 1417 (10th Cir. 1990).

24 IRS Action on Decision (AOD) 1991-015.

25 IRC § 513(a); Reg. § 1.513-1(a).

26 Reg. § 1.513-1(d)(10), (2).

27 Reg. § 1.513-1(d)(1), (2). *E.g.,* Rev. Rul. 75-472, 1975-2 C.B. 208.

28 Rev. Rul. 78-51, 1978-1 C.B. 165.

29 *San Antonio Bar Association* v. *United States,* 80-2 U.S.T.C. ¶ 9594 (W.D. Tex. 1980).

30 *Texas Apartment Association* v. *United States,* 869 F.2d 884 (5th Cir. 1989).

31 Rev. Rul. 78-52, 1978-1 C.B. 166.

32 Rev. Rul. 66-338, 1966-2 C.B. 226.

33 Rev. Rul. 61-170, 1961-2 C.B. 112.

34 IRS Priv. Let. Rul. 8503103.

35 *E.g., Oklahoma Cattlemen's Association, Inc.* v. *United States,* 310 F. Supp. 320 (W.D. Okl. 1969).

36 IRS Priv. Let. Rul. 7902006.

37 IRS Priv. Let. Rul. 9023081.

38 Reg. § 1.513-1(d)(3).

39 Rev. Rul. 73-386, 1973-2 C.B. 191, 192.

40 Rev. Rul. 76-94, 1976-1 C.B. 171.

41 Reg. § 1.513-1(d)(4)(ii).

42 E.g., Rev. Rul. 78-98, 1978-1 C.B. 167.

43 Reg. § 1.513-1(d)(4)(iii).

44 Reg. § 1.513-1(d)(4)(iv).

45 IRC §§ 1, 11.

46 IRC § 512(b)(12).

47 IRC § 512(a)(1).

48 Reg. § 1.512(a)-1(a).

49 *E.g., Rensselaer Polytechnic Institute* v. *Commissioner,* 732 F.2d 1058 (2d Cir. 1984), *aff'g,* 79 T.C. 967 (1982).

50 IRC § 512(b)(10), (11).

51 Form 990-T.

52 IRC § 6154(h); Form 990-W.

53 IRC § 512(b)(7), (8), and (9).

54 IRC § 512(a)(5).

55 IRC § 513(a)(1).

56 *Executive Network Club, Inc.* v. *Commissioner, supra,* Chapter 7, endnote 23.

57 IRC § 513(a)(2).

58 IRC § 513(a)(3).

59 Rev. Rul. 71-581, 1971-2 C.B. 236.

60 IRC § 513(a)(2).

61 IRC § 513(d)(2).

62 IRC § 513(d)(3).

63 IRC § 513(e).

64 IRC § 513(f).

65 IRC § 513(g).

66 IRC § 513(h)(1)(A).

67 IRC § 513(h)(1)(B).

68 IRC § 512(b)(1)-(3), (5).

69 Reg. § 1.513-1(b).

70 Reg. § 1.512(b)-1(c)(5).

71 *E.g., Harlan E. Moore Charitable Trust* v. *United States,* 9 F.3d 623 (7th Cir. 1993). The IRS has basically given up on this battle (AOD 1994-001).

72 *Disabled American Veterans* v. *Commissioner, supra,* Chapter 7, endnote 27.

73 *Sierra Club, Inc.* v. *Commissioner, supra,* Chapter 7, endnote 26.

74 *Sierra Club, Inc.* v. *Commissioner, supra,* Chapter 7, endnote 25.

75 This approach was tacitly endorsed in *Texas Farm Bureau* v. *United States,* 53 F.3d 120 (5th Cir. 1995).

76 IRC § 512(b)(13).

77 IRC § 368(c).

78 Reg. § 1.512(b)-1(1)(4).

79 IRC § 514.

80 See *supra* note 68.

81 IRC § 512(b)(4).

82 *E.g.,* IRS Priv. Ltr. Rul. 9506046.

83 IRC § 513(h)(1)(B).

84 IRS Tech. Adv. Mem. 9502009.

85 Form 990 or Form 990EZ.

86 Form 990-T.

CHAPTER 11

1 IRC § 512(b)(13).

2 IRC § 368(c).

3 Reg. § 1.512(b)-1(1)(2).

4 IRC § 512(b)(5).

5 IRS Priv. Ltr. Rul. 9438029.

6 IRC § 337(b)(2)(B).

7 Form 1120.

8 *Id.,* Schedule K, lines 4, 5.

9 Form 990.

10 *Id.,* Part VI, line 80.

11 Form 990-T.

12 Form 990, Part IV, line 54.

13 *Id.*, Part V.

14 *Id.*, Part VI, question 80.

15 *Id.*, Part IX.

16 *Id.*, Schedule A, Part VII.

17 IRC § 6113.

18 IRC § 6711.

19 IRC § 512(a)(1).

20 IRS Tech. Adv. Mem. 8939002.

21 IRC § 168(h).

22 IRC § 168(h)(6)(F)(ii)(I).

23 *E.g.,* IRS Priv. Ltr. Rul. 8505044.

24 IRC § 509(a)(3)(A).

25 Reg. § 1.509(a)-4(e)(1).

26 IRS Priv. Ltr. Rul. 9305026.

27 IRC § 4943.

28 IRC § 4943 (d)(3)(B).

29 IRC §§ 4942 (j)(4), 4943 (d)(3)(A).

CHAPTER 12

1 Reg. § 601.101(a).

2 IRC § 7802(a).

3 IRC § 7802(b).

4 IRC § 7601(a).

5 Internal Revenue Manual 7(10)69 (Examination Guidelines Handbook).

6 IRC § 7602(a).

7 IRC § 7602(a)(1) or (2).

8 Examination Guidelines Handbook § 164.

9 Reg. § 601.105(b)(2) and (3).

10 Examination Guidelines Handbook § 166.

11 Reg. §§ 601.105(b)(5) and 601.201(n)(9).

12 Reg. § 601.105(b)(4); Examination Guidelines Handbook § 169.

13 Examination Guidelines Handbook § 333 (Hospital Audit Guidelines), reproduced by the IRS for broader dissemination in Ann. 92-83, 1992-22 I.R.B. 59. In general, see Chapter 35 § 2 of Hyatt and Hopkins, *The Law of Tax-Exempt Healthcare Organizations* (1995; New York: John Wiley & Sons, Inc.).

14 Hospital Audit Guidelines § 333.1(1)-(8).

15 *Id.* § 333.2(1)–3(6).

16 *Id.* § 333.4(1)–(3).

17 *Id.* § 333.4(4)–(8).

18 42 U.S.C. § 1320a-7b(b).

19 Hospital Audit Guidelines § 333.5.

20 *Id.* § 333.6.

21 See *supra,* endnote 13.

22 *Id.* § 333.7.

23 These 11 forms are 720 (quarterly federal excise tax return), 990 (annual information returns) of related tax-exempt organizations (such as the hospital's development foundation or an auxiliary), 990 (prior and subsequent returns of the hospital under audit), 990-T (prior and subsequent unrelated business income tax returns of the hospital under audit), 1120 (corporate income tax return, for a taxable subsidiary), 1120 POL (income tax return for certain political organizations), 2290 (highway use tax), 5578 (annual certification of private school), 5768 (lobbying election), 8282 (donee information return), and 8300 (report of cash payments over $10,000 received in a trade or business).

24 Hospital Audit Guidelines § 333.8.

25 IRC § 7121.

26 Reg. § 301.7121-1(a).

27 Rev. Proc. 68-16, 1968-1 C.B. 770.

28 Ann. 94-112, 1994-37 I.R.B. 36.

29 OMB Circular A-21.

30 IRC § 170(1).

31 IRC § 170(e)(3).

32 IRC § 117(d)(5).

Index

Accelerated assessment rules, Q 5:10
Accelerated remainder trusts, Q 8:18
Acquisition indebtedness, Q 8:15
Action organizations, Q 4:4, Q 4:20, Q 4:25,
    Q 5:2
Advance ruling period, Q 6:9, Q 6:10
Advance rulings, Q 6:9, Q 6:10
Affinity card programs, Q 10:24
Agents, Q 10:17
American Council on Gift Annuities, Q 8:9
Annual information return:
    preparation of, Q 9:17
    questions in, Q 3:8, Q 4:34–Q 4:36, Q 7:15
Anticipatory assignment of income, Q 7:4
Appraisal requirement, Q 1:43, Q 7:13, Q 9:7,
    Q 12:26
Appreciated property, Q 8:4
Articles of incorporation, Q 1:5, Q 6:18
Articles of organization, Q 1:5
Associate member dues, Q 10:31
Auctions, charity, Q 9:5–Q 9:12
Audits, IRS:
    balance sheet analysis, Q 12:18
    colleges and universities, Q 12:22–Q 12:29
    financial analyses, Q 12:17
    fund-raising, Q 7:4
    in general, Q 12:1–Q 12:29
    health care organizations, Q 12:12–Q 12:21
    initiation, Q 12:4, Q 12:5, Q 12:23
    likelihood of, Q 12:11
    results of, Q 12:10
    scope of, Q 12:6, Q 12:20, Q 12:24–Q 12:29
    types of, Q 12:7

Bargain sale, Q 8:9, Q 8:21
Bifurcation, Q 4:26, Q 10:25, Q 11:2, Q 11:13

Bishop Estate, Q 9:19
Board of directors:
    board of trustees, termed, Q 2:14
    classes of members, Q 1:23
    conflicts of interest, Q 2:28–Q 2:38
    good faith standard, Q 2:42
    expenditures, supervision of,
        Q 2:15–Q 2:26, Q 3:8, Q 3:11
    function of, Q 2:4
    immunity of, Q 2:41
    indemnification of, Q 2:41
    insurance for, Q 2:41
    liability of, Q 2:39–Q 2:42
    meetings of, Q 2:26
    members of, Q 1:23, Q 2:2, Q 2:3,
        Q 2:7, Q 6:23, Q 6:26, Q 9:16, Q 11:5
    minutes of meetings, Q 2:13
    mistakes by, Q 2:39
    origin of, Q 2:1, Q 2:5, Q 2:6
    organizational meeting, Q 1:5
    self-perpetuating, Q 2:1
    voting by, Q 2:11, Q 2:12
Bonuses, Q 3:9–Q 3:12
Business, definition of, Q 10:6–Q 10:12
Business expense deduction rules,
    Q 4:1, Q 4:6, Q 4:27–Q 4:31, Q 5:20
Business leagues:
    lobbying by, Q 4:27–Q 4:31
    purpose of, Q 1:39
    supporting organization for, Q 6:21
Bylaws, Q 1:5, Q 6:25
Byrd Amendment, Q 4:8

Campaign, definition of, Q 5:1, Q 5:7
Candidate, definition of, Q 5:6
Capital gain property, Q 1:43

INDEX

Catholic Church, Q 9:19
Celebrity, value of role of, Q 7:12
Cemetery companies, Q 1:41
Certificate of authority, Q 1:14
Certification programs, Q 11:13
Chapters, Q 1:24, Q 1:25, Q 4:9, Q 4:15
Charitable gift annuities, Q 8:9
Charitable giving:
  auctions, gifts to, Q 9:7
  auctions, by means of, Q 9:8
  audit issues, Q 12:26
  eligible donees, Q 1:41
  foreign charities, Q 11:13
  money, gifts of, Q 1:42
  planned giving, Q 1:44, Q 8:1–Q 8:31
  property, gifts of, Q 1:43
  restricted gifts, Q 9:3
  right to use property, gifts of, Q 9:2, Q 9:7
  rules in general, Q 7:5
  securities, valuation of, Q 9:4
  services, gifts of, Q 9:1
Charitable lead trusts, Q 8:8
Charitable organizations:
  definition of, Q 1:38, Q 1:39, Q 1:41
  donees, qualification as, Q 1:41
Charitable remainder trusts:
  advantages of, Q 8:21
  definition of, Q 8:6
  disadvantages to, Q 8:22
  donors to, Q 8:19
  in general, Q 8:4–Q 8:6
  gift properties, Q 8:14–Q 8:17
  make-up feature, Q 8:13
  options, transfer of, Q 8:16
  remainder interest beneficiaries, Q 8:12
  short-term trusts, Q 8:18
  taxation of, Q 8:5
  trustees of, Q 8:20
Charitable sales promotions, Q 7:25
Charitable solicitation acts:
  charitable sales promotions, Q 7:25
  contracts, contents of, Q 7:28
  effectiveness of, Q 7:36, Q 9:19
  elements of, Q 7:20
  exceptions, Q 7:27
  fees, limitations on, Q 7:24
  in general, Q 7:20–Q 7:38
  legends, Q 7:20
  management system for, Q 7:37
  police power of the states, Q 7:3, Q 7:31
  prohibited acts, Q 7:26
  registration requirements, Q 7:20
  reporting requirements, Q 7:20
  sanctions, Q 7:34
Chartering, Q 1:24
Churches, Q 5:4, Q 5:5, Q 5:11–Q 5:13, Q 9:12
Closely held corporations, Q 2:6
Closing agreements, Q 4:12, Q 5:10, Q 12:21

Colleges:
  audits of, Q 12:22–Q 12:29
  lobbying by, Q 12:27
  political activities of, Q 12:28
  unrelated business rules, Q 10:29, 12:28
Commensurate test, Q 2:16
Commercial activities, Q 6:12, Q 10:11,
  Q 10:12
Commercial co-venturers, Q 7:25
Commercial-type insurance, Q 8:9,
  Q 10:12
Community benefit standard, Q 12:13
Community foundations, Q 6:7
Compensation arrangements, Q 3:8–Q 3:14
Competitive bidding, Q 2:26
Conflict of interest policies:
  breach of, Q 2:35
  charitable gifts in connection with,
    Q 2:36
  enforcement of, Q 2:31
  purchases in connection with, Q 2:37,
    Q 2:38
  statement, contents of, Q 2:30
Conflicts of interest:
  audit issue, Q 12:26
  definition of, Q 2:28
  disclosure of, Q 2:29, Q 2:33, Q 2:34
  identification of, Q 2:32
  penalties for, Q 2:35
Consideration, Q 7:7
Constitution, Q 1:5
Control of organizations, Q 1:3,
  Q 1:22, Q 1:23, Q 4:26, Q 11:1, Q 11:3
Convenience doctrine, Q 7:16, Q 10:23
Conversions, Q 4:13, Q 4:19, Q 4:25
Coordinated examination program, Q 12:7,
  Q 12:8
Corporate sponsorships, Q 10:29
Corporations, charitable gifts by, Q 1:42,
  Q 1:43
Cost consciousness test, Q 2:18–Q 2:23

Declaration of trust, Q 1:5
Definitive rulings, Q 6:11
Directors:
  borrowing by, Q 2:24, Q 3:15
  function of, Q 2:4
  identity of, Q 1:8, Q 1:12
  liability of, Q 2:39–Q 2:42
  origin of, Q 2:1, Q 2:7, Q 2:8
  purchases from, Q 2:25
  rentals from, Q 2:25, Q 3:16
  rentals to, Q 3:16
Disqualified persons, definition of,
  Q 2:27, Q 3:2, Q 3:14, Q 6:8, Q6:23
Doing business, Q 1:13, Q 1:14
Donative intent, Q 9:8
Donative organizations, Q 6:7

Donor recognition, Q 3:21
Dual use test, Q 10:21

Employee compensation, Q 2:17
Endowment funds, Q 11:19
Episcopalian Church, Q 9:19
Equal protection doctrine, Q 4:33, Q 7:27
Excess benefit transactions, Q 3:14
Excess business holdings, Q 11:24
Executive committees, Q 2:4
Exempt functions, Q 1:1, Q 2:16, Q 5:4,
    Q 5:16, Q 10:3
Ex officio, definition of, Q 2:1, Q 9:16, Q 11:3
Expenditure responsibility, Q 6:6
Expenditures of funds, Q 2:15–Q 2:26
Expenditure test, Q 4:15–Q 4:23
Exploitation test, Q 10:21

Facts and circumstances test, Q 2:2, Q 2:5,
    Q 6:7, Q6:13, Q 7:19
Federal election laws, Q 5:23
Federal Regulation of Lobbying Act, Q 4:1,
    Q 4:8, Q 4:34
Federal telemarketing laws, Q 7:19
Fiduciary, definition of, Q 1:18, Q 1:21, Q 2:4
Fiduciary responsibility, Q 1:18, Q 1:19,
    Q 1:21, Q 2:39, Q 11:7
Fifth Amendment, U.S. Constitution, Q 5:13
First Amendment, U.S. Constitution, Q 4:1,
    Q 5:13, Q 7:3
Flow-through rule, Q 4:27
Foreign state, Q 1:13, Q 1:14
Formation, state of, Q 1:13
Forms:
    720, Q 12:19
    990, Q 3:8, Q 3:12, Q 4:34–Q 4:36,
        Q 5:24, Q 5:25, Q 6:5, Q 7:15,
        Q 9:1, Q 9:2, Q 9:12, Q 10:33,
        Q 11:10, Q 12:19
    990EZ, Q 10:33
    990PF, Q 4:34, Q 5:24, Q 6:6
    990-T, Q 10:22, Q 10:33, Q 11:10, Q 12:19
    990-W, Q 10:22
    1023, Q 6:4, Q 6:9, Q 6:11, Q 7:14
    1024, Q 1:31
    1120, Q 11:10, Q 12:19
    1120-POL, Q 5:24, Q 12:19
    2290, Q 12:19
    4720, Q 4:36
    5578, Q 12:19
    5768, Q 4:16, Q 4:22, Q 12:19
    8282, Q 12:19
    8300, Q 12:19
    8734, Q 6:9
    9215, Q 7:4
For-profit organization, definition of, Q 1:1
Foundation managers, Q 3:2
Fragmentation rule, Q 10:7

Fraternal organizations, Q 1:41
Free speech, Q 4:1, Q 7:3
Front-page-of-the-newspaper test, Q 2:18,
    Q 2:24, Q 2:36
Functionally related business, Q 11:24
Fund-raising:
    disclosure by noncharitable organizations,
        Q 7:18
    regulation, by federal government, Q 7:1,
        Q 7:4–Q 7:19
    regulation, by state governments, Q 7:2,
        Q 7:3, Q 7:20–Q 7:38
    related foundation, use of, Q 1:40, Q 11:13
    supporting organization, use of, Q 6:17, Q
        11:13
    unrelated business rules, Q 7:16, Q 10:32

Good faith estimate, Q 7:10, Q 9:9, Q 9:10
Good faith standard, Q 2:42
Grantor trust rules, Q 8:6, Q 8:20, Q 8:22
Group exemption, Q 1:25

Hard money, definition of, Q 5:22
Health care organizations:
    audits of, Q 12:12–Q 12:21
    closing agreements, Q 12:21
    unrelated business activities, Q 10:28
Hotels, expenditures for, Q 2:22

Identification number, Q 1:25
Immunity, Q 2:41
Incidental gifts, Q 7:11
Income interests, Q 8:2
Incorporation, Q 1:6, Q 1:25, Q 2:41, Q 6:23,
    Q 11:4
Incorporators, Q 1:7, Q 1:8, Q 1:12
Indemnification, Q 2:41
Individuals, charitable gifts by, Q 1:42,
    Q 1:43
Injunction, IRS, Q 5:10
Insiders, Q 2:17, Q 2:27, Q 3:1, Q 3:2,
    Q 12:14
Institutions, Q 6:3
Insurable interest, Q 8:10
Insurance, Q 2:41, Q 9:13
Intangible religious benefits, Q 7:11
Intermediate sanctions, Q 2:17, Q 3:8, Q 3:14
Internal Revenue Service organization,
    Q 12:1
    audits by, Q 12:1–Q 12:29
Intervention, definition of, Q 5:3
Inventory, gifts of, Q 1:43, Q 12:26

Joint ventures:
    audit issue, Q 12:15
    involvement in, Q 3:17, Q 7:25

Key districts, Q 12:1

Labor organizations, Q 4:30, Q 5:2
Lawyers:
    compensation of, Q 1:27
    role of, Q 1:26, Q 2:17
    selection of, Q 9:18
Legal standard of operations:
    charitable organizations, Q 1:16, Q 1:17
    nonprofit organizations in general, Q 1:15
Legislation, definition of, Q 4:2
Life insurance, gifts of, Q 8:10
Liability:
    in general, Q 1:11
    personal, Q 1:11, Q 2:40–Q 2:42
Loans by charitable organizations, Q 2:24,
    Q 3:15
Lobbying:
    appropriateness of, Q 4:3, Q 9:20
    audit issue, Q 12:27
    business leagues, by, Q 4:27–Q 4:31,
        Q 11:13
    call to action, Q 4:6
    definition of, Q 4:1, Q 4:6, Q 4:7, Q 4:31
    direct, Q 4:6
    exceptions to, Q 4:11, Q 4:17
    excessive, Q 1:35, Q 4:5, Q 4:18
    expenditure test, Q 4:15–Q 4:23
    grass roots, Q 4:6
    planning in connection with, Q 4:14,
        Q 4:23
    private foundations, by, Q 4:10
    reporting requirements, Q 4:34–Q 4:36
    social welfare organizations, by,
        Q 4:13, Q 4:24–Q 4:26, Q 11:13
    substantial part test, Q 4:9–Q 4:14
    tax-exempt organizations, in general,
        Q 4:4, Q 4:8
    veterans' organizations, by, Q 4:32, Q 4:33
Low-cost articles, Q 7:11, Q 10:23

Mailing lists, Q 10:23, Q10:24
Meals, expenditures for, Q 2:23
Memberships, Q 1:23, Q 1:37, Q 1:39, Q 11:3
Minutes of board meetings, Q 2:13
Modifications, Q 10:23, Q 10:24

Net earnings, Q 3:1
New Era for Philanthropy Foundation,
    Q 9:19
Nonprofit organizations:
    control of, Q 1:3, Q 1:22, Q 1:23
    definition of, Q 1:1, Q 3:1
    incorporation of, Q 1:6
    legal standard of operations, Q 1:15–Q 1:17
    members of, Q 1:23
    ownership of, Q 1:2
    starting, Q 1:5, Q 1:13
    stock-based, Q 1:2, Q 1:13, Q 1:23
Not-for-profit activities, Q 1:4

Office of Management and Budget, Q 4:8
Officers:
    function of, Q 2:4, Q 2:9
    identity of, Q 1:8, Q 1:12, Q 2:10
Operational tests, Q 3:4, Q 6:15
Ordinary income property, Q 1:43
Organizational tests, Q 1:5, Q 6:15, Q 6:18

Partial interests, Q 8:1, Q 8:2
Participation, definition of, Q 5:3
Partnerships:
    direct involvement in, Q 3:17
    subsidiaries in, Q 11:21
Percentage limitations, charitable giving,
    Q 1:42, Q 1:43, Q 8:17
Per se private inurement, Q 3:10
Planned giving:
    charitable gift annuities, Q 8:9
    charitable lead trusts, Q 8:8
    charitable remainder trusts, Q 8:4–Q 8:6,
        Q 8:12–Q 8:22
    definition of, Q 1:44, Q 8:1
    farms, Q 8:11
    income interests, Q 8:2
    life insurance, Q 8:10
    personal residences, Q 8:11
    pooled income funds, Q 8:7, Q 8:23–Q 8:30
    remainder interests, Q 8:2–Q 8:4
    split-interest trusts, Q 8:3
    tax advantages, Q 8:4
Police power of the states, Q 7:3, Q 7:29,
    Q 7:31
Political action committees, Q 5:15, Q 5:17,
    Q 5:21, Q 9:20
Political activities:
    audit issue, Q 12:27
    business leagues, by, Q 5:17
    definition of, Q 5:1, Q 5:3, Q 5:9, Q 5:10
    individuals, by, Q 5:5
    private foundations, by, Q 5:14
    religious organizations, by, Q 5:4,
        Q 5:11–Q 5:13
    reporting requirements, Q 5:24, Q 5:25
    social welfare organizations, by, Q 5:16
    tax-exempt organizations, in general, Q 5:2
Political organizations, Q 5:15–Q 5:18,
    Q 5:21, Q 11:13
Political organizations tax, Q 5:18
Pooled income funds:
    advantages of, Q 8:29
    disadvantages to, Q 8:30
    donors to, Q 8:26
    in general, Q 1:40, Q 8:7, Q 8:23–Q 8:30
    gift properties, Q 8:24
    rates of return, new funds, Q 8:25
    remainder interest beneficiaries, Q 8:23,
        Q 8:28
    trustees of, Q 8:27

Postal laws, Q 7:19
Preparatory time, Q 10:16
President, role of, Q 2:9
Primary, definition of, Q 10:1
Principal-agent relationship, Q 10:17
Private benefit:
  audit issue, Q 12:14
  charitable giving and, Q 3:21
  consequences of, Q 3:6
  definition of, Q 3:4, Q 3:5, Q 3:18
  excessive compensation as, Q 2:17
  incidental, Q 3:22
  primary, Q 3:19
  secondary, Q 3:20
Private foundations:
  classification as, Q 6:6
  definition of, Q 2:6, Q 6:2
  lobbying by, Q 4:10
  political activities by, Q 5:14
  subsidiaries of, Q 11:24
Private inurement:
  audit issue, Q 12:14, Q 12:16
  consequences of, Q 3:6
  definition of, Q 1:1, Q 1:2, Q 3:1, Q 3:5
  excessive compensation as, Q 2:17,
    Q 3:8–Q 3:14
  joint ventures, involvement in, Q 3:17
  loans as, Q 3:15
  organizations involved, Q 3:3
  partnerships, involvement in, Q 3:17
  per se, Q 3:10
  provision of services as, Q 3:17
  rentals as, Q 3:16
  transactions, in general, Q 3:7
Professional fund-raisers:
  annual return, role in preparing, Q 9:17
  definition of, Q 1:18, Q 7:22
  regulation, combatting of, Q 9:29
Professional solicitors, definition of, Q 7:23
Profit-making:
  entity level, Q 1:1
  ownership level, Q 1:1
Profit motive, Q 10:8, Q 10:9
Prohibited acts, Q 7:26
Proxy tax, Q 4:29, Q 4:30
Prudent person rule, Q 1:16, Q 1:19, Q 2:18,
  Q 2:26
Public charities:
  definition of, Q 6:1, Q 6:3
  institutions, Q 6:3
  lobbying by, Q 4:9–Q 4:36
  political activities by, Q 5:2–Q 5:15
  publicly supported organizations,
    Q 6:7–Q 6:14
  supporting organizations, Q 6:15–Q 6:28
Public charity status:
  acquisition of, Q 6:4
  advantages of, Q 6:6

loss of, Q 6:13, Q 6:14
maintenance of, Q 6:5
Public office, definition of, Q 5:8
Publicly supported charities:
  donative organizations, Q 6:7
  in general, Q 6:7–Q 6:14, Q 6:12
  service provider organizations, Q 6:8
Purchases by charitable organizations,
  Q 2:25, Q 2:26, Q 2:37, Q 2:38

Qualified appreciated stock, Q 1:43
Qualified conservation contributions, Q 8:11
Quid pro quo contributions, Q 1:43, Q 7:7,
  Q 7:8, Q 9:10, Q 12:26

Reasonableness standards, Q 1:1, Q 1:6,
  Q 1:20, Q 2:17, Q 2:18, Q 2:22,
  Q 2:23–Q 2:26, Q 2:39, Q 7:3
Recognition of tax exemption:
  concept of, Q 1:31, Q 1:35
  exemptions from, Q 1:32
Registered agent:
  function of, Q 1:10
  identity of, Q 1:9, Q 1:12, Q 1:14
  liability of, Q 1:11
Registration, fund-raising, Q 1:5, Q 7:20
Regularly carried on test, Q 10:12–Q 10:17
Related foundations, Q 1:40, Q 2:14, Q 11:13
Religious Freedom Restoration Act, Q 5:13
Remainder interests, Q 8:2–Q 8:4
Rentals by charitable organizations, Q 2:25
Reporting requirements:
  charity auctions, Q 9:12
  fund-raising, Q 7:20
  lobbying, Q 4:34–Q 4:36
  political activities, Q 5:24, Q 5:25
  subsidiaries, Q 11:10, Q 11:11
Research, Q 4:31, Q 10:23, Q 12:14, Q 12:23
Restricted gifts, Q 9:3
Royalty exception, Q 7:16, Q 7:17,
  Q 10:24, Q 10:25

Same state test, Q 10:21
Scandals, Q 9:19
Scientific property, gifts of, Q 1:43
Secretary, role of, Q 2:9
Securities, valuation of, Q 9:4
Self-dealing:
  definition of, Q 2:27
  forms of, Q 2:24, Q 2:25
Self-defense exception, Q 4:10, Q 4:17
Service provider organizations, Q 6:8
Size and extent test, Q 10:21
Social welfare organizations:
  lobbying by, Q 4:24–Q 4:26
  purpose of, Q 1:38
  supporting organization for, Q 6:21
Soft money, definition of, Q 5:22

Special events, Q 9:5, Q 9:12
Specification requirement, Q 6:18
Split-interest trusts, Q 8:3
Spouse travel, Q 2:21
Starting a nonprofit organization, Q 1:5
Starting a planned giving program, Q 8:31
Step transaction, Q 7:4
Stock-based nonprofit organizations, Q 1:2,
    Q 1:13, Q 1:23, Q 11:3
Subsidiaries:
  capitalization, Q 11:22
  control mechanisms, Q 11:3
  definition of, Q 11:1
  first-tier, Q 10:27, Q 11:8
  formation of, Q 11:4, Q 11:12
  in general, Q 11:2, Q 11:5, Q 11:23
  liquidations, Q 11:9
  maintenance of relationship, Q 11:6, Q 11:7,
    Q 11:16–Q 11:19
  partnerships in, Q 11:21
  private foundations, of, Q 11:24
  reporting requirements, Q 11:10, Q 11:11
  revenue taxation, Q 11:8
  second-tier, Q 10:27, Q 11:8
  supporting organizations, as, Q 11:15
  tax-exempt, Q 4:26, Q 11:12–Q 11:19
  taxable, Q 11:20–Q 11:24
  uses of, Q 11:13, Q 11:20, Q 11:21
Substantial, definitions of, Q 2:16, Q 4:5,
    Q 4:30, Q 5:9, Q 6:7, Q 6:16, Q 10:2,
    Q 10:18–Q 10:21
Substantial contributor, definition of, Q 6:8
Substantial part test, Q 4:9–Q 4:14
Substantiation rules, charitable gift, Q 1:43,
    Q 7:6, Q 9:9
Supporting organizations:
  board of directors of, Q 6:22, Q 6:25
  functions of, Q 6:17
  in general, Q 6:15–Q 6:28, Q 11:15
  noncharitable organizations, for, Q 6:21
  operational test, Q 6:15
  organizational test, Q 6:15
  relationships, Q 6:16
  reporting requirements, Q 6:27
  taxable subsidiaries of, Q 11:23

Tangible personal property, gifts of, Q 1:43,
    Q 8:17, Q 9:7
Tax-exempt entity leasing rules, Q 11:21
Tax exemption:
  acquisition of, Q 1:31, Q 7:14, Q 9:19,
    Q 11:14
  forfeiture of, Q 1:37

reacquisition of, Q 1:35
retention of, Q 1:33
revocation of, Q 1:16, Q 1:34, Q 2:17, Q 4:12
scope of, Q 1:30, Q 1:36
Tax-exempt organization, definition of,
    Q 1:28–Q 1:30
Title-holding corporations, Q 10:2, Q 11:13
Travel expenditures, Q 2:20, Q 2:21
Treasurer, role of, Q 2:9
Trust agreement, Q 1:5
Trustees, Q 2:1, Q 8:20, Q 8:27

Unfair competition, Q 10:4, Q 10:5, Q 11:21
United Way of America, Q 2:18, Q 9:19
Universities:
  audits of, Q 12:22–Q 12:29
  unrelated business rules, Q 10:29
Unrelated business activities rules:
  associations, application to, Q 10:31
  auctions, application to, Q 9:6
  audit issues, Q 12:20, Q 12:28
  business, definition of, Q 10:6–Q 10:12
  colleges, application to, Q 10:29
  convenience doctrine, Q 7:16, Q 10:23
  exceptions, Q 10:23–Q 10:28, Q 11:8
  fund-raising programs, application to,
    Q 7:16, Q 10:32
  health care organizations, application to,
    Q 10:28
  modifications, Q 10:23, Q 10:24
  museums, application to, Q 10:30
  rationale for, Q 10:4
  regularly carried on test, Q 10:12–Q 10:17
  related businesses, Q 10:18–Q 10:21
  royalty exception, Q 7:16, Q 7:17, Q 10:24,
    Q 10:25
  substantially related test, Q 10:18–Q 10:21
  tax calculation, Q 10:22, Q 10:33
  universities, application to, Q 10:29
Unrelated debt-financed income rules, Q 8:9,
    Q 8:15, Q 12:26
User fees, Q 7:36

Veterans' organizations:
  charitable donees, as, Q 1:41
  lobbying by, Q 4:32, Q 4:33
Volunteers, Q 4:35, Q 9:13–Q 9:16
Voter education activities, Q 5:4

Watchdog agencies, Q 2:29, Q 7:38
Winding-down time, Q 10:16